The Roots of the World

VERITAS
Series Introduction

"The truth will set you free" (John 8:32)

In much contemporary discourse, Pilate's question has been taken to mark the absolute boundary of human thought. Beyond this boundary, it is often suggested, is an intellectual hinterland into which we must not venture. This terrain is an agnosticism of thought: because truth cannot be possessed, it must not be spoken. Thus, it is argued that the defenders of "truth" in our day are often traffickers in ideology, merchants of counterfeits, or anti-liberal. They are, because it is somewhat taken for granted that Nietzsche's word is final: truth is the domain of tyranny.

Is this indeed the case, or might another vision of truth offer itself? The ancient Greeks named the love of wisdom as *philia*, or friendship. The one who would become wise, they argued, would be a "friend of truth." For both philosophy and theology might be conceived as schools in the friendship of truth, as a kind of relation. For like friendship, truth is as much discovered as it is made. If truth is then so elusive, if its domain is *terra incognita*, perhaps this is because it arrives to us—unannounced—as gift, as a person, and not some thing.

The aim of the Veritas book series is to publish incisive and original current scholarly work that inhabits "the between" and "the beyond" of theology and philosophy. These volumes will all share a common aspiration to transcend the institutional divorce in which these two disciplines often find themselves, and to engage questions of pressing concern to both philosophers and theologians in such a way as to reinvigorate both disciplines with a kind of interdisciplinary desire, often so absent in contemporary academe. In a word, these volumes represent collective efforts in the befriending of truth, doing so beyond the simulacra of pretend tolerance, the violent, yet insipid reasoning of liberalism that asks with Pilate, "What is truth?"—expecting a consensus of non-commitment; one that encourages the commodification of the mind, now sedated by the civil service of career, ministered by the frightened patrons of position.

The series will therefore consist of two wings: (1) original monographs; and (2) essay collections on a range of topics in theology and philosophy. The latter will principally be the products of the annual conferences of the Centre of Theology and Philosophy (www.theologyphilosophycentre.co.uk).

Conor Cunningham, *Veritas Series Editor*

Available from Cascade Books

[Nathan Kerr	*Christ, History, and Apocalyptic: The Politics of Christian Mission*][1]
Anthony D. Baker	*Diagonal Advance: Perfection in Christian Theology*
D. C. Schindler	*The Perfection of Freedom: Schiller, Schelling, and Hegel between the Ancients and the Moderns*
Rustin Brian	*Covering Up Luther: How Barth's Christology Challenged the* Deus Absconditus *that Haunts Modernity*
Timothy Stanley	*Protestant Metaphysics After Karl Barth and Martin Heidegger*
Christopher Ben Simpson	*The Truth Is the Way: Kierkegaard's* Theologia Viatorum
Richard H. Bell	*Wagner's Parsifal: An Appreciation in the Light of His Theological Journey*
Antonio Lopez	*Gift and the Unity of Being*
Toyohiko Kagawa	*Cosmic Purpose*, translated and introduced by Thomas John Hastings
Nigel Zimmerman	*Facing the Other: John Paul II, Levinas, and the Body*
Conor Sweeney	*Sacramental Presence after Heidegger: Onto-theology, Sacraments, and the Mother's Smile*
John Behr et al. (eds.)	*The Role of Death in Life: A Multidisciplinary Examination of the Relation between Life and Death*
Eric Austin Lee et al. (eds.)	*The Resounding Soul: Reflection on the Metaphysics and Vivacity of the Human Person*
Orion Edgar	*Things Seen and Unseen: The Logic of Incarnation in Merleau-Ponty's Metaphysics of Flesh*
Duncan B. Reyburn	*Seeing Things as They Are: G. K. Chesterton and the Drama of Meaning*
Lyndon Shakespeare	*Being the Body of Christ in the Age of Management*
Michael V. Di Fuccia	*Owen Barfield: Philosophy, Poetry, and Theology*
John McNerney	*Wealth of Persons: Economics with a Human Face*
Norm Klassen	*The Fellowship of the Beatific Vision: Chaucer on Overcoming Tyranny and Becoming Ourselves*
Donald Wallenfang	*Human and Divine Being: A Study of the Theological Anthropology of Edith Stein*
Sotiris Mitralexis	*Ever-Moving Repose: A Contemporary Reading of Maximus the Confessor's Theory of Time*

---

1. Note: Nathan Kerr, *Christ, History, and Apocalyptic*, although volume 3 of the original SCM Veritas series, is available from Cascade as part of the Theopolitical Visions series.

Sotiris Mitralexis et al. (eds.)	*Maximus the Confessor as a European Philosopher*
Kevin Corrigan	*Love, Friendship, Beauty, and the Good: Plato, Aristotle, and the Later Tradition*
Andrew Brower Latz	*The Social Philosophy of Gillian Rose*
D. C. Schindler	*Love and the Postmodern Predicament: Rediscovering the Real in Beauty, Goodness, and Truth*
Stephen Kampowski	*Embracing Our Finitude: Exercises in a Christian Anthropology between Dependence and Gratitude*
William Desmond	*The Gift of Beauty and the Passion of Being: On the Threshold between the Aesthetic and the Religious*
Charles Péguy	*Notes on Bergson and Descartes*
David Alcalde	*Cosmology without God: The Problematic Theology Inherent in Modern Cosmology*
Benson P. Fraser	*Hide and Seek: The Sacred Art of Indirect Communication*
Philip John Paul Gonzales	*Exorcising Philosophical Modernity: Cyril O'Regan and Christian Discourse after Modernity*
Caitlin Smith Gilson	*Subordinated Ethics: Natural Law and Moral Miscellany in Aquinas and Dostoyevsky*
Michael Dominic Taylor	*The Foundations of Nature: Metaphysics of Gift for an Integral Ecological Ethic*
David W. Opderbeck	*The End of the Law? Law, Theology, and Neuroscience*
Caitlin Smith Gilson	*As It Is in Heaven: Some Christian Questions on the Nature of Paradise*
Andrew T. J. Kaethler	*The Eschatological Person: Alexander Schemann and Joseph Ratzinger in Dialogue*
Emmanuel Falque	*By Way of Obstacles: A Pathway through a Work*
Paul Tyson (ed.)	*Astonishment in Science: Engagements with William Desmond*
Darren Dyk	*Will & Love: Shakespeare and the Motion of the Soul*
Matthew Vest	*Ethics Lost in Modernity: Reflections on Wittgenstein and Bioethics*
Hanna Lucas	*Sensing the Sacred: Recovering a Mystagogical Vision of Knowledge and Salvation*
Philip Gonzales et al. (eds.)	*Finitude's Wounded Praise: Responses to Jean-Louis Crétien*
Martin Koci et al. (eds.)	*God and Phenomenology: Thinking with Jean-Yves Lacoste*
Steven E. Knepper (ed.)	*A Heart of Flesh: William Desmond and the Bible*
James Madden	*Thinking About Thinking: Mind and Meaning in the Era of Techno-Nihilism*

The Roots of the World

The Remarkable Prescience of G. K. Chesterton

DUNCAN REYBURN

CASCADE *Books* • Eugene, Oregon

THE ROOTS OF THE WORLD
The Remarkable Prescience of G. K. Chesterton

Copyright © 2025 Duncan Reyburn. All rights reserved. Except for brief quotations in critical publications or reviews, no part of this book may be reproduced in any manner without prior written permission from the publisher. Write: Permissions, Wipf and Stock Publishers, 199 W. 8th Ave., Suite 3, Eugene, OR 97401.

Cascade Books
An Imprint of Wipf and Stock Publishers
199 W. 8th Ave., Suite 3
Eugene, OR 97401

www.wipfandstock.com

PAPERBACK ISBN: 979-8-3852-2609-2
HARDCOVER ISBN: 979-8-3852-2610-8
EBOOK ISBN: 979-8-3852-2611-5

Cataloguing-in-Publication data:

Names: Reyburn, Duncan [author].

Title: The roots of the world : the remarkable prescience of G. K. Chesterton / by Duncan Reyburn.

Description: Eugene, OR: Cascade Books, 2025 | Series: Veritas | Includes bibliographical references and index.

Identifiers: ISBN 979-8-3852-2609-2 (paperback) | ISBN 979-8-3852-2610-8 (hardcover) | ISBN 979-8-3852-2611-5 (ebook)

Subjects: LCSH: Chesterton, G. K. (Gilbert Keith), 1874–1936—Religion. | Desmond, William. | Plato. | Aristotle. | McLuhan, Marshall, 1911–1980.

Classification: PR4453.C4 R49 2025 (paperback) | PR4453.C4 (ebook)

VERSION NUMBER 02/19/25

Scripture quotations marked (KJV) are taken from The Authorized (King James) Version. Rights in the Authorized Version in the United Kingdom are vested in the Crown. Reproduced by permission of the Crown's patentee, Cambridge University Press

For my beloved parents, Lindsay and Yvonne, who gave me roots.

He answered and said unto them, When it is evening, ye say, It will be fair weather: for the sky is red. And in the morning, It will be foul weather to day: for the sky is red and lowring. O ye hypocrites, ye can discern the face of the sky; but can ye not discern the signs of the times?

—Jesus, *The Gospel According to St. Matthew* 16:2–3 (KJV)

But what does the word "hope" represent? It represents only a broken instantaneous glimpse of something that is immeasurably older and wilder than language, that is immeasurably older and wilder than man; a mystery to saints and a reality to wolves.... It is true that the philosophical meaning of the word, in the conscious mind of man, is merely a part of something immensely larger in the unconscious mind, that the gusty light of language only falls for a moment on a fragment, and that obviously a semi-detached, unfinished fragment of a certain definite pattern on the dark tapestries of reality.

—G. K. Chesterton, *G. F. Watts* (1904)

Contents

Acknowledgements | xi

1. Being Prophetic | 1
    The Wind in the Trees | 1
    The Question in the Predictions | 11
    The Roots of the World | 16

2. Being True | 26
    G. K. Chesterton Through William Desmond's Fourfold | 26
    The Univocal Sense of Being | 36
    The Equivocal Sense of Being | 43
    The Dialectical Sense of Being | 53
    The Metaxological Sense of Being | 59

3. Being Formed | 73
    G. K. Chesterton Through Plato's Forms | 73
    Reinstating the Form | 75
    Reclaiming the Ideal | 82
    Restoring Analogy | 93

4. Being Informed | 110
    G. K. Chesterton Through Aristotle's Fourfold | 110
    The Material Cause | 119
    The Efficient Cause | 125
    The Final Cause | 130
    The Formal Cause | 144

5. Being Conformed | 148
    G. K. Chesterton Through Marshall McLuhan's Tetrad | 148
    The First Law of Mediation: Extension | 162
    The Second Law of Mediation: Obsolescence | 166
    The Third Law of Mediation: Retrieval | 173
    The Fourth Law of Mediation: Reversal | 181

6. Being Transformed | 186
    Chesterton's (Formal) Cause | 186
    Chestertonian Prescience | 196
    A Chestertonian Renascence | 201

Bibliography | 209
Index | 217

Acknowledgements

Thank you, Keith Borien, for organizing the shipment to South Africa of many back copies of *The Chesterton Review*, as well as several books on and by Chesterton. I am grateful to the late Fr. Jerome Bertram, who was a kind presence at the Oxford Oratory before the Chesterton Library was moved to the University of Notre Dame in London, and who helped get Keith's shipment to me. More indirectly, I am indebted, as are so many Chesterton scholars, in various ways, to the late Aidan Mackey, for collecting many of the journals and books that are now in my care. I am grateful to the University of Notre Dame for inviting me to speak at the inaugural conference and opening of the Chesterton Library in London, *G. K. Chesterton, Polymath*, held in October 2022. Fr. Jim Lies and Joanna Byrne, and unnamed sponsors, deserve special thanks for getting me there. This event spurred me to complete this book. I am grateful to my fellow Chestertonian panelists at that conference, with whom, and others there, I first shared some of the thoughts contained in these pages: Martijn Cremers, Hadas Elber-Aviram, Felipe Fernandez-Armesto, Michael Hurley, Matthew Ingleby, Mark Knight, Rebekah Lamb, Alison Milbank, Luke Seaber, Michael Shallcross, Michael Ward, and Judith Wolfe. I am grateful to *The Chesterton Review*, currently under the leadership of Dermot Quinn and Gloria Garafulich-Grabois, for supporting my research over the years. I am grateful to friends with whom I have discussed many of the ideas contained in these pages and who have encouraged me along the way, especially, Miguel Romero-Ramirez, Stephen Costello, Dale Ahlquist, Marno

Kirstein, and Gideon Nel. I am grateful to Danie Goosen, whose reading recommendations and conversations have shaped my thinking in more ways than I can describe.

I am thankful the University of Pretoria, which granted me funding to acquire research material needed for this book. To Adrienne Warricker and Fundiswa Buthelezi at the Library of the University of Pretoria, thanks to both of you for assisting me. I am thankful to my colleagues whose dedication to our shared task ensured that I could find time to work on this book. A special thanks to Lee Cerling, at the University of South Carolina, who read an early version of this book and offered excellent suggestions. Thank you very much, Robin Parry, my editor, and others at Wipf and Stock, for supporting my work. I am grateful to the Rijks Museum, in the Netherlands, for sending me a digital copy of the painting *Forest Landscape by Moonlight* (1861) by Georg Eduard Otto Saal to be the cover of this book.

I am immensely grateful to my family, for keeping me rooted. My deepest thanks to my parents, Lindsay and Yvonne, to whom this book is dedicated, for laying the foundations upon which my life has been built; thank you also for being the greatest contributors to my personal Chesterton library. Huge thanks to my mother-in-law Beulah Neethling, for extra help and support. Immense gratitude to my dear wife, Linda. Thank you, my love, for your love and devotion, for sharing this one wild life with me, and also for many excellent suggestions on this book. And lastly, thank you to my daughters, Isla and Sophia, for being filled with wonder. My girls, my prayer for you is that you will always know, no matter how the world around us may crumble, there are some realities, rooted in God, that, while often mysterious, remain firmly planted, unmovable, and trustworthy.

1

Being Prophetic

The Wind in the Trees

"I AM SITTING UNDER TALL trees," Gilbert Keith Chesterton writes in a moment of reverie, "with a great wind boiling like surf about the tops of them, so that their living load of leaves rocks and roars in something that is at once exultation and agony."[1] He notices the wind tug at the trees "as if it might pluck them root and all out of the earth like tufts of grass."[2] Those trees strain, tear, and lash, "as if they were a tribe of dragons each tied by the tail."[3] Witnessing this, Chesterton wonders about what is causing what. A child might judge that the trees are moving the wind—a whimsical possibility. The whole modern world, which is childish in many ways, seems convinced of something like this. The brain causes the mind, say the moderns, just as they contend that things cause thoughts and material conditions cause moral problems. Sometimes such interpretations seem to fit. The visible can appear to command the invisible, as when stubbing your toe drives you to feel pain or when reading the average student essay is enough to nudge you towards despairing for the future of humanity.

But Chesterton is not convinced that this is the best way to understand what is happening here. *It is the wind that moves the trees*, say the ancients; and Chesterton trusts them more than the moderns. "The wind is up above the world before a twig on the tree has moved. So there must always be a

---

1. Chesterton, *Tremendous Trifles*, 59.
2. Chesterton, *Tremendous Trifles*, 59.
3. Chesterton, *Tremendous Trifles*, 59.

battle in the sky before there is a battle on the earth. Since it is lawful to pray for the coming of the kingdom, it is lawful also to pray for the coming of the revolution that shall restore the kingdom. It is lawful to hope to hear the wind of Heaven in the trees."[4]

It is impossible to read Chesterton's work without being astonished at extraordinary prescience. He paid close attention to the movements of the trees of the world while making every effort to discern which way and how hard the wind was blowing to stir those movements. He saw how what was happening around him was not just relevant to his own age but also to ours. So many of his predictions, outlandish ones included, have already come true. And yet he was no ordinary speculator. As Friedrich Jünger suggests, when the speculator or science fiction writer's forecasts come true, he typically fails to live up to the title of prophet and visionary because he lacks the "necessary wisdom, and the language with which wisdom speaks."[5] This cannot be said of Chesterton, who was not only accurate in his predictions but also wise in his judgments.

His friend Emile Cammaerts wrote of him, "The prophetic touch, the desire to warn, to advise, and to convince, meets us at every turn in Chesterton's works."[6] He possessed "the prophet's fertile eloquence, his burning zeal, and his sincere consistency."[7] Working in almost every genre and writing on a staggering range of subjects, he demonstrated a saintly level of consistency. His prophetic vision was and remains conspicuous in his unceasing concern with the "fate of the soul."[8] His wisdom sets his prescience apart from the conjectures of writers like Edward Bellamy, H. G. Wells, and Jules Verne. He saw, or ventured to see, not just the surface of things to come but their essence—or, sometimes, how things, happenings, and probable happenings signalled of a loss of essence. He considered not only the exultation and agony of the trees swaying in the wind but also the nature and shape of the wind itself. He knew the order of things, which explains his love for the ordinary. He knew the origins of things, which explains his originality.

The etymology of the word *prescience*, which I have used to refer to this one aspect of Chesterton's perception that I have elected to home in on, echoes two key ideas that are worth some attention if the purpose of this book is to be understood. *Pre* is a prefix meaning *before* or *prior to* and, when attached to science (*praescientia*), connotes anticipating something

---

4. Chesterton, *Tremendous Trifles*, 61.
5. Jünger, *Failure of Technology*, 1–2.
6. Cammaerts, *Laughing Prophet*, 31.
7. Cammaerts, *Laughing Prophet*, 32.
8. Cammaerts, *Laughing Prophet*, 24.

in advance of its occurring. Deeper than the epistemological dimension of this prefix, however, is an ontological attunement that precedes and even supersedes all implied possibilities. It suggests the priority of being over knowing, the priority of metaphysical foundations over interpretation, the priority of knowing over judging, and the priority of judging over acting. It therefore also hints at the ancient metaphysical priority of act over potency. By implication, *prescience* indicates a wakefulness to the true origins and order of things and not just the divulgation and imposition of theoretical models on the world. Considering Chesterton's prescience cannot only be about knock-on effects and superficial consequences. Chesterton strives for an intense sense of the invisible truth and meanings of things behind their appearances.

The suffix *science* is also part of the word *prescience*. It comes from the Latin words *scientia*, meaning *knowledge*, or *scire*, meaning *to know*. The word *science* did not once automatically refer to natural science as it tends to now and so it did not always suggest the nominalist, voluntarist, Baconian equation of knowledge with power that took root in modernity. Science does not have to be confined to physicalism. I take the word to mean something closer to its older form: seeking out *being* as other to thought and not just as confirming or refuting conceptual hypotheses. The kind of knowledge I have in mind is not experimental knowledge. *Prescience* still rightly implies far-sightedness, foresight, and foreknowledge. Some beautiful old words echo, often mythically, these more familiar terms: vaticination, haruspication, psychism, pythonism, and prevision. But we find that the etymology of the word *prescience* points to more than just knowing in advance. The word implies, first and most importantly, being present to and dedicated to what is real and true, happening and developing. What emerges out of the happening of being gains its meaning and significance from this happening and what this happening depends on.

This fits Chesterton's unique perception. He was not primarily a predictor of possible futures but a faithful metaphysician and a dedicated Catholic theologian, albeit a lay theologian, even before his conversion to Catholicism in 1922. It should be no surprise, therefore, that his artful prophecies differ from those of his many contemporaries, who were taken in by the soteriology of modernity in a way he never was. He was certainly fascinated, as many in his time were and as many of us are, with how certain events would play out as time wore on. But he did not perceive things as others did, and so he saw much more than many others could. He was considered a prophet even in his own time,[9] and he thought of himself as

---

9. Cammaerts, *Laughing Prophet*; Maycock, "Introduction," 29.

a prophet.[10] Because of his wisdom, he can be a prophet for us today.[11] To have a clearer sense of why we can call Chesterton a *prophet*, it will help to have some examples of his foresight. Here, therefore, is a sweeping and rapid overview, the chief aim of which is simply to introduce the nature, scope, and reliability of many of his forecasts.

Regarding the more immediate future before him and the people of his age, Chesterton predicted that communism in Russia would ascend and fall.[12] He foresaw the transformation of the Russian Revolution into a stifling and often insane bureaucracy.[13] He knew that in time there would be a revival of the old idea of empires but he also foresaw what many are noticing today, the return of "small nationalities" based on localized sentimentality.[14] He observed the trend towards globalization, often with distrust and alarm, but refused to accept that this meant the erasure of nationalism.[15] He would not have been surprised at the establishment of the European Union in the 1940s, nor would he have been caught off guard by the recent so-called Brexit, the withdrawal of the United Kingdom from the European Union in 2020, or the arrival on the world's stage of various dissident political movements, populisms, and postliberalisms.

Towards the end of his life, he was among the first to warn the world against the malice of Hitler.[16] He was especially worried about the likelihood of violence against Jewish people.[17] His speculations about how the Second World War would start on the Polish border proved correct.[18] He knew that it would be the most widespread and catastrophic war to date, much worse than the Great War.[19] While "reading through a mass of essays with the idea of selecting them to make a book," Frank Sheed noted with amazement his realization that "as far back as the middle twenties up to his death in 1936," Chesterton's mind "had been dominated by the present war," World War Two.[20] Chesterton "took it for granted" that the war was not

---

10. Chesterton, *Collected Works, Volume 5*, 405.
11. Ahlquist, *G. K. Chesterton*, 173–77; Mackey, *G. K. Chesterton*.
12. Chesterton, *Illustrated London News*, 12 July 1919.
13. Chesterton, *Illustrated London News*, 1 February 1919.
14. Chesterton, *Illustrated London News*, 14 July 1906.
15. Chesterton, *Illustrated London News*, 1 July 1933.
16. Chesterton, *Illustrated London News*, 19 December 1931.
17. Chesterton, *Illustrated London News*, 28 February 1914; 4 September 1920.
18. Chesterton, *Collected Works, Volume 5*, 525.
19. Chesterton, *Illustrated London News*, 2 December 1933.
20. Sheed, "Compiler's Note," in Chesterton, *End of Armistice*, 5.

just possible or probable but "humanly speaking certain to arrive."[21] Note the phrase "humanly speaking." While considering Chesterton's prescience, we are not dealing with absolute certainties; we are dealing with what he thought likely.

Chesterton foresaw that technologies would transform the way warfare was conducted; and that this would result in civilians getting caught up in violence as much as soldiers.[22] But he also saw how technologies would affect almost all other areas of life and not just the experience of war. As Dale Ahlquist notes, while technology "is always advertised as being for our betterment,"[23] Chesterton showed us not to overlook its limitations and downsides. What is built to help may also harm; what is created to assist may manufacture monotony and death.[24] "By all means go on progressing, if it amuses you," Chesterton said; "Go on inventing machines for anything or everything. But always remember that you are not only inventing machines; you are inventing riddles."[25]

Noting that "Progress" is "Parricide"[26] and the "mother of Problems,"[27] for instance, he observed that the same "modern industrial civilisation, which aims at rapidity, also produces congestion."[28] Mirroring this thought he contended, "The modern world is a crowd of very rapid-racing cars all brought to a standstill and stuck in a block of traffic."[29] He knew where the accelerationism of modernity would lead.[30] "Civilization has run on ahead of the soul of man," he said, "and is producing faster than he can think and give thanks."[31] He was clear that a culture too concerned with supply and demand would only create a society bereft of virtue. "Idolatry is committed," he noted, "not merely by setting up false gods, but also by setting up false devils; by making men afraid of war or alcohol, or economic law, when they should be afraid of spiritual corruption and cowardice."[32] In this, he predicted the way many modern leaders would wield the human capacity for

21. Sheed, "Compiler's Note," 5.
22. Chesterton, *Collected Works, Volume 5*, 64.
23. Ahlquist, *G. K. Chesterton*.
24. Chesterton, *Illustrated London News*, 21 March 1925.
25. Chesterton, *Illustrated London News*, 6 April 1935.
26. Chesterton, *Illustrated London News*, 28 April 1934.
27. Chesterton, *Illustrated London News*, 6 April 1935.
28. Chesterton, *Illustrated London News*, 23 December 1922.
29. Chesterton, *Illustrated London News*, 29 May 1926.
30. Chesterton, *G. K.'s Weekly*, 19 June 1926.
31. Chesterton, *Daily News*, 21 February 1902.
32. Chesterton, *Illustrated London News*, 11 September 1909.

fear, in particular, as a technique for steering their citizens towards political ends without proper benefits.

In 1926, close to forty years before the so-called sexual revolution, Chesterton rightly claimed that the "next heresy" was going to be "simply an attack on morality, and especially sexual morality."[33] This prediction is one of a range of predictions I consider in more detail in the pages that follow. Even without much context, however, it is striking in its pellucidity. Against the guesswork of many others in his time, Chesterton sensed that this specific attack was not going to come from Socialists or the offspring of Bolshevists, although he raged against such groups. "The madness of tomorrow is not in Moscow but much more in Manhattan,"[34] he suggested. As would be confirmed by more recent sociologists, he emphasized how many unwelcome alterations to the Western mind would rest on "a fashionable fatalism founded on Freud"[35] that would "at once exalt lust and forbid fertility."[36] He thus spelt out the manipulative and destructive influence of his distant contemporary, Freud's psychoanalytically minded, mass-manipulating nephew Edward Bernays, without ever having heard of him. In general, he thought psychoanalysis, which would infect humanities departments in universities around the world decades after his death,[37] was likely to become popular despite being a "science conducted by lunatics for lunatics."[38] He observed not only the fraudulence of Freud's work but also the fact that its fraudulence would not prevent it from becoming influential.[39]

Chesterton saw that so-called reproductive rights would become a major issue, although they would not be right or in favor of reproduction.[40] As women became increasingly involved in statecraft, he perceived that birth and marriage would be interfered with more than ever before.[41] He suggested, along these lines, that birth control, which he called "birth prevention,"[42] would become a political focus and that abortion and other forms of anti-natalism would dominate political progressivism.[43] As Sohrab

33. Chesterton, *G. K.'s Weekly*, 19 June 1926.
34. Chesterton, *G. K.'s Weekly*, 19 June 1926.
35. Chesterton, *Illustrated London News*, 29 May 1920.
36. Chesterton, *Well and the Shallows*, 172.
37. Trueman, *Rise and Triumph of the Modern Self*.
38. Chesterton, *Illustrated London News*, 23 June 1928.
39. See Rieff, *Triumph of the Therapeutic*.
40. Chesterton, *G. K.'s Weekly*, 12 November 1932.
41. Chesterton, *Collected Works, Volume 4*, 143.
42. Schall, *Schall on Chesterton*, 131.
43. Chesterton, *G. K.'s Weekly*, 17 January 1931.

Ahmari asserts in his foreword to a recent edition of Chesterton's *What's Wrong with the World*, originally published in 1910, Chesterton foresaw what has become known in recent years as "woke capital,"[44] referring to the strange collusion of contemporary leftist victimocratic identity politics and liberal-democratic capitalism that targets and decimates local relational bonds and institutions while monetizing and commercializing the remaining shrapnel.

Chesterton knew that progressivism and capitalism were bedfellows that would produce unnatural offspring.[45] He was also conscious that the politicization of sex would lead to confusion instead of fulfilling the desire for equality or the happiness of both sexes. Sexlessness, the refusal to acknowledge the God-ordained design of sexual difference, would be the result of the battle of the sexes.[46] Once cut off from its spiritual roots, equality would lead not to fairness but to a culture of lies and the popularizing of consumable otherness.[47] Chesterton was sure that, in the name of equality, standards would be attacked and what Pope Benedict XVI would later name a "dictatorship of relativism" would become the norm.[48]

He anticipated many of the less obvious but still harmful consequences of feminism, including those that would prove more detrimental than helpful for women.[49] The feminists of his time mistook an introjected negation of the feminine and a powerful resentment of paternal grace for a triumph over tyranny.[50] The result of attacking patriarchy indiscriminately would not be freedom but servility. This is something, noted by Chesterton at the very start of the first wave of so many feminist waves, that more metaphysically astute feminists now, in both secular and religious contexts, are beginning to realize.[51] There is no single unified feminism nowadays, but Chesterton's critique of feminism was well ahead of its time in making explicit how the result of that ideology would be injustice against everyone.[52] Feminism has tended to be dangerously allied to a larger trend in modernity that obliterates or seizes the common in the name of nominalist particulars. The

---

44. Ahmari, "Foreword," xii.
45. Chesterton, *Collected Works, Volume 5*, 45.
46. See Chesterton, *What's Wrong with the World*.
47. Chesterton, *G. K.'s Weekly*, 26 July 1930.
48. Jankunas, *Dictatorship of Relativism*.
49. Chesterton, *Collected Works, Volume 4*, 149.
50. Mackey, *G. K. Chesterton*, 19–20.
51. See Favale, *Genesis of Gender*; Harrington, *Feminism Against Progress*; Perry, *Case Against the Sexual Revolution*.
52. Reyburn, "Death of the Feminine and the Homelessness of Man."

modern trend, in other words, is concerned with reconstituting the world according to a degraded human image; and the world is now lurching ever more rapidly towards posthumanism because too few recognize how vital it is to receive the world imaginatively as a gift.

Chesterton foresaw that states would begin to interfere more and more in private affairs, often in the name of freedom.[53] There is an atmosphere in America, he suggested, that could end up punishing people for kissing or making a person a convict for wearing a necktie. "There is an American atmosphere in which people may someday be shot for shaking hands, or hanged for writing a postcard."[54] In our time, examples of this shadow side of liberalism are abundant but Chesterton already suspected what was coming long ago. The threat of policing every aspect of private life was often on his mind. He perceived that an increasing and indiscriminate openness, like that promoted by Karl Popper,[55] would give rise to an astonishing degree of pedantry as trust would be replaced by micro-managerialism.[56] Chesterton saw, as Tocqueville and Dostoevsky did before him, that the rise of individualism provided no immunity against anarchy, and that it did not even offer any defense against despotism. Anarchy and authoritarian overreach are closely allied. "Anyone who is not an anarchist agrees with having a policeman at the corner of the street," he said, "but the danger at present is that of finding the policeman half-way down the chimney or even under the bed."[57] In recent years, we have seen this realized in the obsolescence of privacy through constant surveillance, whether in places like London or Beijing, or via the internet.[58] Society has become transparent to an absurd degree, although it is not an unconditional transparency.[59] Its upshot is that what ought to be hidden is proclaimed from the rooftops while what ought to be made known is buried in the backyard. A more recent example, fulfilling Chesterton's prediction that healthcare could start to resemble an oppressive regime, is found in many actions taken by governments and organizations around the globe during the SARS-CoV-2 pandemic.[60]

Not coincidentally, on a slightly different subject, Chesterton predicted that the misleading interventions of the media were likely to become

53. Chesterton, *Illustrated London News*, 24 March 1923.
54. Chesterton, *Collected Works, Volume 21*, 164.
55. See Popper, *Open Society and Its Enemies*.
56. See Reno, *Return of the Strong Gods*.
57. Chesterton, *Collected Works, Volume 21*, 169.
58. See Zuboff, *Surveillance Capitalism*.
59. See Han, *Transparency Society*.
60. See Berenson, *Pandemia*.

increasingly inimical to people.[61] Journalism would rot from colluding with the rich and powerful.[62] In his day, he already recognized that journalism was "popular mainly as fiction. Life is one world, and life seen in the newspapers is another."[63] He was alert to the fact that this was likely to continue and grow as technologies assumed a more significant role in the lives of people.[64] However, his concern was not only with news media. He noted entertainment as another hazard. Being a man of letters, Chesterton was aware that the sheer scale of media distortions, or just scale on its own, would become a force, if not *the* force, to contend with in the future. As a consequence, he wanted to offer a balancing, if controversial, voice within the media environment he inhabited. He was often combative in a tame world and jolly in an overly serious one. He embodied a desire to highlight tensions in everyday expressions that were downplayed or forgotten.

As an autodidact, Chesterton was mindful that centralizing education policy would play a significant role in shaping society for the worse. The trouble was that bureaucrats had more say over what was taught than parents did. The same is true in many places now. "The purpose of Compulsory Education," Chesterton opined, "is to deprive the common people of their common sense."[65] He predicted the rise of a pluralism that would welcome all kinds of new faiths in the name of tolerance while being hateful towards Christianity.[66] Pluralization would be far from neutral. It would not only seek to invalidate but would ridicule Christian claims while recently invented so-called religions without any solid metaphysical and theological foundations would be flaunted without restraint or subtlety.

Chesterton thought an increase in populist politics was likely, I have said, but he was not worried about what was popular as much as he was certain that the mob would be misled by rich elites. In this and more, he anticipated the rise of oligarchy and demagoguery that has been the mark of so much politics in recent years. He knew how dangerous crowds could be in what Gustave Le Bon had called "the era of crowds."[67] Nevertheless, since he appreciated the common man, his critical eye was on those who wanted to manipulate the masses. He predicted a time when people would be "howled down for saying that two and two make four" and hanged for "saying the

---

61. Chesterton, *Illustrated London News*, 7 April 7 1923.
62. Chesterton, *Illustrated London News*, 5 November 1917.
63. Chesterton, *G. K.'s Weekly*, 26 July 1930.
64. Chesterton, *G. K.'s Weekly*, 26 July 1930.
65. Chesterton, *Illustrated London News*, 7 September 1929.
66. Chesterton, *Illustrated London News*, 13 January 1906.
67. See Le Bon, *Crowd*.

grass is green."[68] This hyperbolic prediction rested on his intuition that some people with more power and influence could drive consenting multitudes to silence dissenters who spoke the truth, even the plain truth. He predicted further expansions of capitalism and the rise of environmental degradation. He foresaw how the frivolous legalization of divorce would ensure frivolous marriages, temporary unions, and, ultimately, the breakdown of the family. He saw how this would wreak havoc on society by giving the state even more power to interfere in the personal lives and choices of its people. He could tell that revelling in luxuries would render whole swaths of Western civilization more passive and manipulable than ever.[69] He predicted the arrival of the first movies but knew that the reign of entertainment was unlikely to stop there. Like Moses, who witnessed his people bowing to a statue of a beast instead of worshipping the God who freed them, he perceived that the worship of the image in the West was inadvertent suicide.[70]

I am well aware that some would contest certain judgments about the precise nature of some of these predictions. Nevertheless, the point has been made. Chesterton's perspicacity about the signs of his own time and foreseeing the future remains impressive. It would be fairly unremarkable if he had been right about only a few things in a very select sphere. But repeatedly and on a wide range of matters, he made definite pronouncements on what he thought likely, and many of his predictions, all that I have found, have been right. While many of his predictions are undoubtedly generalizations, he managed to get many specifics astonishingly right. Apart from his accuracy about the threat and start of World War Two, and the fact that in recent years a quite literal furore about whether two and two add to four has broken out,[71] consider Chesterton's prediction, in 1930, that high heels would get out of hand at some point in the twenty-first century.

"A fashionable person in the twenty-first century," he wrote, "may end up in shoes with such high heels that he (or, rather, she) practically cannot walk at all."[72] Such a fashionable person "may carry the same tendency so far as to walk on stilts, or to be unable to walk on stilts."[73] Well, right at the start

68. Chesterton, *Illustrated London News*, 14 August 1926.
69. Chesterton, *New Renascence*, 19–22.
70. Chesterton, *New Renascence*, 19–22.
71. See Murray, *War on the West*.
72. Chesterton, *Illustrated London News*, 17 May 1930. For the sake of neatness, stylistic continuity, and symmetry with my previous book, I have elected to follow Chesterton's usage of the masculine singular pronoun to refer to the generic person. I am aware, as Chesterton was, that this is sometimes imperfect but the decision was contextual and grammatical, rather than political.
73. Chesterton, *Illustrated London News*, 17 May 1930.

of the twenty-first century, a fashion designer won the Guinness Book of World Records award for the highest-heeled shoes commercially available. At twenty inches, they were a lot like the stilts Chesterton predicted. And when the exhibitionist singer Lady Gaga wore similar stilt-like shoes designed by Noritaka Tatehana in 2011, she could barely walk and needed help to stand. What a powerful symbol of the modern lack of good judgment this is and what a profound demonstration of Chestertonian prescience.

The Question in the Predictions

How was G. K. Chesterton able to be so prescient? The most straightforward answer, which is by no means yet an explanation, must be that he possessed a profound understanding of causation. This answer may animate some misunderstandings that I would like to clear away immediately. For starters, we should notice that Chesterton's prescience and his conception of causality cannot be explained only by his commitment to logic; his understanding of mental relations. He was undoubtedly a brilliant logician, and much of his insightfulness is found in his ability to explain his thinking with admirable rational precision. He often pointed out the errors made by his interlocutors by incisive reasoning and was able to note the implications of shoddy thinking better than so many other thinkers. But he was familiar with the fact that logic can mislead as well as lead. Logical possibility does not equal logical necessity. His natural mode of thinking was therefore not so much logical—as an unfolding of negations, affirmations, and sublations within a disembodied conceptual space—as it was analogical, unfolding along the lines of non-identical repetitions in harmony with a powerful sacramental imagination and symbolic awareness.

 He cautioned against the view that logic alone can get us to the truth. We may claim, for example, that the two ears on one person added to the two ears on another person make four ears. We may also claim that the sixteen ears on one person plus the sixteen ears on another person make thirty-two. Both statements are perfectly logical, but the latter is untrue despite being logical. In the end, the discovery of the truth is not just about logic but is closer to a direct experience. "You can only find truth with logic," Chesterton noted, "if you have already found the truth without it."[74] Indeed, many of his predictions are not strictly logical. They do not follow a neat procession of causes and effects explainable by an inferential rationale. Prescience, as I have defined it, requires an ability to notice not just logical sequences but also things that contravene the laws of logic, as many evil human actions

---

74. Chesterton, *Daily News*, 25 February 1905.

do. Foresight must necessarily involve an understanding of psychology as something complex and often unsystematic, as well as fallen. Human beings are not at all like the keys of a piano that when pressed produce a predictable response. A sound understanding of psychology would account for this.

With this in mind, we can also dismiss the idea that Chesterton's prophetic insights are owed to something like a science of history, in the narrow modern sense of *science*. He was no believer in historical determinism and warned strongly against fatalism.[75] He was against a certain historicism that C. S. Lewis defines as the idea "that men can, by use of their natural powers, discover the inner meaning in the historical process."[76] "It is a beautiful and even blissful thought," Chesterton once joked, "that, whatever happens will never be what the scientific futurists and fatalists have proved to be inevitable and quite certain to happen."[77] "History is the most human of all sciences," he insisted.[78] It must retain its status as an exploration of humanity and not of a machine with human parts.[79] While reflecting on the emergence of Bolshevism, Chesterton noted that sociologists tended not to be sufficiently mindful that history hangs on three dogmas: "(1) That humanity is far too complex to have such calculations made about it. (2) That humanity is afflicted by original sin. (3) That the will of man is free."[80] Given these simple truths, we have to recognize just how precarious prediction is. There are "too many men and too many moods" to give us any clue into even the simplest of human actions.[81]

The so-called pendulum theory of history was especially bothersome for Chesterton because a pendulum is a dead thing. People would need to be similarly dead to swing about like that—perhaps caught in an ideological rut that frees them from the terrible stigma of being considered capable of coherent thinking and decision-making. Such a theory substitutes "an idea of fatalistic alteration for the medieval freedom of the soul seeking truth."[82] As far as such a theory goes, modern thinkers who hold to it would be forced to be merely reactive, endlessly protesting without having any sense

75. Chesterton, *Illustrated London News*, 13 August 1910; 16 March 1912; 19 April 1913; 29 May 1920; 10 July 1920; 25 November 1922; 15 August 1923; 10 November 1923; 5 January 1924; 24 July 1926; 14 September 1929; 19 October 1929; 26 October 1929; 2 August 1930; 4 June 1932; 10 March 1934; 9 February 1935; 30 March 1935.

76. Lewis, *Essay Collection*, 213.

77. Chesterton, *Illustrated London News*, 1 July 1933.

78. Chesterton, *Daily News*, 22 June 1912.

79. Chesterton, *Daily News*, 5 October 1912.

80. Chesterton, *Illustrated London News*, 15 April 1933.

81. Chesterton, *Illustrated London News*, 15 April 1933.

82. Chesterton, *Collected Works, Volume 4*, 142.

of finality or form; they would be compelled to regard everything, people included, as inanimate and soulless. Such a theory of history presents to any mind a potentially degraded view of people, themselves as well as others. No wonder Chesterton would want nothing to do with it. Even if people become habituated to operating like machines from time to time, and even if the aggregation of mass movements is somewhat possible, he refused to let this fact shut down the possibility of sincere truth-seeking.

Mercifully, therefore, we find no ironclad, logical, materialistic laws of historical development or pendulum brandishing in Chesterton's work. He regarded as outright "folly" any "materialist theory of history."[83] He was especially disparaging of the "Teutonic" tendency, like that of the socialist revolutionary Karl Marx or the conservative revolutionary Oswald Spengler, to suggest that we could know history's laws as we know the laws of Newton.[84] He was mindful that we cannot be sure in advance how things will turn out without being plagued by methodological conundrums and errors.[85] We will be consistently boggled by the complexities of human interactions and decisions, which confound any pre-decided rationalist mold. History is messy; and given how messy the world is now, the future is unlikely to be neat and tidy.

There are good reasons for not being overly confident in one's predictions. Political violence becomes the likely tool of those who want to ensure that things turn out as their theories of history predict—as if an earthly city can be transformed into the perfect synthesis of all human tensions, contests, and antagonisms. Social engineering becomes dangerously common among utopians. Typically, the mob, as a mental abstraction, is created when people are reduced to being mere atoms at the mercy of impersonal forces and incentives. One implication of taking one's predictions too seriously, together with an immanentizing of a deterministic eschatology, is a technical reordering of the so-called mob, which manifests a confusion of means and ends, with methods triumphing over teleology, materiality and moralism triumphing over virtue, and will triumphing over reality and the knowledge of reality. Ironically, the materialist view of history proves the subordination of matter to mind as historical materialists seek to impose their theories on the world.

It is fair to ask, then, how, without having a science of history, even while being so emphatically against any attempt to pinpoint how history worked, was Chesterton able to so astutely discern and predict so much of

---

83. Chesterton, *Illustrated London News*, 21 November 1925.
84. Chesterton, *Illustrated London News*, 21 November 1925.
85. Chesterton, *Illustrated London News*, 17 April 1926.

what lay ahead of him? If it was not a science of history or brilliant logic that helped him predict the future, might we suggest that he was then simply divinely gifted with prophecy? People who share his faith, as I do, will have no trouble regarding him as a uniquely gifted man and acknowledging that every good thing about him was divinely appointed. In the letter of St. James, we are reminded, "Every good gift and every perfect gift is from above, and cometh down from the Father of lights, with whom is no variableness, neither shadow of turning."[86] It is perfectly reasonable, given how he saw his present and our future, to welcome the idea that Chesterton's prescience was God-given. Taking such an answer at face value would make for a brutal ending to this book. Even if such an ending may bring relief to the reader, it would be unsatisfactory as a conclusion. It would create an unacceptable rift between nature and grace to assume that Chesterton's prescience was by divine will alone. It would relegate his prescience to the realm of pure revelation. If that is the kind of prescience he possessed, we can ask nothing further of it; pure revelation is inscrutable. But I do not think his prescience can be so abruptly separated from natural theology. Even if he was graced with a prescience that we cannot imitate or understand perfectly, we can learn from attending to the unique way of perceiving that grounded his forecasting.

We do not contradict the possibility of a grace given to this wondrous journalist, even if we can provide a more reasoned account of his prescience. But humility is required of us. We must not make any attempt to take for ourselves a gift that was not meant for us. We should not imitate the motive of Adam and Eve who plucked and ate what had been expressly forbidden, the fruit of the Tree of the Knowledge of Good and Evil—a symbol here of taking hold of something before its appointed time.[87] The early Christians rightly warned against being too eager to examine omens and other signs of future happenings because of the temptation of idolatry.[88] If most of us are unlikely to be as perceptive about both the present and the future as Chesterton was, we can seek to more fully appreciate the gift he had and to understand its significance. St. Paul encourages his readers to seek spiritual gifts and the gift of prophecy above all.[89] But he also warns that if we exercise prophecy without the gift of love, celebrating the Creator and the gift of created being that he gives, we reduce ourselves to nothing.[90]

86. James 1:17.
87. Genesis 3.
88. Stewart-Sykes, *On the Two Ways*, 37; Didache, ch. 3.
89. 1 Corinthians 14:1.
90. 1 Corinthians 13:2.

Thankfully, Chesterton modelled both humility and charity. His gift of prophecy reflects his love of God, people, and creation. We see this in how he aimed to seek out, preserve, and restore what is good, as well as in his celebration of the unique personhood of people rather than in some attempt to love some vague abstraction called humanity. "The tendency of our whole society today," he advised his readers in 1912, "must be curiously considered if we are to really see it—and stop it. For it is quite impossible for us not to want to stop it, if at once we really see it."[91] Understanding causality as Chesterton did means recognizing that it concerns conserving and/or discontinuing certain qualities in being, and attending to the part we have to play in the drama of being. Chesterton was no passive observer of history; he was willing to take a stand and fight for what is right. His desire was to think through what it means to participate in the life of God and the life of the world. For him, prophecy was not about declaring as final what could be changed. Prophecy was and is, first and foremost, concerned with doing God's work. The prophet may warn us of hell, for instance, but only because he wants us to notice that the kingdom of heaven is at hand. He may warn us of catastrophe so that we may be better equipped to avert it. He sees what is amiss because his eyes are fixed on what is right.

Even when Chesterton was both self-conscious and confident about his predictions, he refused to succumb to historical determinism. He was often hopeful that his more alarming predictions would be proven wrong. "Like all healthy-minded prophets," Chesterton wrote in *Utopia for Usurers* (1917), "I can only prophesy when I am in a rage and think things look ugly for everybody. And like all healthy-minded prophets, I prophesy in the hope that my prophecy may not come true."[92] There is to Chesterton's prophecies often an atmosphere of pessimism, and even a sense, here and there, of what Spengler had referred to as "the decline of the West," from a book Chesterton had read.[93] However, as we find in *The New Renaissance: Thoughts on the Structure of the Future*,[94] essays published in *Vanity Fair* between 1920 and 1921, he was clear that he was remarking on a trend, tendency, or possibility. He could see a certain trajectory, but he refused to mistake what was *possible* or *likely* for what is *inevitable*. If decline were happening in one way or another, it would by no means suggest that decline should have the last word. Where Chesterton saw doom in the future, he

---

91. Chesterton, *Daily News*, 3 February 1912.
92. Chesterton, *Collected Works, Volume 5*, 405.
93. Chesterton, *Illustrated London News*, 3 September 1932.
94. See Chesterton, *New Renascence*.

nevertheless believed that doom could be averted. He hoped to help others to avoid making compromises that would prove disastrous.

Although I have not yet answered the question of how Chesterton was able to be so prescient, we already have some clues to an answer. Chesterton did have a remarkable sense of causality while refusing to see causality in simplistic terms. He did not reduce causality to cause and effect, as many of his materialistically minded contemporaries did, although he maintained something of the logic of cause and effect in noting how certain qualities, evident in certain structures, patterns, and pictures, carry with them certain expected consequences. His attention was omnidirectional, even multi-causal. He did not see one thing only but saw everything as embedded within a vast complex of reality, including intermingling truths and meanings. Moreover, he saw that complex of reality, truths, and meanings in relation to their compliance with or deviation from a clear set of principles and forms. His prescience was an extension of his perceptiveness. Many of the examples of what he thought would happen reflect what he saw happening already in his own time. The McLuhanite dictum could easily apply to Chesterton: "I've always been careful never to predict anything that had not already happened."[95] Chesterton did not see what was happening in his time apart from the obscure and sometimes invisible context. We might say that he was prescient because being prescient was beside the point; it was a byproduct of attending to the point, the principle, and the very truth of things. He saw the future because he was concerned more with often invisible actualities than with visible and easily imaginable possibilities. He attended to the wind in the trees, so to speak. He also attended to the roots of the trees and to the invisible roots of the world.

The Roots of the World

Chesterton felt it was essential to understand the nature and role of the invisible in the play of the visible. Another of his parables shows this. It was first published in *The Daily News* on August 17, 1907,[96] and later reproduced in *Lunacy and Letters* in 1958, where it was given the title that I am borrowing for this book, "The Roots of the World."[97] The story concerns a little boy who is allowed to pick flowers from the garden next to his house. However, he is expressly prohibited from uprooting them. As is somewhat expected when little boys are told not to do something, the story's protagonist finds

---

95. Marshall McLuhan, interview with Tom Wolfe, *TVOntario*, August 1970.
96. Chesterton, *Daily News*, 17 August 1907.
97. Chesterton, *Lunacy and Letters*, 1.

himself at the mercy of an uncontainable urge to defy his elders. He is not convinced by the many reasons the grownups give to dissuade him. Instead, those reasons pique his interest. One day, he decides to give an especially intriguing plant a good tug. Already in the opening of this story, the overt presence of a negation gets given priority in the boy's mind in the form of a verbal interdiction: *Don't uproot the shrubbery!* This negation is a reminder of what Chesterton, before writing this parable, termed the "negative spirit,"[98] which refers to the modern tendency to despise limits. Because of this negative spirit, the boy's attention is constricted. He sees the plants in that garden, especially that one particular plant, not as things to be understood and enjoyed but as things to be used, manipulated, and mangled. In his idolatry, he forgets the whole world around him. He turns the particular against the universal.

For the boy, the fact that the rule has no reasonable foundation and no experiential resonance supports his rebellious actions. Rules and reasons do not matter to him. Against any attempt to discover and understand the world, his desire to dominate it overcomes him. Because of this, he sees lawmakers as rivals to be challenged. He regards the natural law as an irrational and arbitrary enemy to be overcome. In the modern era, where so many laws are irrational and arbitrary, perhaps this is an understandable assumption. But it is wrong. The absence of context renders the command not to wreak havoc on the flora unintelligible. He does not recognize the plants or the garden as part of a larger world of meaning. He regards them as isolated and, to use a term from phenomenology, *unworlded*. He falls for a modern hermeneutic of suspicion that wants to falsify everything before having a positive reply for anything.

As the boy begins to tug at the base of that one plant's stem, things around him start to crumble. His forgetting of the world spells the devastation of the world. For starters, his own house is ruined, the king's castle falls down miles away, and watchtowers erected along the coastline crumble into the ocean. Symbolically speaking, all hierarchies are levelled, all organic social relationships are thrown into chaos. But the plant remains stubbornly in place. Perplexed and exasperated, the boy stops what he is doing and waits for the destruction of his district to be repaired. Although his innocence falters, he accepts that it is not worth his trouble to persist in his rebellion. That the world around him has been crumbling suggests to the boy that the plants and the garden belong to a larger world. Their roots were and remain interwoven into the fabric of reality. Perhaps those injunctions delivered to the boy had a context.

---

98. Chesterton, *Collected Works, Volume 1*, 47–53.

Sadly, the boy grows up and neglects the wisdom of his innocence. He finds that his original curiosity about that plant has not faded. The boy, by now a man, tells his people, "Let us have done with the riddle of this irrational weed. In the name of Truth let us drag it up."[99] With an army of strong men, he takes hold of the plant and tugs at it night and day but it does not budge. Miserably, the combination of age, determination, and force produces destruction that far exceeds what happened when the man was only a child. As is typical for anyone preoccupied with wrecking the world, he believes he is acting in the name of "Truth."[100] However, since he is relying primarily on flimsy imaginary presuppositions, he perpetuates only disintegration and unreality. His use of scientific force to test reality becomes an echo and imitation of the negative injunction he was offered early on. Among other things, the Great Wall of China falls, the Pyramids in Egypt are reduced to rubble, and Paris's Eiffel Tower topples, as does the Statue of Liberty in New York. St. Paul's Cathedral in London is levelled, and Japan experiences such severe earthquakes that it sinks into the sea like Atlantis.

With the protagonist's rage exacerbated by his failure to achieve his original goal, he moves to technologize his original desire. He gets elephants and steam engines to help him rip up the plant. But even after the moon's orbit changes and after the sun grows dimmer, after war upon revolution upon cosmic ruination, the plant looks nonplussed. It remains unmoved and undamaged, although the same cannot be said of the environment it lives in. The misguided protagonist of the story, at last, approaches his elders and reprimands them. "You gave me a number of elaborate and idle reasons why I should not pull up this shrub," he says. "Why did you not give me the two good reasons: first, that I can't; second, that I should damage everything else if I even tried it on?"[101] At last, the boy has grown up. The adolescent spirit of rage and revolt has been tamed by consequence. The clear voice of reason is heard in the end as it becomes clear that it is not possible to win against the roots of the world.

In this parable, the roots of the world represent the invisible as enduring and unchanging. If moderns tend to be preoccupied with surfaces and superficial changes, the prophetic mind is preoccupied with what is deep, hidden, and often inarticulable. This unchanging invisible world may be dynamic, as implied by the metaphor of the wind in the trees, but it remains permanent. To know what is real, to seek to understand the invisible context, presumes that the order of the merely apparent is secondary. The roots

---

99. Chesterton, *Daily News*, 17 August 1907.
100. Chesterton, *Daily News*, 17 August 1907.
101. Chesterton, *Daily News*, 17 August 1907.

of the world are more real than the trees and the branches. The invisible wind is more real than the movement of the trees in the wind.

Frank Sheed contends, referring to Chesterton, "When a man is as right as that in his forecasts, there is some reason to think he may be right in his premises."[102] Chesterton had solid premises against which he could measure the world he saw. We likewise need a fixed vision, an unmoving star, and clear premises to guide us through a world of illusions and fluctuations.[103] The world is always changing, often unexpectedly and significantly. And, as hermeneutical thinkers are especially aware, consciousness is historically shaped. One cannot therefore read Chesterton without becoming aware of how context-dependent were the concerns he wrote about. We cannot read *Eugenics and Other Evils* (1922), for example, without becoming aware of the world in which and for which that book was written.[104] The word *eugenics*, coined by Francis Galton in the year Chesterton was born,[105] is not widely used now. Still, while eugenics technologies have altered and while the language on the subject has changed, the principles that governed Chesterton's writings on the subject have not changed at all. His arguments there remain pertinent for our time, even if they would need to be slightly adjusted to be understood now. Similarly, careful historical inquiry into the feminist cause of Chesterton's time shows us why he said what he did about the feminism of his own day. Although women in the West no longer campaign for suffrage, it would be an error to assume that what Chesterton said about feminism is therefore no longer applicable in its entirety. After all, many of the philosophical tenets of the Suffragettes are still with us, residues of a bygone age. While various kinds of feminism have come and gone, as if it is an ideological movement that has yet to figure out its own premises and arguments, Chesterton's consistent search for deeper principles makes his writings pertinent for us too.

But a fixed vision is not enough. The world is filled not only with stabilities but with combinations, patterns, and mixtures, as well as anomalies. As Chesterton contends, to recognize the truth of anything, it helps to recognize that thinking is a romance. Thoughts are romantic. This proposal is not irrelevant to the question of Chesterton's prescience. "It takes two thoughts to make a world," he says. "One thought without the next, and balancing thought, is as barren as Adam without Eve. It repeats itself; but it

---

102. Ahlquist, *G. K. Chesterton*, 177.
103. Chesterton, *Collected Works, Volume 1*, 249.
104. Chesterton, *Collected Works, Volume 4*, 294–418.
105. Galton, "On Men of Science," 227–36.

cannot reproduce itself. It breeds no new thoughts."[106] Note the stress here on a *balancing thought*. It is no foundation for insight, and no support for prescience or relevance, to treat thoughts merely promiscuously. Combining ideas at random according to arbitrary nominalist whims may produce some interesting diversions, but such an approach will only occasionally allow for insight. Mixing "anything and everything" is no sign of sane sense.[107]

Against flights of fancy, Chesterton wants to see the actuality and not merely the possibility. This is to say, it matters what one's foundation is with regard to thinking. To be as prescient as he was requires a foundation in what is real and true. In more metaphysical language, one needs to have a sense of how the thought of *actuality* and the thought of *potentiality* dance together. The modern tendency, unfortunately, as commonly reinforced by contemporary liberal-democratic ideology, is to emphasize *potentiality* often at the expense of *actuality*. This produces more degeneration than generativity. To perceive clearly, we need to get the tension between the actual and the potential right, keeping in mind the concrete aspects of existence and temporality.

This is one step closer to articulating where we should begin to understand Chesterton's gift for prophecy. But to get even closer, it helps to consider another short Chestertonian story, which goes that there "was once a man who, when he was told that his salary would be doubled at the tenth year of his work, said he would begin with the tenth year."[108] Chesterton explains that "the modern rational world is very like that man; like that man it thinks itself very practical when it is only very greedy. It is too greedy ever to be practical."[109] People ought to know that "in all arguments there is a first principle and a first deduction and a second deduction," and so on.[110] But the presentist trend or recency bias in Chesterton's day, and today as well, is to say, "'Let us begin at the fourth deduction. Let us begin at the sixth proposition. Do not let us begin at theory, for that is beginning at the beginning. Let us begin at practice. Let us begin at the end.'"[111] Again, this points to the importance of context and knowing what is real. It suggests, furthermore, that we should have a way of thinking through the meaning of such things. We must not only understand individual premises, in other words, but also the laws of a situation, symbols, gathering principles,

---

106. Chesterton. *Daily News*, 28 December 1912.
107. Chesterton, *Illustrated London News*, 15 December 1928.
108. Chesterton, *Daily News*, 7 July 1906.
109. Chesterton, *Daily News*, 7 July 1906.
110. Chesterton, *Daily News*, 7 July 1906.
111. Chesterton, *Daily News*, 7 July 1906.

patterns, pictures, and stories of meaning. First principles are forms and not just content. They refer to the mediation of being and not just to objects of immediate perception.

The loss of first principles is indicated by the moods of the boy in Chesterton's parable of the roots of the world. The boy takes action but ignores the necessity of understanding. He is a pragmatist, so he does not know what he is doing or undoing. He is a pragmatist who does not realize that pragmatism is, at best, only a preliminary guide to truth.[112] In the long run, his pragmatism cannot work. It is like promoting good etiquette without any reference to the good of others that etiquette is meant to serve. And so, against the modern trend of beginning without considering beginnings, Chesterton explains: "For this reason I have always engaged, and always shall engage, whenever opportunity offers, in any sort of discussion on the first principles of human existence."[113] Unfortunately, controversies and controversialists tend to begin "not with any primary principle" but rather "with a great motley mass, not only of mere assumptions, but often of mere associations. They start with everything they are used to, without even finding out what it is."[114] Chesterton's preoccupation with first principles allows him to reorientate himself constantly. From his approach, we can learn how we might reorientate ourselves today. Where do we find ourselves now? Where are we headed? Where should we be going? What principles should we recover, preserve, abandon, modify, and revolutionize? To ask such questions and to dare to answer them requires a bold idealism, which Chesterton is only too delighted to supply.

Chesterton calls for idealism, which he takes to mean "considering everything in its practical essence. Idealism only means that we should consider a poker in reference to poking before we discuss its suitability for wife-beating; that we should ask if an egg is good for practical poultry before we decide that the egg is bad enough for practical politics."[115] We should know what things are, in their essence, before we can understand how they may be understood or misunderstood, used or abused. "When things will not work, you must have the thinker, the man who has some doctrine about why they work at all."[116] In Chesterton's writings, we find not only a desire to ensure a right proportion between act and potency but a desire to reestablish a right relationship between *theoria* (contemplation) and *praxis* (action). It may

---

112. Chesterton, *Collected Works, Volume 1*, 239–40.
113. Chesterton, *Daily News*, 7 July 1906.
114. Chesterton, *Illustrated London News*, 21 November 1925.
115. Chesterton, *Collected Works, Volume 4*, 43.
116. Chesterton, *Collected Works, Volume 4*, 43.

seem counterintuitive but contemplation ought to be first. We must first, as the Thomistic tradition holds, know what is true; only then will we be capable of being wise about what we ought to do.

As Chesterton contends, by referring to a famous quote by Virgil, to perceive things rightly requires, "*rerum cognoscere causas.*"[117] This further clarifies his concern with first principles. We need to know the *causes* of things. "This is the essential idea," he writes elsewhere, "that all good argument consists in beginning with the indispensable thing and then disputing everything else in the light of it. It is of great working value in many modern discussions, if its general principle is understood."[118] One potent example of Chesterton's understanding of this idea and its importance is found in an essay published in 1934. There he discusses various aspects of German politics and especially some disturbing developments around the figure of Hitler. Chesterton begins by referring to the analogy of a "photographic negative."[119] Photographic negatives are negatives without being negations and without being reflective of the negative spirit. Together with the process of creating a photograph, they are, paradoxically, negatives that affirm. They symbolize an insight for Chesterton that if you want to understand anything, whether fashion, fanaticism, or fascism, the last thing you should do is to look at the thing itself. Do not attempt to conceive of things in isolation from the world around them, for doing so ensures that you land up only with misconceptions. The "right way to understand Fascism," he claims, "is *not* to look at the Fascists."[120] As with any drama in existence, "there is always something at once inadequate and exaggerated about the figures that actually take the stage, when it has been thus cleared for action."[121] The "wiser way" to understand what is happening on the world's stage "is to look at the state of the stage [itself], and all that led to the clearance."[122] Chesterton offers the somewhat parallel example of the French Revolution, which he contends can be understood only "if you study it a long time before it occurred."[123] The intelligibility of things is not in things alone but in their enworldedness; in how they inhabit their worlds across time.

To understand things as enworlded is equal to knowing the *principle*. Chesterton explicitly links first principles to causality. This stress on first

---

117. Chesterton, *Collected Works, Volume 4*, 43.
118. Chesterton, *Illustrated London News*, 7 November 1908.
119. Chesterton, *Illustrated London News*, 16 June 1934.
120. Chesterton, *Illustrated London News*, 16 June 1934; emphasis added.
121. Chesterton, *Illustrated London News*, 16 June 1934.
122. Chesterton, *Illustrated London News*, 16 June 1934.
123. Chesterton, *Illustrated London News*, 16 June 1934.

principles and causes is echoed in an essay in which he considers the possibility that America will negatively influence the culture of British people in the future.[124] He observes the importance of attending not only to events and things but to the "forms" of things.[125] To perceive things well, their *forms* have to be compared with another *form*, namely the form, the photographic negative, of reality. If we want to discover influences on and intimations of the future, we must know more than just the "logic" of events, as modern determinists would. We must consider how forms interact with formal causality, by mirroring or deviating from or even denying it. We can know, for instance, what a revolution stands for by the world of meaning it wants to overturn and the aims it wants to achieve, as well as by the aimless anarchies it wants to establish.[126]

Above I mentioned Chesterton's example of how high-heeled shoes would get out of hand in the future. Perhaps he is parodying the second-rate prophets of his time. Even so, he hits on the important point, that one might easily imagine shoes becoming less practical because of a common feature of the modern world. Modern people, Chesterton says, tend to neglect "the sacred duty of Thinking About Boots."[127] Here he suggests a possibility not by taking a trend as a rule, as so many of his contemporaries did, but by taking it as a violation of a rule. It may be a transgression of a rule emerging, in part, out of an unconscious desire to figure out what the rule is supposed to be. As with the boy in the story of the roots of the world, certain oppositions may, in the end, prove instructive.

Practically and metaphysically speaking, "Thinking About Boots" would mean walking "backwards in your moral and philosophical boots till you find the ancient archetypal boots from which all boots have come."[128] Many moderns fail to carry out the arduous legwork of such thinking. They fail to walk a mile in their own shoes, so they mistake wisdom for retrogression. Arriving at a deformation of boots is endemic in the modern forgetting of the form of boots. The collateral benefit of understanding this is that it becomes easier to speculate about various possible deformations. Once you have a sense of the divine idea, to use Platonist language, any matter gains a meaning that might otherwise be overlooked. This is just one instance of many instances where Chesterton, the prophet who dismissed

---

124. Chesterton, *Illustrated London News*, 2 February 1924.
125. Chesterton, *Illustrated London News*, 1 March 1924.
126. Chesterton, *Illustrated London News*, 21 November 1908.
127. Chesterton, *Illustrated London News*, 17 May 1930.
128. Chesterton, *Illustrated London News*, 17 May 1930.

so many sham prophets, has proven so strikingly prescient. He saw clearly ahead because he saw the form, which Aristotle called the *formal cause*.

I am well aware that Chesterton is not alone in being so prescient. A host of other thinkers have had many brilliant insights into their own time and into the future, many of whom have nothing to do with Chesterton. Certainly, many prescient thinkers would not agree with Chesterton's metaphysical assumptions, although arguably their prescience is owed to their having some residue of a metaphysics akin to the one he adopted. Tellingly, though, many of the thinkers who are now widely recognized to have been so prescient about what was to come are, if only in a qualified sense, Chestertonians. I think here especially of C. S. Lewis, Marshall McLuhan, and René Girard. Even where these thinkers differ from Chesterton, a similar preoccupation with formal causality in their work is unmistakable to anyone who knows what to look for. To see this is to know that a discussion of formal causality is by no means just an abstract issue. It is not merely theoretical. The quintessential Chestertonian question is how to come into contact with reality. Put otherwise, how might we better understand the roots of the world? We need, as Chesterton suggests, a telescope by which we can see the star we live on,[129] and it is just such a telescope that I present in this book.

I view Chesterton's writings through four lenses or hermeneutical refractions provided by four thinkers. I do this not only to highlight certain facets of Chesterton's work that might otherwise remain concealed but also to build on the foundation he has established for us. Two of the thinkers I involve as conversation partners preceded Chesterton, Plato and Aristotle, and two of them came after him, the Catholic philosophers Marshall McLuhan and William Desmond. I begin with Desmond, before discussing Plato, Aristotle, and finally, McLuhan. With the lenses in question polished and the telescope constructed, and with the light of Chesterton considered through the work of these other minds, we can begin to better see as he saw and so also better understand what he understood. Put otherwise, my method involves a certain education of attention; it helps us to focus on the nature of formal causality in Chesterton so that we may gain a clearer sense of what sort of world we live in, as compared to what sort of world we ought to live in, and what sort of world we might expect to live in tomorrow, next week, or perhaps well into the future. Still, what I offer here is by no means a manual on how to be prophetic. I can provide only a few clues into this grand Chestertonian art, one that was caught up in his unique being and character. However, I remain adamant to the end, as Chesterton did, that

---

129. Chesterton, *Tremendous Trifles*, v–vi; Chesterton, *Defendant*, 12–13.

predicting the future should always remain a secondary concern at best. We should not get so caught up in looking ahead that we fail to see the truth that is right in front of us.

2

Being True

G. K. Chesterton Through William Desmond's Fourfold

WILLIAM DESMOND OFFERS THE first lens through which I consider Chesterton's attention to formal causation. Here, it is worth bringing to mind Desmond's conception of metaphysics, and especially his fourfold, as a way of being true to reality. The question of being and the mediation of being in Desmond's work opens a way for articulating what Hugh Kenner refers to as Chesterton's "metaphysical intuition of being."[1] It illuminates his generous and jubilant posture towards first principles and causes. Chesterton was mindful, and I want to be similarly mindful, that the word *being* often carries with it a rather vague atmosphere, unlike the atmosphere implied by the *ens* of Aquinas.[2] However, if the paradox may be forgiven, the idea is profoundly concrete. Being true regards attuning ourselves rightly to reality and participating rightly, with our whole lives, in the order of creation.

Ultimately, as I show here, this requires a meeting of tensions that are not reducible to univocal precision, scattered equivocal indecision, or dialectical assimilation. For Chesterton, true mediation is essentially *metaxological*, a notion explained below. That so many of Chesterton's predictions have proven true, sometimes on a global scale, should not cause us to forget that his own sense of where things were going was informed by his local context and immediate concerns. To understand Chesterton's perspective as mainly metaxological is to remain humble about the nature of his claims about the future.

---

1. Kenner, *Paradox in Chesterton*, 1.
2. Chesterton, *Saint Thomas Aquinas & Saint Francis of Assisi*, 138.

In the wake of the scientific revolution and certain deadening forms of modernist presumption, the trend has been to sever the bond between objectivity and subjectivity. Consciousness in the modern West has been informed by trends that follow this severance.[3] Subjectivity and objectivity are commonly viewed as opposite, even at odds, rather than being component parts of an already reconciled whole. The hard sciences have sided with objectivity against subjectivity. The human sciences have done the opposite.[4] Errors of all kinds follow from this bifurcation of perception and being into two seemingly incompatible worlds of meaning, especially when one side of the dichotomy is elected over the other for arbitrary reasons. But this is not how Chesterton experienced the world. Arguably, this is not how anyone experiences the world, despite rationalizations to the contrary. Divorcing subjectivity and objectivity, value and fact, is entirely theoretical and yet this particular "superstition"[5] has become widely accepted as true.

Chesterton was likely drawn to the medieval world and so often accused of being a medievalist, as if that were such a terrible thing, because his sense of the world was more like that of St. Francis of Assisi, Geoffrey Chaucer, or St. Thomas Aquinas, even with their differences, than that of the average intellectual of his own time. He was a medievalist because of an affinity with the medieval mind, which saw no contest between the inner man and the outer world. For him, the world was haloed and personal, not impersonal; it participated in God and was not abandoned to its own separateness. Chesterton therefore stands as an example of how to recover a more unified and holistic perception and conception of a world always already charged with God's grandeur and guided by his providence. Chesterton's writings show a heedfulness of truth and reality that may jar with the expectations of those whose perspective has been infected by modern materialism. Still, there is no escaping how his unique way of attending to the world, especially to formal causality, ensured such relevant speculations not only about his present but also about the future that is our present. His medievalism cannot be separated from his realism and his prophetic voice. In contrast, modernism is inseparable from a dull, mechanical, and ultimately misleading way of attending to reality. No one misunderstands the future more than the modernist who is obsessed with it.

To attend to the question of what is real and how perception is part of reality is to seek to reposition ourselves by an alert awareness of being, even

---

3. See Barfield, *Saving the Appearances*.
4. Philips, *Obedience Is Freedom*, 5–6.
5. Chesterton, *Collected Works, Volume 4*, 229–51.

if, since we are finite, such awareness can only be limited and incomplete.[6] We are who we are by our unique relationship with and attention to reality. To ask the question of being, the question of what fundamentally *is*, is also to question our posture towards it, as well as to question how we ought to be true to it. Chesterton draws our attention to the fact that attention itself, maximally considered as a resonance between our being and being itself, is reality for us; how we attend to the world with our whole selves determines what truth and meaning we find in it. In theological terms, what and how we worship shapes our attunement to existence.[7] While subsequent chapters reveal aspects of Chesterton's work that are Platonist, Aristotelean, and Thomistic, he shares with Desmond an appreciation for our intimacy with the *why* of being that fits well with an Augustinian desire for ultimacy. Desmond echoes what Chesterton calls the "Romance of Orthodoxy."[8]

Casting Chesterton as a metaphysician may seem at first to be a hyperbolic category error. No doubt, it is risky. He preferred to be thought of as just a journalist. However, this preferred title is significant for its metaphysical implications. Chesterton does not present us with a neat set of abstractions or a careful analytic of being even while he is aware of metaphysical concerns. What he does, joyfully and so astutely, is draw our attention to common miracles, ordinary wonders, and the way that our thinking might reveal or conceal such things. Given his attention to the everyday, he presents us with what I want to call a *journalistic metaphysics*, which bears no resemblance to so much anti-metaphysical journalism today. His way of interpreting the world is closely akin to philosophical hermeneutics because it has an existentialist focus without existentialist excesses.[9] He does not, for instance, place existence over and above essence as Sartre does. Still, there are good reasons for considering Chesterton a philosopher and metaphysician even if he is one with no portfolio.[10]

Metaphysicians preoccupy themselves with the question of being. Metaphysics ponders the significance and meaning of being.[11] This implies understanding why there is being and not nothing[12] and why meaning persists despite gestures towards meaninglessness. Why, to reference a

---

6. Desmond, *Being and the Between*, 3.
7. Psalm 115:4–8.
8. Chesterton, *Collected Works, Volume 1*, 329.
9. See Reyburn, *Seeing Things as They Are*.
10. See Lauer, *Philosopher Without Portfolio*.
11. Desmond, *Being and the Between*, 3.
12. Desmond, *Being and the Between*, 4.

Chestertonian thought, is this "the best of all impossible worlds"?[13] Such abstract concerns are far from trifling. After all, the person who takes no trouble to prudently answer the question of being will find the question settled for him by default, and probably not at all satisfactorily. If a person turns out to be an incompetent metaphysician, it would prove disastrous to renounce the call of metaphysics entirely. To do so would mean denying the claim being has on us, for being always makes a claim on us. Metaphysical thinking, as perpetually "relative to the question of being," involves an attempt to articulate "the milieu of mindfulness within which this question can be heard."[14] Reality wants to speak and we need to have ears to hear what it is saying.

Desmond approaches the *meta* of *metaphysics* as a twin concern with the *beyond* of being, implied by the old question of why there is being and not nothing, and the idea of being *in the midst* of being. To be is to be interested in being. We make sense of things and find sense in things while always already being immersed in being. We understand the drama of being as actors on the stage, not as detached spectators viewing everything from a distance. Metaphysics thus always begins *in media res*; in the midst of real things.[15] This sense of the gigantism of being should foster humility in us.[16] Hopefully, this will not be a misplaced humility that denigrates certainty and undermines reason. It should be a humility that recognizes our contingency even as we notice signals of transcendence and permanence. We are relative to the roots of the world and we are relative to God. We see through a glass darkly, and yet we do see.[17]

Arguably, this sense of contingency has always been part of any reasonable metaphysical awareness. To aspire to understand the loftiest things by no means denies our human vulnerabilities. Unfortunately, in recent history, metaphysics has become almost a dirty word in the mouths of some philosophers, which may simply mean that even if metaphysics remains important on reasonable grounds, it has simply become unfashionable. Perhaps the consecrated has been rendered profane by the secular order. For some, the word connotes everything that's been wrong with philosophy so far.[18] However, the impugning of metaphysics has relied on a misguided reframing of metaphysics as a violence-loving tyrant, as too pompous and self-assured.

13. Chesterton, *Charles Dickens*, 213.
14. Desmond, *Being and the Between*, 3.
15. Desmond, *Being and the Between*, 5.
16. Chesterton, *Defendant*, 129–38.
17. 1 Corinthians 13:1–13.
18. Simpson, *Religion, Metaphysics, and the Postmodern*, 2–3.

Such a cynical perspective by no means captures what decent metaphysicians are concerned with. The essence of metaphysics is not violence but peace; it is order, not disorder; it is truth, not power. Being is not fundamentally a state of perpetual rivalry but suggests a harmonious, if often perplexing, world of relations. It is up to thinkers to discern this. The aim of metaphysics is not to dissolve particularity but to clarify what reality is like. Desmond's "dissident" metaphysics[19] shows this by insisting on bridging the personal and the universal.[20] The aim is not to enslave being or to be enslaved to the demands of being but to be true to the betweenness, the cruciform nature, of being. The aim is to be true to being as an intimate immensity.

To claim what Plato calls the *metaxu*, the middle, is to encourage a mindfulness of one's betweenness. Man is both divine breath and worldly dirt, both angel and beast. And yet, he is also, in his uniqueness within the created order, neither. To think metaphysically is therefore to admit a powerlessness before the world of meaning even while we recognize our strength and desire to seek out and, to some measure, hold and be held by the truth of real things. We imagine the beyond from the between. Our intimacy with truth is therefore also considered from the between. It is only possible to arrive at the universal from the middle. Chesterton claims that this very sense of the between is at the heart of his philosophy. Famously, he tells a parable about a man who sets off to discover a new country only to arrive back in his home country under the mistaken impression that it is somewhere new. He makes the "most enviable mistake" of planting his homeland's flag in the soil of his homeland.[21] This story suggests "the main problem for philosophers,"[22] as Chesterton sees it. The problem is how we can admit astonishment at the world while also feeling at home in it. Wonder and constancy ought to exist alongside each other, and neither should exist at the expense of the other. "How," Chesterton asks, "can this queer cosmic town, with its many-legged citizens, with its monstrous and ancient lamps, how can this world give us at once the fascination of a strange town and the comfort and honour of being our own town?"[23] How can our awe of reality harmonize with our intimacy with reality? How can primal astonishment survive welcome?

---

19. Simpson, *Religion, Metaphysics, and the Postmodern*, 2–3.
20. Desmond, *Intimate Universal*, 1–19.
21. Chesterton, *Collected Works, Volume 1*, 212.
22. Chesterton, *Collected Works, Volume 1*, 212.
23. Chesterton, *Collected Works, Volume 1*, 212.

Chesterton knows how difficult it is to articulate a philosophy that would be "true from every standpoint."[24] But we still need a philosophy that takes seriously the "double spiritual need" for a "mixture of the familiar and the unfamiliar."[25] We need a philosophy that allows for both without diluting either. Such a philosophy could not be a string of abstractions but would be a romance. It would be felt as well as thought, lived as well as contemplated. Such a romance would be true to our need for "an active and imaginative life, picturesque and full of a poetical curiosity, a life such as western man at any rate always seems to have desired."[26] This means having a sense of the strange and the secure. It does not mean that no one is allowed to make any claims of universality. Universality is not only permitted but encouraged given that our participation in reality does not mimic the shrunken universality of the lunatic who has access only to his solipsistic point of view.[27]

More than two decades after penning these thoughts in *Orthodoxy* (1908), Chesterton suggests that perception follows Aquinas's understanding that a thing perceived "becomes a part of the mind."[28] More concretely put, "the mind actually becomes the object."[29] However, "it only becomes the object and does not create the object. In other words, the object is an object; it can and does exist outside the mind, or in the absence of the mind."[30] In the process, the object "enlarges the mind of which it becomes a part. The mind conquers a new province like an emperor; but only because the mind has answered the bell like a servant."[31] This confirms Chesterton's awareness of perception as intertwined in betweenness. "The mind has opened the doors and windows," he writes, "because it is the natural activity of what is inside the house to find out what is outside the house. If the mind is sufficient to itself, it is insufficient for itself. For this feeding upon fact *is* itself; as an organ it has an object which is objective; this eating of the strange strong meat of reality."[32]

The primary way to avoid sacrificing the real to false universality is to notice that metaphysics and metaphysical thinking are intimately intertwined and already reconciled. Our job is to discover this reconciliation

---

24. Chesterton, *Collected Works, Volume 1*, 212.
25. Chesterton, *Collected Works, Volume 1*, 212.
26. Chesterton, *Collected Works, Volume 1*, 212.
27. Chesterton, *Collected Works, Volume 1*, 222.
28. Chesterton, *Saint Thomas Aquinas & Saint Francis of Assisi*, 169.
29. Chesterton, *Saint Thomas Aquinas & Saint Francis of Assisi*, 169.
30. Chesterton, *Saint Thomas Aquinas & Saint Francis of Assisi*, 169.
31. Chesterton, *Saint Thomas Aquinas & Saint Francis of Assisi*, 169.
32. Chesterton, *Saint Thomas Aquinas & Saint Francis of Assisi*, 169.

rather than to create it *ex nihilo*. One cannot answer the question of being without noticing that reality and mediation are interdependent. One cannot answer the question of being apart from an openness to the nature of the question. Being, as understood and articulated, is coextensive with the God-given consciousness that understands and articulates it. But being is also in excess of this consciousness. We know the world but we always know that there is more to be known and beyond which there is more than we can know. We feel the call of metaphysics but this call is a mystery that is both endlessly knowable and irreducible to our knowing.

To know being is to know that being transcends our minding of being. Being and mediation are enmeshed; the universal and the intimate are entwined. In intimacy, we recognize that being transcends our immediate attention. While contemplating the world we notice that we are not the source of what we are contemplating and we are not the source of our ability to contemplate it. Every *what* implies *whys* that cannot be fully spelled out, just as every stillness before being welcomes happenings not anticipated.[33] Even our wildest and most fantastical imaginings are dependent on what we have not authored. It is still possible, however, to have a sense of the universal without neglecting "the community of being that transcends any abstract universal."[34] In metaphysical mindfulness, the determinate, the indeterminate, and the overdetermined play and dance together.

Being is no object over and against us, nor are we meant to be over and against it. The strict dualism between being and the minding of being is a conceptual error derived from misrecognizing the indeterminate and patient clearing within an original ontological intimacy. Such a misrecognition confuses an opening within being for a determinate and sometimes unbridgeable chasm. Being is an advent. It happens to us, with us, as us, and within us, calling us to move beyond ourselves into a reality that is more solid than any fancy. Being is also an adventuring. It grants wonder to the wandering wonderer. "Metaphysical thinking," Desmond writes, "is precipitated in the between. We find ourselves in the midst of beings."[35]

Desmond describes the awareness of this mindful opening towards and consequent mediation of being through a fourfold structure of categories, explored in more depth below as a way to think through Chesterton's journalistic metaphysics.[36] It would be wrong, however, to regard these categories as merely convenient conceptual containers. They point to specific

---

33. Chesterton, *Daily News*, 31 March 1906.
34. Desmond, *Being and the Between*, 4.
35. Desmond, *Being and the Between*, 5.
36. Desmond, *Being and the Between*, 5.

attitudes or postures towards reality and not only to ways of defining it. They also suggest ways of speaking of the interplay of act and potency. The fourfold includes the univocal, equivocal, dialectical, and metaxological senses of being. Desmond regards the metaxological as the pinnacle of a metaphysician's awareness. It refers to a certain logic or communication (*logos*) of the between (*metaxu*). This metaxology finds being doubly mediated and is therefore like Chesterton's paradox, which is a double (*para*) glory (*doxa*) and not just an adjacent (*para*) opinion (*doxa*). This is not a nominalist naming that splits the subjective and the objective but the middle voice, like Owen Barfield's middle voice,[37] that includes and transcends the objective and subjective, as well as active and passive postures towards being. On one side of this mediation, "our perplexity shows us to be *distanced* from the truth we seek."[38] We are somehow "*other* to the truth of being" and therefore, by divine rule, also lacking in being. We are not the world we are in but only part of it. On the other side of this mediation, we are driven beyond any lack by something other within us that transcends perplexity and is not mere lack. To refer to the words of Christ, we are in the world and yet not of it.[39]

Thus, even at our most perfect, we remain hilariously insufficient. We are finite and dependent creatures, vulnerable even when we are unaware of our vulnerability. And yet our insufficiency is not the starting point for our metaphysical awareness. We begin with a sense of that foundational power of being that precedes and supersedes us, as well as the fact that it is always already with us and in us.[40] Something in us has to comprehend our lack and this cannot be mere lack. From the beginning, being is given to support our consideration of being. The tension between lack and fullness echoes Chesterton's articulation of that double sense of adventure and home. In Desmond's words, "Metaphysical perplexity is a *tense togetherness* of being at a loss *and* finding oneself at home with being."[41] He insists, "We must not fail to keep in mind both of these sides. This doubleness is both our plenitude and poverty, our grandeur and frailty, our highest call to nobility and perennial reminder of infirmity."[42] As Chesterton says, the between-being man is both "a microcosm" and "the measure of all things," although not in

---

37. See Di Fuccia, *Owen Barfield*.
38. Desmond, *Being and the Between*, 6.
39. John 15:19; 17:14–16.
40. Desmond, *Being and the Between*, 6.
41. Desmond, *Being and the Between*, 6.
42. Desmond, *Being and the Between*, 6.

Protagoras's sense.[43] He is "a creator" with nearly godlike capacities but also "a kind of cripple."[44] To attend properly to the world of people must therefore mean attending to what it means that we are superior to all things. We are called to exercise dominion over creation. But we are also utterly dependent upon creation, and are therefore called to be humble and grateful.

As we might expect, a metaxological mindfulness challenges any strictly monodirectional drive in our desire to know that would move us from a simple question to a plain answer.[45] It also challenges any conception of causality as merely moving from cause to effect or from a simple action towards a simple consequence or reaction. The question of being cannot be posed and then answered so simplistically while we dust our hands off in a moment of gleeful self-congratulation. As Chesterton is aware, "everything hides a face."[46] The immediate does not account for itself but always points beyond itself to more. What presents itself as an answer is often "the back of things."[47] It may be yet another shadow or appearance that demands further searching and questioning.[48]

A cruciform, metaxological posture finds that any answer we get renews our questions, reframes them, and breathes new life into them. Our perplexity is not dispelled by answers but reawakened.[49] The welcome of being is not the numbing of perplexity but the source of its revitalization. This is why the question of being must be asked endlessly and why first principles and causes must be returned to without ceasing; it is why children, closer to the innocence and wonder that gives rise to all wondering, ask questions without stopping and want things repeated without end.[50] They do not tire of their metaphysical perplexity as easily as grown ups do. The aim of metaphysical thinking is not to dispel wonder but to stir it and deepen it. Being presents itself always as a gratuitous abundance of meaning in search of the truth. It is not determinate or indeterminate only but also overdeterminate; it is always in excess of itself and reveals surplus meanings that cannot be contained within a finite and easily replicable identity.[51] As Simpson notes while reflecting on Desmond's work, "This excessive or gratuitous surplus

---

43. Chesterton, *Everlasting Man*, 35.
44. Chesterton, *Everlasting Man*, 36.
45. Desmond, *Being and the Between*, 6.
46. Chesterton, *Man Who Was Thursday*, 247.
47. Chesterton, *Man Who Was Thursday*, 247.
48. Chesterton, *Man Who Was Thursday*, 247.
49. Desmond, *Being and the Between*, 6.
50. Chesterton, *Collected Works, Volume 1*, 264.
51. Simpson, *Religion, Metaphysics, and the Postmodern*, 23.

of given being calls at once for a metaphysical thinking that is an act of gratitude for such gratuity."[52] This sounds remarkably Chestertonian.

I am aware that Chesterton does not articulate his thinking as Desmond does. Still, Desmond's recovery of metaphysics beautifully echoes Chesterton's perpetual concern with ensuring that we are not the sole imaginers and managers of meaning even while we retain our drive to be creative in our knowledge of the truth. Being and meaning are primary; they precede our awareness and understanding. Chesterton therefore preempts Desmond, who writes, "The advent of metaphysical thinking is in a primal astonishment. Astonishment itself is primal."[53] Being cannot be accounted for by mere cause and effect; and all accounts must remain incomplete to remain faithful to being. The ancient philosophers insisted that philosophy, as a love of wisdom, begins with wonder. Such a beginning is not a once-off but is, like the created order itself, an ongoing fact at the root of the love of wisdom. We begin with wonder and to wonder we must return.

With this in mind, we should endeavor to retain a sense of the primacy of otherness over self-consciousness as we seek to connect with what is other via what we already know. Moreover, we ought to be mindful that mediation is no enemy of being true to being but is the grace that allows us to encounter being and to be encountered by being. We feel a call to get beyond ourselves but this is only because the call precedes and grounds us. With this in mind, and with an awareness of a "two-fold mediation in beholding,"[54] Desmond proposes his fourfold. He recalls Aristotle's contention that being can be said variously, as well as the Aristotelian awareness that the multifaceted communications of being are bound together by analogy. However, he focuses specifically on how we might get beyond the erroneous assumption that immediacy, whether univocal or equivocal, suffices to allow us to encounter reality. He also notices that modern dialectical mediation fails to allow for the wonder that gives rise to our wondering.[55] In modern dialectic, the middle gives way too quickly to the same. To explore how metaphysics can best articulate its encounter with being.[56] I take each category in Desmond's fourfold in its turn, showing how it can begin to illuminate Chesterton's attention to formal causality.

---

52. Simpson, *Religion, Metaphysics, and the Postmodern*, 23.
53. Desmond, *Being and the Between*, 8.
54. Desmond, *Being and the Between*, 9.
55. Desmond, *Being and the Between*, xiii, 34.
56. Simpson, *Religion, Metaphysics, and the Postmodern*, 28.

The Univocal Sense of Being

There's an old legend about a man living in Soviet-era Russia who was suspected of stealing from the factory he worked at. Because of this, at the command of the factory manager, the man's wheelbarrow was searched by security guards. His wheelbarrow was filled with odd bits of rubbish and various personal belongings, but nothing else. And so, after many spot searches, his guilt could not be established. Years later, long after the factory had closed, one of those security guards happened to bump into that man in the street. He explained to the man that he couldn't help wanting to know, now that there would be no consequences, if he was indeed stealing from the factory. The man smiled and admitted that, yes, he was the thief. He had been stealing wheelbarrows. He had hidden what he was stealing in plain sight. The visibility of the wheelbarrows had made them invisible. "If a man had to hide a dead body," Chesterton jokes in one of his stories, "he would make a field of dead bodies to hide it in."[57]

As the legend shows and as Chesterton is aware, it is easy to believe that what we see and expect to see is all there is. We forget that we do not merely see things; we see them according to a set of attitudes, convictions, perceptual filters, and conditions of understanding that are so obvious to us that we have forgotten they are there at all. We find ourselves daily caught up in habits of thought and settled ways of acting in the world. We listen to and utter phrases without necessarily noticing their extravagance. We utter so many dead metaphors, for instance, that we fail to notice them as metaphors. We typically communicate while assuming that our meaning should be readily apparent to those we are speaking to, even when they do not necessarily share our assumptions. Sometimes, we ourselves may not be aware of the assumptions between our words. In our standard expressions, in other words, we tend to gravitate towards a way of thinking univocally about the truth. We ensure, in this way, that we are not just confused by what we do not know but that we are also confused by what we know without knowing that we know it.

The univocal sense of being, in Desmond's vocabulary, implies this urge we all have to render being as determinately intelligible as possible.[58] This is already suggested in the word *univocal*, which implies a unified, singular voice without which an encounter with reality cannot be articulated. The univocal sense may suggest that we do not see the back of things after all, and that we do not even see only the front; we see the whole. Admittedly,

---

57. Chesterton, *Father Brown*, 154.
58. Desmond, *Being and the Between*, 16.

we need something of this sense of the overt and the undeniable to cope with our everyday lives. It is the most practical sense of being we can adhere to. But problems arise when this is the only sense of being we trust. Our search for meaning naturally seeks out sameness against a backdrop of multiplicity.[59] We adore certainty and quiver anxiously in the face of the inexplicable. As a result, we gravitate towards univocity as we do towards familiar faces and friendly places. As a way of apprehending and speaking of the world of meaning, univocity emphasizes a cozy immediacy, immediate unity, identity, simplicity, and uniformity. It gives priority to the represented over the presented. Univocity prizes immediate obviousness over nuance, closeness over necessary distance, and efficiency over excellence. It gives priority to flattened-out or formulaic conclusions over depth, subtlety, nuance, and an analogical sense of universality. It attends to specifics but at the expense of continuity. This is not always inevitable but the univocal sense of being, especially when excluding the other senses of being, tends to view the world as manipulable by our concepts and theories.

Univocity tends to ignore the halo on being; it forgets that things always suggest more than themselves. But any attempt to remove the halo on being can act as an inadvertent and often unwelcome reminder of the equivocal sense of being discussed below. The more we try to confine being to a univocal attitude and pronouncements, the more we are likely to feel, quite rightly, that being cannot be trapped within conceptual confines. Being has a wildness to it. It will forever escape our single-mindedness. One of the consequences of sticking too rigidly to the univocal sense, even when it begins to hint at a rebellion against its own univocity, real patterns in being become difficult, if not impossible, to discern. The formal cause is therefore somewhat foreclosed to aggressive univocalizers. Such univocalizers will see patterns since consciousness is naturally receptive to patterns. However, to remove the halo on being is to inevitably end up with mistaken patterns; that is, with juxtapositions that fail to add definition, correlations that deny causation, panchrestons, and straw men, as well as other logical fallacies and ontological misapprehensions. Because the univocal sense prioritizes parts over the whole, it becomes easier for any grain of truth to be warped and set up as a fetish.

Funnily enough, the univocal emphasis on oneness can take on a variety of shapes.[60] For instance, univocity can be aesthetic, logical, ontological, mathematical, transcendental, pantheistic, and so on. In all of

---

59. Desmond, *God and the Between*, 49.

60. Desmond, *Desire, Dialectic, and Otherness*, 6; Desmond, *Being and the Between*, xii; Desmond, *Perplexity and Ultimacy*, 12.

these different univocities, each of which offers an anchor for the univocal mind, an attempt is made to expel difference. The multiplicities in being are rebelled against by univocity. The very idea of mediation, despite its demonstrable inescapability, is denied authority. Being and intelligibility are wrongly perceived as coextensive in their determinacy. Put more crudely, the univocalizer sees an incontestable identity between what he knows and what is real. Similarly, to perceive and speak univocally is to desire no excess to escape perception and speech. The univocalizer would say, "To be is to be intelligible; to be intelligible is to be determinate; to be determinate is to be univocal."[61] There is an immediate unity here between thought and things and between the self and the other. Certainly, what is known and understood can seem to be all there is and what escapes knowledge can seem to cease to be real. This is perhaps nowhere better exemplified than by any anti-theistic rationalist who denies reality to anything that cannot be accounted for within an unquestioned univocal frame. Such a person might offhandedly deny miracles, not primarily because they are improbable but because they cannot be scientifically proven. In principle, then, to think of being univocally is to assume that being can be known fully and without any remainder.[62]

More positively, however, univocity suggests an immediacy to our earliest immersion in the world and pays homage to our desire to let this sense of immediacy persevere. But when retained without question or questioning, especially as a result of a particular constriction of attention, it suggests only a limited mindfulness of this immersion. Univocity is, perhaps surprisingly, only comprehensible as an abstraction that emerges in response to the ongoing interplay of identity and difference, as well as being and becoming.[63] We may want to believe in the obviousness of what we perceive and the obviousness of what we communicate. However, any obviousness we encounter in the world has already been mediated. Univocity is always mediated, although it relies on our forgetting of that mediation. It does this in favor of the comfort of confident certainty. At its worst, univocal certainty becomes a substitute for truth. Univocity has to be forgetful of mediation to persist in its stubborn slide into brittle fundamentalism.

Univocity is conclusive even if it has not accounted for all the facts. It knows somehow even when it does not know how it knows. It confidently words the between in terms that apparently require no interpretation. It sticks closely to the facts and the available information, as well as to

---

61. Desmond, *God and the Between*, 50.
62. Simpson, *Religion, Metaphysics, and the Postmodern*, 29.
63. Desmond, *Being and the Between*, 47.

unquestionable doctrines, as if there were no between at all. It is a deadening of any sense of the between that produces such rigidity. A decline in poetic speech fosters this literalistic mode of attention to the world.[64] This does not mean that metaphors disappear, only that metaphorical awareness is dampened. Mediation persists but the univocal mind wants to downplay or radically suppress this often awkward and unwieldy dimension of reality, especially since mediation challenges egotism and idolatry. Univocity tends to prize what is obvious to perception. Whatever is most apparent to the univocalizing mind is all there is and all that matters. Why would anyone look further, if this is the case?

At its best, however, the univocal sense of being can still be true to being, albeit in a limited sense. As we make our way through the world, as I have already suggested, we rely on simple identifications and straightforward speech. Often, it is according to the univocal sense that our understanding first takes shape, although the halo on being is still present in our earliest experiences. A small child, Chesterton notices, is often amazed when someone opens a door in a story and does not need anything more magical to happen to be amazed.[65] The univocal sense is something we rely on even as adults. Our shopping lists and directions to new places should not be difficult to interpret for purely functional reasons. Rules, appliance instructions, and scientific descriptions necessarily quiet down all other senses of being. We may provide definitions and simple methods, for instance, to delimit what we know and to prevent misunderstanding. Given our common reliance upon univocity, we may be surprised when we are interpreted in a way we had not intended. Such occasions are noteworthy if only because they show us that what we regard as self-evident and free of mediation is always reliant on mediations that we have become accustomed to. To be able to communicate univocally requires a prior mindfulness of being that is not univocal.

The richness of perception has to be whittled down to the univocal, not built up from fragments composed of univocal elements. An already-present transcendence in our minding of being has to be filtered for us first before we can forget the inescapability of mediation. Again, the univocal is an important facet of life and of our articulations of meaning. It is a way to confront and appreciate the limits that accompany our movements in the world. But there are significant dangers when the univocal sense of being predominates, as Chesterton warns us. It is one thing to be able to occasionally speak univocally but quite another to assume that this is the only way

---

64. See Barfield, *Poetic Diction*.
65. Chesterton, *Collected Works, Volume 1*, 257.

of speaking. To render the univocal sense absolute is to insist that figures do not only *need* no ground but somehow also *have* no ground. When separated from the between, the univocal sense betrays being. It fails to think of being as other to thought, and so it can only fail to attend properly to causation. Univocity, in its most alarmingly absolute form, tends to reduce causality to monocausality. This is one of modernity's favorite errors, although moderns do not tend to think of it as an error. Many, if not most, instances of reducing causality to cause and effect are instances not only of refusing mediation, which is central to understanding causality, but of reducing a complex of causes to a single, usually efficient, cause.

The epitome of absolutizing univocity is found in the person Chesterton calls the maniac, who "believes in himself" without realizing that "complete self-confidence is a weakness."[66] He is thoroughly worldly and this is why he cannot understand the world.[67] He is a "man of science" who is convinced that we should begin only with the "facts."[68] Chesterton is quick to note that the ancient masters of religion were just as set on facts as the modern masters of science, only they refused to limit facts to being merely material things.[69] Sin is a fact as much as a piranha. Virtue is a fact as much as a cabbage or the number 9. The mind is a fact as much as the brain, and looking for the mind inside the brain is like looking for flight inside the wings of a sparrow or a song in the syrinx of a nightingale. Facts cannot be reduced to mere elements in being but should include principles of design, patterns, and proportions as well.[70] Facts without form deform since they can easily be turned against the whole. The manifest, in univocal or equivocal form, can be instrumentalized against the hidden. The one that Chesterton calls a maniac fails to take into account all the facts because he only accepts some facts while rejecting all others. He sees only what he expects to see and therefore misses everything else that is presented to him. His mind is shut to the superabundances of being and so he loses contact with being itself. In short, he is oblivious to formal causality.

"To the insane man," Chesterton writes, "his insanity is quite prosaic, because it is quite true. A man who thinks himself a chicken is to himself as ordinary as a chicken. A man who thinks he is a bit of glass is to himself as dull as a bit of glass."[71] What is troublesome here is the "homogeneity of

---

66. Chesterton, *Collected Works, Volume 1*, 216.
67. Chesterton, *Collected Works, Volume 1*, 216.
68. Chesterton, *Collected Works, Volume 1*, 216.
69. Chesterton, *Collected Works, Volume 1*, 217.
70. Chesterton, *Illustrated London News*, 22 February 1930.
71. Chesterton, *Collected Works, Volume 1*, 218.

his mind."[72] Everything is flattened out, diluted, and devalued. Everything conforms to a formula but fails, possibly because of this, to conform to a form. The world is relieved of depth and richness. It becomes a mere abstract diagram in the mind of a nutter. In discussing this maniac, Chesterton frequently contrasts him with the poet, a symbol of metaxological sanity. This is a vital contrast for understanding his work as a whole. The poet helps us to see why Chesterton takes issue with the maniac. In essence, the poet is not interested in forcing the world to conform to his tapered prejudgements. The poet refuses to cling to some technique that would claim to solve being before encountering it. He refuses to regard being as something to be solved. Consciousness is not reducible to problem-solving. The poet wants a world to live in, a world that is larger than his capacity to understand it. He wants a world that brims with fascination. He wants to encounter things that he did not invent and interpret things that confound his immediate impressions. And he wants others to be able to do the same.

Perhaps against expectation, it is the feeling of being dwarfed by the world and being at its mercy that grants to the poet a sense of belonging and security. Perplexity offers welcome. The poet is aware of the world in a particular way. He feels what comes into consciousness and is mindful of the life within the happening of being. He undergoes being and does not merely grasp it. He refuses to reduce being to having. He identifies with being not as a scientist identifies an object but as a creator who identifies with the dynamism within the creative process and as a creature who feels grateful that he was made. In other words, he stands between being and becoming; and between letting be and receiving. He regards being as a gift, generously offered.

The maniac, in contrast, reduces the gift to the given. What is given is just there as given. The maniac has placed himself above the world and above reason and is therefore plagued by distortions and disquiet. He fails to identify with the happening of being and only notices its products. He notices only what already fits his frame of mind. The result can only be "mental exhaustion," or worse.[73] While the poet can fit his head into the heavens without any trouble, the maniac attempts the impossible; he tries to fit the heavens into his head and, as a consequence, his head splits.[74] By restricting himself only to a univocal attunement to being, he inadvertently refuses to understand anything. Crucially, the contrast between the poet and the manic is not offered by Chesterton as a way to simplistically split the world

---

72. Chesterton, *Collected Works, Volume 1*, 218.
73. Chesterton, *Collected Works, Volume 1*, 220.
74. Chesterton, *Collected Works, Volume 1*, 220.

into two types of people. There are different kinds of poets, with varying talents and capacities, just as there would also be varieties of lunatics. Often poets have to resist their own inner lunatic, just as lunatics must recover their inner poet. Nevertheless, this division highlights two general postures towards reality, one that desires to be true to being in the fullest possible way and another that replaces being true to being with being true only to one's conception of being.

Chesterton is still well aware that a homogeneous way of attending to the world can and does come up with brilliant explanations for things. The maniac can often explain everything by the few facts he has selected from the vastness of reality. However, he cannot explain them in a large way. He can see a lot as figures appear to him everywhere. But formal cause is sacrificed. His mind moves "in a perfect but narrow circle."[75] While we can admit that the maniac's explanation can account for "a great deal," we must also notice how much it leaves out of its explanations.[76] To attend to things simply or simplistically, it must insist on a great deal too many omissions. What is the essence of such insanity? It is simply "reason without root, reason in the void."[77] It is reason closed off from formal causation.

Chesterton wants us to see that "the moment we have the fact we cannot help feeling as if it [is] something more than a fact."[78] Let us not denigrate facts, then; let us rather be mindful of how facts fit in a world.[79] We cannot help but feel, when we are true to our poetic, porous selves, that the fact belongs in and to a context. To borrow a distinction from Gestalt psychology, the *figure* belongs within and to the *ground*, just as the ground belongs to the figure. "The street appears lazy in the book of facts," says Chesterton, "but is busy and fruitful in the book of life."[80] "Statistics, for example, never give the truth" on their own "because they never give the *reasons*."[81] They are not accounts of cause and are, in this, not accountable to the whole. Facts are formless and can only be intelligible when informed. For this reason, Chesterton encourages his readers to attend to what is *meant* and not just to what is *said*. Against the rise of various forms of scientism, literalism, and the rising tide of univocalization in the modern world, we need to recover the primary poetic sense that we are often socialized to filter out. We

---

75. Chesterton, *Collected Works, Volume 1*, 222.
76. Chesterton, *Collected Works, Volume 1*, 223.
77. Chesterton, *Collected Works, Volume 1*, 224.
78. Chesterton, *Illustrated London News*, 18 November 1905.
79. Chesterton, *Collected Works, Volume 5*, 241.
80. Chesterton, *Illustrated London News*, 18 November 1905.
81. Chesterton, *Illustrated London News*, 18 November 1905.

do this quite naturally already and often simply need to become aware that we do this. Ontologically speaking, we are already poets. We are artists and creators.[82] We read between the lines all the time. We feel our way through the world in ways that conscious attention does not always notice.

Given the bad habits of thought and action that moderns are prone to, Chesterton wants to wake us up to a more mystical and creative mindfulness. We must discover that even the univocal sense is dependent on much more than univocity to be what it is. As Chesterton's character Basil Grant says in *The Club of Queer Trades* (1905), "how facts" can "obscure the truth. . . . Every detail points to something, certainly; but generally to the wrong thing. Facts point in all directions . . . like the thousands of twigs on a tree. It is only the life of the tree that has unity and goes up—only the green blood that springs, like a fountain, at the stars."[83] How can we find this unity? We begin to get a preliminary but not final sense of this "life of the tree" in a second sense of being named and discussed by Desmond.

The Equivocal Sense of Being

One way to think of the univocal sense as that unmediated sense of determinate meaning, especially as having gained ascendency in the wake of modernity, is as a flight from the equivocal sense of being. The certainty offered by univocity acts as a refuge from the uncertainty spurred on by equivocity. As with the univocal sense of being, the equivocal sense denotes a default of immediacy and obliviousness to mediation. As with univocity, this seeming lack of mediation cannot exist apart from mediation. It involves misinterpreting mediated immediacy as if it is unmediated immediacy. It similarly reflects a corrupted desire to retain meaning as a given and as a possession, rather than as a gift. But unlike the univocal sense, the equivocal sense attends to plurality instead of unity, difference instead of similarity, and ambiguity instead of clarity.[84] It reminds us of the inescapability of difference, which takes more shapes than words could ever capture. It is suggestive without necessarily clarifying what is being suggested. Equivocity discloses reality as always existing by implication. However, what is implied is irresolvable when equivocity reigns. It may be rather confusing since order is not obvious to the equivocal, or perhaps equivocating, mind.

---

82. Chesterton, *Everlasting Man*, 34.
83. Chesterton, *Club of Queer Trades*, 16.
84. Desmond, *Desire, Dialectic, and Otherness*, 6.

Equivocity resists unity and celebrates the dispersal and fracturing of being into exceptions that deny the presence of any rule.[85] We find this prominently in anti-metaphysical and post-metaphysical philosophies, which resist imposing rules on reality, while also resisting finding rules in reality. Perhaps this would be fine if the aim were to allow being to declare, in its own language, the order it conforms to. Perhaps this would be wholesome if the aim were to get past the order of efficient causality to seek out formal causality, as seems to be the case with a philosopher like Martin Heidegger, whose work constantly ricochets from the univocal to the equivocal and back again. However, such an intention does not necessarily lead to the sacramental awareness that formal causality calls for. It merely substitutes one kind of constricted consciousness, or even unconsciousness, with another. To attend to equivocity, which is a fact of being as much as univocity, is to notice how otherness is amply manifest even while it "recedes into unintelligibility."[86] The community of mind and being is lost here, and skepticisms and subjectivisms reign, often to the point of refusing to allow intelligibility to be discovered. Falsification is the obsession of the unreflective equivocalizer. The specificity of the univocal sense of being gives way to a vague impressionism of unnameable possibilities, as the emergent picture, a gesturing towards dialectical sublation, disappears. Definability is resisted and meaning gives way to entropy.[87]

The equivocal sense can be true to being by allowing for those perplexities we encounter. Existence is in flux and therefore is always calling our attention to its impermanence and alterability. Things and thoughts and words do not keep still. Difference is not an illusion. Contingency haunts the equivocal much more than it does the univocal. Becoming does sometimes appear to challenge being's claims of stability. It may often seem to us that being is merely the result of some strange human desire for persistence. Being may even seem to us, as Nietzsche proposes, something that one must posit or impose on the anarchic, always-becoming, always-conflicting, splintering world of disintegrating meanings.[88] Truth and meaning, if not in a state of degeneration, may seem to be in hiding. This conditions the temptation to grab onto an answer too quickly, as a man drowning in a maelstrom might grab onto any debris he finds, even if the debris in question cannot provide the salvation he hopes for.[89]

85. Desmond, *Perplexity and Ultimacy*, 12–23.
86. Simpson, *Religion, Metaphysics, and the Postmodern*, 29.
87. Chesterton, *In Defense of Sanity*, 65.
88. Nietzsche, *Late Notebooks*, 75.
89. Poe, *Descent into the Maelstrom*, 33–35.

Mind and being can be at odds. And they are at odds as far as equivocity dominates. We experience shattering and disintegration from time to time, although familiar being still draws us towards coherence. While we may find awe in the equivocal, we may also experience horror in it, as Chesterton explores especially in his *The Man Who Was Thursday* (1908), which he deliberately and emphatically gives the subtitle: *A Nightmare*. In that novel, the protagonist Gabriel Syme, his name implying an angelic (Gabriel) unity (Syme, a pun on *same*), bemoans the impenetrability of existence. So little in his experience of the world feels coherent. He desires univocity but gains only equivocity. The "secret" and the whole trouble with the world, he discovers, is that "we have only known the back of the world. We see everything from behind, and it looks brutal. That is not a tree, but the back of a tree. That is not a cloud, but the back of a cloud."[90] As Chesterton's mouthpiece, Syme asks the reader, "Cannot you see that everything is stooping and hiding a face?"[91] The face, that welcoming face that would still our fears, does sometimes escape us. In that novel, Syme is looking for Sunday, for a Sabbath for thought. He is looking for the formal cause, although he cannot find this sense of rest in the between while equivocity reigns.

I have already mentioned this idea but here it gains a different significance. Chesterton alerts us to a concern with mistaking the back of things for the front; as he does this, he also alerts us to the bother of having no clear anchor for the equivocal. In a nightmare, the real world is inaccessible. Everything becomes a simulacrum behind which there is no foundation and behind which what is real becomes indiscernible. Nevertheless, if we are attentive enough, we can still feel that truth must be discoverable. Here, we confront a similar problem to what we find with unmediated univocity. Ruptures and breakages and all appearances of dilapidation coalesce into patterns. Even chaos can be mapped, as we discover in everything from mythology to mathematics. As Chesterton says, we can only recognize change against a background that is unchanging.[92] This shows us that mind and being can never be wholly alienated from each other in their essence. Difference is perceived because of a shared unity, even if that unity is only dimly perceived. We may try to ignore mediation, but our ignorance is not enough to shut mediation out permanently. Even our ignorance is mediated. Equivocity declares a relation to being, and therefore despite all of its protesting and tantrum-throwing, and against its evocation of anxiety, nightmare, and dread, it gestures towards mediation and sense-making. It implies the very

---

90. Chesterton, *Man Who Was Thursday*, 247.
91. Chesterton, *Man Who Was Thursday*, 247.
92. Chesterton, *Collected Works, Volume 1*, 79.

reality it seems to suppress or oppress. Meaning is inevitable because, while truth can be denied, it cannot be conquered by the mind.

Just as univocity can result from an unconscious flight from equivocity, equivocity can result from avoiding univocity. The two senses are mimetic doubles, each emulating the other's desire to escape the deeper truth of being. In their rivalry, they are secret allies in that they both attend to the world in its most easily detectable appearance, as if mediation is absent and as if we know the truth of being without help. This highlights again the attitude of the person who is perceiving the world. How we attend to the world is of inestimable importance. Perception is a moral act because it shapes what we find in the world. These two senses of being that we have covered so far allow for a sense of the importance of our attitude to being in different ways. Being clear and resolute, univocity claims to know reality in its self-identity. Being ambiguous and dissolute, equivocity claims that it is impossible to know reality. However, this emerges also in connection with a specific conception of identity.[93] Univocity assumes the self-evidence of knowledge. Equivocity assumes the self-evidence of ignorance. Unaware of its own faith, it "doubts the organ of conviction."[94] Against both, nothing is ever so self-evident. Self-evidence is supported by habituation, acedia, pride, and many other things. Our attitudes shape our beliefs; our beliefs greatly determine what revelations we are willing to receive.

Surprisingly, Chesterton often sides with the equivocal to challenge, if only incompletely, the recalcitrant reign of the univocal sense on its own unmediated terms. He toys with this risky counter-univocity and its nihilistic intimations, recognizing how it gestures beyond itself. Things become "commonplace" when intimations of "sacrifice or peril," as well as "mystery" and "romance," are "lacking."[95] The "commonplace" or univocal "interpretation upon things," Chesterton notes, "is to trace it to that spirit which often calls itself science but which is more often mere repetition."[96] It is often the process of transforming specific things, which can be loved in their specificity, into a mere catalogue of things. Chesterton is especially fond, as in this example, of taking aim at scientific univocity. To be clear, he is by no means against science. He is against "making the world" as "small" as the maniac does.[97] He observes this especially in circles where science is paid univocal attention. As Cecil Chesterton points out in his criticism of his brother,

---

93. Simpson, *Religion, Metaphysics, and the Postmodern*, 30.
94. Chesterton, *Collected Works, Volume 1*, 236.
95. Chesterton, *Illustrated London News*, 13 January 2017.
96. Chesterton, *Illustrated London News*, 13 January 2017.
97. Chesterton, *Collected Works, Volume 1*, 54–62.

Gilbert uses the words "science" and "scientist" as "terms of flippant abuse."[98] Stanley Jaki rightly argues, however, that Chesterton was no opponent of science itself.[99] He attacked what we today call *scientism*, a derogatory term purportedly defined by his friend George Bernard Shaw as an irrational trust in the "omnipotence of scientific knowledge and methods and in their applicability to everything." Scientism insists on itself as a gargantuan category error. It requires an excessive trust in the power of scientific technique and scientific ways of knowing and offers a misguidedly unwavering commitment to the univocal sense of being at the expense of contact with reality through the other senses of being. Against this, Chesterton says that the "rebuilding of a bridge between science and human nature is one of the greatest needs of mankind."[100] Such bridge-building is impossible, however, if we think that only univocity is true to being.

Scientism, which is still surprisingly persistent today despite having been derided and discredited for well over a century, stands against such bridge-building. It implies that "only the scientific or quantitative method yields valid knowledge and reliable value judgements."[101] Again, the trouble is not science but the way that science is used to smuggle in a materialistic and nihilistic ideology. All that the ideologically minded scientist cannot pin down is scapegoated as necessarily untrue or may be regarded as some or other irrelevant equivocity. Still, an appeal to unscientific equivocities of being may help to destabilize and relativize scientism, even if equivocity alone is insufficient to triumph over this limited perception of being. The popular slogan today—"*Follow the science!*"—is a good example of what Chesterton warns his readers of: "Let any one run his eye over any average newspaper or popular magazine," he suggests, and let him "note the number of positive assertions made in the name of popular science, without the least pretense of scientific proof, or even of any adequate scientific authority."[102] What he says here is still with us today in so many appeals in popular journalism to so-called experts. The invocation of scientific univocity as a deity to be trusted at the expense of reflective thinking is very much at the expense of formal causality.

Chesterton's concern is elegantly captured in his recollection of his childhood visits to the Crystal Palace, an impressive symbol of the modern project. There Chesterton found "something negative . . . arching over all

98. Cecil Chesterton, *Gilbert K. Chesterton*, 124–25.
99. See Jaki, *Chesterton*.
100. Chesterton, *Defendant*, 75.
101. Jaki, *Chesterton*, 9.
102. Chesterton, *All Is Grist*, 130–31.

our heads, a roof as remote as the sky . . . impartial and impersonal. . . . Our attention was fixed on the exhibits, which were all carefully ticketed and arranged in rows; for it was the age of science."[103] To his young mind, this compartmentalization and instrumentalization of reality was worryingly clinical. It predicted so many ways that science has continued to mechanize the world and render it impersonal while also edging dangerously towards mechanizing and depersonalizing people.[104] Among other things, this is a crime against romance. "The romance of conscience has been dried up into the science of ethics," Chesterton writes.[105] "The cry to the dim gods, cut off from ethics and cosmology, has become mere Psychical research. Everything has been sundered from everything else, and everything has grown cold."[106] Although he does not use these exact terms, he clearly sees univocity and equivocity colluding against the formal cause here. Echoing his above-mentioned assessment that the modern world creates a fragmentary perception, devoid of creative relationality, Chesterton observes, "This world" is rendered as "one wild divorce court."[107]

It is no wonder he wants to dissent against the rigid grasp of unmediated univocity. Thus, while he recognizes the limits of equivocity, he often drives home the point that maniacal univocalizers are wrong to have settled on an answer too quickly and too arrogantly. To use his image noted above, a dead body buried in a field of dead bodies may not have arrived in that field in the same way as all the other dead bodies. It matters to actively seek out difference and non-identical repetitions where identical repetitions have lulled awareness to sleep. As suggested by the case of scientism, certainty becomes idolatry and ideology under the reign of univocity. Univocalizers, in a trance of intellectual self-satisfaction and metaphysical boredom, forget that questions always outnumber answers and that excess meanings escape neat categorizations. Human reason is powerful but limited. Chesterton shows us a world that cannot be reduced to any formula and where any attempt to do so must be challenged. We live in a mystery and have been created to experience occasional bafflement and bewilderment. A loss of wonder should alert us to the truth that something has gone dreadfully wrong. Univocity is often a significant cause of the loss of wonder.

To confound univocity, Chesterton frequently defamiliarizes elements of the world. He draws the reader's attention to the trouble with relying

---

103. Chesterton, *Collected Works, Volume 3*, 100.
104. Chesterton, *Collected Works, Volume 1*, 113.
105. Chesterton, *Daily News*, 31 March 1906.
106. Chesterton, *Daily News*, 31 March 1906.
107. Chesterton, *Daily News*, 31 March 1906.

only on univocity, which has a nasty habit of universalizing the particular. He points, for instance, to the uniqueness of flowers even within their own species.[108] Against the lunatic's tendency to mechanize perception and so also to demand an "ugly uniformity,"[109] Chesterton wants to transport us from intellectual fatigue and false pattern-making into a world in which we can encounter the actual picture we are looking at.[110] Against a scientific determinism that would dull perception rather than wake it up, he wants to disrupt our attention so that we can refocus it on the world and not just on the narrow conclusion we have arrived at before careful contemplation.[111] In other words, the aim is to restore to attention an openness to real otherness, a desire to not have the world be remade according to mere human expectations. It is, more seriously, a step towards restoring a sense of the sacramental; that is, contact with God. Arguably, Chestertonian defamiliarization rests on the metaxological sense of being but the key here is that, as Chesterton uses it, this mediated equivocity is, at first, known only to him and not to the reader encountering it in his work. Chesterton aims, in many instances, to use the reader's direct experience of unmediated equivocity to point to a higher, mediated sense of being. He breaks with custom but not with the natural law, dramatized in his novel *Manalive* (1912).[112]

Chestertonian defamiliarization, as Alison Milbank argues and explains, echoes the idea articulated especially by the literary critic Viktor Shklovsky.[113] Defamiliarization conforms to no strict method even if it may turn into a method of a kind. A predictable method would risk undermining the primary concern that drives defamiliarization. In Chesterton, we find blunt statements of fact, careful attention to detail, drama, exaggeration, various expressions of humor, questions, jokes, and other conceptual tools at his disposal to disrupt our sense of the overly familiar. All such variations suggest a guiding attitude that intends to break the spell of univocal habit, which prevents us from being mindful of the between. Such attention to variations works by restoring differences. This attitude highlights those dissimilarities that are right in front of us, especially in unmediated form. Such differences are recognized as transcending rigid algebraization and automatic thinking. Chesterton presents them to us often without explanation,

---

108. Chesterton, *Poet and the Lunatics*, 41.
109. Chesterton, *Illustrated London News*, 30 October 1920.
110. Chesterton, *Illustrated London News*, 24 September 1932.
111. Chesterton, *Collected Works, Volume 1*, 227.
112. Chesterton, *Manalive*.
113. Milbank, *Chesterton and Tolkien as Theologians*, xv, 32; Reyburn, *Seeing Things as They Are*, 205–12.

and for a few moments we find ourselves confounded, with no easy way to make sense of what we are being shown.

I think especially of his story, in *The Poet and the Lunatics* (1929), about the crimes of Gabriel Gale, his name suggesting an angelic force of wind, perhaps an analogy for the Holy Spirit or Pentecost. In that story, we find the mild-mannered and sensible poet-protagonist acting completely out of character. He appears to have gone mad. He wildly discards social convention and even seems to try to kill a man. But Chesterton shows by the end of the story that our assumptions about Gale's apparent insanity have been wrong. He was sane all along; so sane that even madness could become the most reasonable recourse.[114]

If, as Chesterton notices, we have a propensity for worshiping law, the right response is to relativize the law.[115] If the equivocal sense of being were the only true way of speaking of being, this would be a move towards anarchy and atheism. We need to keep in mind therefore that we should not relinquish any sense we have of a given order. If anything, Chesterton wants to free us to align ourselves with the right order rather have us fall prey to its counterfeit. The right order would need to account for the fact that there are equivocities in being. Attempts to ignore these amount to being intellectually dishonest. And yet, it is also dishonest to ignore the apparent presence of order. When two roses look alike, we might say it is a coincidence. However, given the fact that one rose looks like myriad other roses and that they all look like flowers and that they are all so beautiful together, we may fairly confidently say that we smell a rather fragrant plot. We may not yet fully understand what the plot is but we know that something is up.

Chesterton does not use defamiliarization to set up an overproduction of difference in the manner of a Derridean scholar in the throes of psychosis. The most radical forms of equivocity may indeed suggest that such an overproduction of difference is possible. But who of us can believe that there are tiny fragments of the real floating about entirely independent of those foundations and principles shared by reality as whole? Who of us can believe in such a radical degree of difference that renders any and all closure unimaginable? Such a belief would require a remarkable leap of faith, a deep trust of a kind that no equivocity could account for. It would require a believing it possible to interpret such alien bits and pieces as intelligible; that is, according to something that persists despite so much difference while being unreflective of what is happening in perception itself. This would be to make equivocity an idol; it would be to think of equivocity in univocal

---

114. Chesterton, *Poet and the Lunatics*, 59–76.
115. Chesterton, *Collected Works, Volume 1*, 246.

terms. In opposition to this, always aware of the call of intelligibility, Chesterton intends to restore a meaningful engagement with reality through a meaningful sense of difference.

Bear in mind that equivocity is true to being only as one way of attending to and speaking of being. It is true to being as relative to being and as relative to the other senses of being. Against ironic postmodern truth-refusal and metamodern oscillations between sincerity and indifference at the expense of truth, Chesterton guides his reader to notice how preconceptions can warp attention and prevent clear perception. This is perhaps nowhere more evident than in his detective fiction, which draws attention to puzzlement and indefiniteness, as well as the unexplained intractabilities of reality. Fitting the metaxological mode of attention at the heart of Chesterton's journalistic metaphysics, his interest is in restoring the adventurous side of life where the comfort of the overly familiar has caused us to lose our primal astonishment and foundational perplexity. How can we feel at home if we have lost a sense of wonder? That would not be home but a prison for the soul. And how can we truly wonder if we have no place of refuge? Without a safe haven, wonder turns into terror.

Chestertonian defamiliarization may be misunderstood as an attempt to restore passivity to the perceiver, given that univocity tends to put people in an active relationship with reality, albeit still unconscious and devoid of reflective reasoning. This is only part of the truth. As suggested, Chesterton wants to resist the "worship of law,"[116] especially the worship of arbitrary human laws, by restoring difference. But the deeper aim of this strategy is to restore the possibility of genuine consciousness and real choice; that means recovering participation in reality. Without fully recovering a feel for mediation, if we stick with equivocity alone, such a restoration can only be incomplete and accidental. Nevertheless, where defamiliarization is a component of an intention to seek out the equivocities of being, we see that the world is separate from us. There is a real boundary between the person and the world he is contemplating. This opens up a flexibility in our awareness and the potential of selecting one thing and not another. While univocity presents the world as an immediately obvious and often merely consumable otherness, equivocity can restore to us a sense that there is an abundance in the world that we cannot master and should not seek to master. While univocity regards being, and therefore possibility, as transparent, equivocity can offer the possibility of recovering a sense of the hidden and mysterious.

Chesterton's awareness of difference and the play of difference in the world of perception is a component of his attunement to formal causality

---

116. Chesterton, *Collected Works, Volume 1*, 246.

and also therefore one reason for his prescience. To allow the equivocal is to allow for possibility in the fullest sense. Being plays tricks on us; it surprises us. It allows more than the immediately given to become apparent, if only in a proto-speculative form. It allows more than one possibility to present itself. This is crucial if we are to notice where happenings may be headed. One might regard the equivocal sense of being as a way to loosen up perception and judgment; it invites the possibility of reading atmospheres and not just things, as well as the possibility of relinquishing one's prejudices about the past and the present, and perhaps also the future. It reminds us to keep imagination alive; for being too rigid in one's minding of being squashes imagination and destroys the very possibility of a level-headed metaphysics. Humble conjectures about the future can be welcomed when the grip of univocity is released, keeping in mind that univocity cannot admit speculation. The equivocal allows for a questioning of certainties via interruptions that floor our expectations. Defamiliarization attunes us to the betweenness of being when a sense of this betweenness has been lost.

In this, however, we must recognize a distinction between Chestertonian defamiliarization and any defamiliarization that cares only to highlight obscurity or absurdism without implying wholeness or ultimate goodness. Such obscurantism alienates us from being; it reinforces the uprooting that is already present in our forgetting of mediation and in our forgetting of being. The point is not to reify irrationality or grant exaggerated superiority to the grotesque or incongruous. The point is to reinvigorate a subdued awareness by an awakened contingency-sense. This can allow for a renewed encounter with truth and reality. It involves the imagination's power to inject new life into "our whole orderly system of life."[117] The main function of imagination, for Chesterton, "is not to make strange things settled," after all, "so much as to make settled things strange; not so much to make wonders facts as to make facts wonders."[118] This amounts, among other things, to seeing facts reestablished within the larger order of being. Already in defamiliarization, in the fact that equivocity generates a sense of the implied in being and in our minding of being, a further sense through which being is encountered might be intuited. Univocity and equivocity submit to the immediate, and therefore suggest a largely unconscious immersion in being. However, the fight is always ultimately for a consciousness or awareness that transcends, while still including, this unconscious immersion.

---

117. Chesterton, *Defendant*, 84.
118. Chesterton, *Defendant*, 84.

The Dialectical Sense of Being

There are various ways to get lost in the woods when discussing the dialectical sense of being. To consider G. W. F. Hegel's dialectic, for example, as Desmond's primary paradigm for modern dialectic, would demand such a complicated map and so many detours that the point of what it might mean with regard to Chesterton and formal causality is likely to be lost. Here, therefore, the dialectical sense of being implies an attempt to recover the univocal sense of being without ignoring equivocity.[119] As Desmond suggests, philosophers tend to "dread the equivocal."[120] The idea that everything is ultimately intractable to the point of being nonsense is frightening. Nevertheless, retreating into the univocal, as I have already suggested, will not do. "We do not reject univocity, but a total retreat to univocity is out," writes Desmond.[121] "We do not reject equivocity, but the nihilistic totalization of equivocity is out. We need to go beyond both, which means acknowledging the contributory truth of both."[122]

The dialectical sense of being attempts this very thing, although not perfectly. It tries to return to the between by acknowledging the mediation of being that sustains the univocal and equivocal senses. It attempts to retrieve unity without sticking to simple sameness nor simple difference. While univocity and equivocity assume certain limits as self-evident, the dialectical sense suggests becoming aware of the limits of each, which is tantamount to going beyond said limits. Because of the reasonable insistence that mediation is inescapable, the dialectical sense finds thought reanimated. It is important to clarify, however, that Desmond has in mind modern dialectic, as in the work of Hegel, not Plato's dialectic. The latter is closer to what Desmond means by the metaxological, just as Quentin Lauer's reference to Chesteronian dialectic[123] is also closer to metaxology.

Modern dialectic can be broadly thought of as attempting a logic of the whole while taking seriously the interplay between the self and the other.[124] Here is a definite recognition of the *between*. However, in the end, this logic settles too readily on the side of self-mediation. Determination seems to conquer indeterminacy even if there is still always more to learn. Modern dialectic, although trying to overcome one-sided articulations of

---

119. Desmond, *Being and the Between*, 143, 175, 178.
120. Desmond, *Being and the Between*, 131.
121. Desmond, *Being and the Between*, 131.
122. Desmond, *Being and the Between*, 132.
123. Lauer, *Chesterton*, 48.
124. Lauer, *Chesterton*, 140–41; Desmond, *Being and the Between*, 3–46.

truth,¹²⁵ suggests a mediation of being that sides with self-mediation over intermediation. This is why it is not an optimal posture towards the between.¹²⁶ Certainly, a dialectical attunement to being is better equipped to attend to formal causality than the other two senses of being already discussed. But it falls short because it remains caught up in an "immanent standard" that is somehow known "in advance of all disputed claims."¹²⁷ Error is regarded not as a deviation from or opposition to a transcendent standard but as a sort of truth that is part of being.¹²⁸ It is sensible to acknowledge that we can learn from mistakes and wrong turns, always trusting that we are called to know the truth. But by being entangled in the immanent, we may fail to recognize the ways that errors of all kinds block the way to truth. A person can take so many dialectical wrong turns that he ends up believing lies. In this, the formal cause, as a sense of the whole, is likely to be at the mercy of the efficient cause and its proneness to self-deception, or subordinate to counterfeit final causes, as potentialities turned against actuality. Dialectic has everything to do with what consciousness itself becomes mindful of. Even where there is an attempt to recover the between and especially a sense of the centrality of mediation to our awareness of being, priority is still given to what the mind identifies. In dialectic, being exists for thought. The consequence of this is that reality can be displaced by so-called understanding, which is judgment at the expense of understanding. This tendency gives ontological priority to the mind's capacity for generating abstractions. There is more than a little of the maniac in this.

Here, to my mind, is where modern dialectic is most worrisome, even if it is better than univocity and equivocity. By rendering being as always for thought, dialectical sublation is unavoidably and necessarily reductionistic. The sublated result survives as an abridgement of the complex process undergone to ensure its arrival on the attentional stage. It also tends to reduce the role of the transcendent, which can be regarded as merely in the service of the immanent. The kaleidoscope of being is desaturated. As one Hegelian notes, "There is nothing more foreign to Hegel than a lamentation for the richness of reality that gets lost when we proceed to its conceptual grasp."¹²⁹ Why would Hegel not lament this? There would be nothing more foreign to Chesterton than indifference to any loss of a sense of the richness and wonder of reality. Although profound in its sheer scope and ambition, the risk

---

125. Hegel, *Phenomenology of Spirit*, §2.
126. Desmond, *Desire, Dialectic, and Otherness*, 6.
127. Desmond, *Being and the Between*, 157.
128. Desmond, *Being and the Between*, 157.
129. Žižek, *Sublime Object of Ideology*, ix–x.

of modern (Hegelian) dialectic, with regard to the subject of this book, is to reduce formal causality to what we happen to be mindful of; and Chesterton's *modus operandi* is to confront us with the limits of our awareness. The dialectical sense tends entertain only the definable and so it risks shutting the door to the ineffable. The latter is vital if we are to allow any room for the spiritual, for miracles and revelations. But it is also vital if we are to allow for things in the immanent realm that we have not properly considered. While we must aim at an account of causality and so should grant a high place to intellection, we should not build yet another Tower of Babel. This is the temptation of dialectical self-absolutization.

Speaking more generally, Desmond points out that the dialectical sense allows for otherness only because it can be contextualized within a determinate and often predetermined frame of reference. It subsumes the interplay of sameness and difference into a higher harmony. The interplay between mind and being serves the ever-present call for a more comprehensive unity. But, again, this unity is on the side of thought itself, which is to say that it is on the side of thought thinking its other and the person's ability to mediate all otherness through thought.[130] Mind gains priority over being. The interplay of univocity and equivocity, once mediated by the dialectical, becomes "an occasion for the self to come to understand itself—to return to itself—to attain greater self-consciousness."[131] In the process, self-mediation, self-consciousness, and self-determination coincide. Is there not, in this, too much egotism?

As with the previous two senses of being, we notice how the dialectical sense is both true to being and untrue to it. It is faithful even while it betrays being. Its truth is most obvious in that it takes seriously the need to account for the instabilities, fluctuations, and uncertainties in being through a more determinate understanding. It is true to our desire to know. It attends closely to the development of concepts through improving articulation and determination.[132] Hegel rightly stresses the importance of lingering over the different moments in the process and tarrying with its various tensions and negativities. He also contests the idea that self-awareness and understanding are possible apart from otherness. Still, his method is strangely absolute. It can be deaf to the very mediation it wants to listen to and can too easily become yet another form of univocal determination as the tensions between univocity and equivocity are dissolved.[133] Otherness, subsumed into self-

---

130. Simpson, *Religion, Metaphysics, and the Postmodern*, 30.

131. Simpson, *Religion, Metaphysics, and the Postmodern*, 31.

132. Desmond, *Ethics and the Between*, 123, 125.

133. Desmond, *Desire, Dialectic, and Otherness*, 124; Desmond, *Being and the Between*, xi–xv, 163; Desmond, *Perplexity and Ultimacy*, 14.

mediation, is transformed into an extension of sameness. As Hajime Tanabe suggests, "Dialectics deprived of its paradoxical character can no longer be authentic dialectics; it degenerates into a mere logic of identity."[134] The dialectical sense fails to take seriously the finitude of the person, while also failing to pay sufficient mind to what is other to thought. As Simpson notes, "Reference to the other is always a subordinate moment to the self-mediating whole."[135] Thankfully, in failing to account for otherness, the dialectical sense of being indicates its own self-subversion. Self-mediation eventually proves unsuccessful if it is sufficiently attuned to being and to the way being mediates itself to us. The desire to repress otherness has to eventually yield to its inability to account sufficiently for that otherness.

As with the previous two senses of being, Chesterton attends to the dialectical, but he remains more playful in allowing for occasional distractions and meanderings than comfortably fit this frame. With Plato, he is comfortable destroying false claims and sees no need to always assimilate them into a higher synthesis. In keeping with his intention to return to first principles, many of his arguments work dialectically in two important ways. First, he is constantly engaged with various interlocutors. He offers points and counterpoints to develop his understanding of things. This is most evident in the many articles he writes to directly respond, often combatively, to those who have read his work and contested what he has said.[136] It is also evident in the way his work factors in the viewpoints he knows his audience is aware of, much as Aquinas does in his work. Then, secondly, Chesterton adopts dialectic when arguing logically with reference to first principles. He works carefully through the interplay of various elements to consider how they imply certain conclusions. He wants arguments that are correct and not merely conclusions that seem right.[137] He is mindful of the interplay of thought and things and often synthesizes what is other than thought to resonate with his metaphysical intuitions.

However, he takes a fairly strong stand against the stubborn linearity and reductiveness of dialectical reasoning. He is critical of the modern formulation that relies too heavily on what is often referred to as the labor of the negative. Probably the best example of this is found in his argument against Marinetti and the futurists, who were "progressive to the extent of being preposterous."[138] They drew on the logic of progress evident in Marx and

---

134. Tanabe, *Philosophy as Metanoetics*, 135.
135. Simpson, *Religion, Metaphysics, and the Postmodern*, 31.
136. See Chesterton, *G. K. Chesterton at the Daily News*, vols. 1–8.
137. Chesterton, *Illustrated London News*, 26 November 1921.
138. Chesterton, *Illustrated London News*, 23 December 1922.

Engels's *Communist Manifesto*, which gives ground for celebrating violence and totalitarian ideology.[139] In their work, Marx, Engels, and Marinetti stand on Hegel's toes instead of on his shoulders by reifying his dialectic, transforming it into a caricature of itself. Dialectical negation can offer a way to energize creative thought, just as the sculptor uses the negation of stone and clay to produce the form of the sculpture. Equivocal difference or negation, so essential to both creativity and reason, can generate a contrasting figure to allow for a clearer view of the form or ground. However, Chesterton notices that even in such cases, negation *presumes* a form; without a form, there can only be destruction and deformation. Dialectical negativity, also considered a moment of instability, may be likened to a potentiality in being that calls for the actualizing power of form. But this form must therefore transcend self-mediation.

The pursuit of novelty by mere negation exemplified by the futurists, a mere rejection of what has gone before, is no guarantee of progress any more than refusing to drink water guarantees that your thirst will be quenched. All that the pursuit of mere novelty does in the end is "narrow the mind to what is novel" and deny for the mind a realization of what we already possess, which is "universal."[140] A more "universal poet" does not need to reject slowness for the sake of speed, as futurists do, but can "admire thunderbolts and wild horses at one time, without losing the power to admire lakes and lilies at another."[141] Chesterton does not assume here that the subjective mind is sufficient to mediate all otherness. The human mind may be capable of thinking itself in itself but this does not make it the rightful sovereign over the mediation of being. The other needs to pitch in to help in the intercommunication of being. Mediation is not, therefore, as lonesome as many moderns make it out to be. Being is an agapeic community, reflective of the Trinitarian structure of reality itself.

And so Chesterton does not ultimately conform to modern dialectical reasoning. This is significant in that modern dialectic, while attempting to attend somewhat to formal causality, still risks attending more to figures than to the ground. John Milbank echoes Lauer in refuting Slavoj Žižek's assumption that Chesterton is an accidental Hegelian.[142] As both Lauer and Milbank propose, Chestertonian dialectic does not side with self-mediation but rather sides with the between. To notice this is to see more clearly what sort of attention Chesterton pays to formal causality. His reasoning does not

---

139. Reyburn, "Repetitions Repeatedly Repeated."
140. Chesterton, *Illustrated London News*, 23 December 1922.
141. Chesterton, *Illustrated London News*, 23 December 1922.
142. Milbank, "Double Glory, or Paradox Versus Dialectics," 110–233.

side with dialectical efficiency but with the openness that seeks out metaxological co-resonances. This means including, against the tastes of Hegel, the unsystematic and the fragmentary, as well as the possibility of aporetic inconclusivity. Hegel is famously considered one of the great systematizers in philosophy while, appropriately, Chesterton can hardly be accused of having any sort of system.

This is good news, in my view, since self-mediation happens to be a problem in a certain historicism, which assumes that the thinker can lay claim to the inner meaning of history. It is no surprise that many Hegelians have assumed that history has a logic that spells out certain inevitabilities. Even as it flags contingencies, it nevertheless suggests finality as history is placed in the service of thought. Not all Hegelians are progressive, obviously, but it is nevertheless striking that Hegel's thought suits a certain type of progressivism rather well. In contrast, Chesterton's attention to history is too playful and participatory to fall into this trap. Indeed, his prescience cannot be estranged from his sense of the between, which allows for the mediation offered by the other. His prescience is found not just in objective observations, although there are many such observations. It can be found in the way that his forecasts resonate poetically and even romantically with readers. This somewhat excuses those of his generalized predictions that still fit with how things have turned out.

Where he predicts, for instance, that censorship in the press is likely to become a problem in the future or that commerce can become fascistic in its own way, we find his meaning reframed by the concerns about censorship and fascism that some of us have now. Our different horizons of meaning meet in the between. Chesterton's interpretation of the future matters, but our interpretation of Chesterton's interpretation counts for something as well. We read him and he reads us in a dance of reciprocal meaning-seeking and meaning-finding. There are surpluses in this, too, and not just sublations. This is because Chesterton's so-called dialectic is paradoxical. Paradox is not merely a stylistic feature in his work, although there is room within paradox for aesthetic and rhetorical effects. It is the natural result of his intuition of being; his sense that being is not merely for thought but is found in life itself. Indeed, Desmond's metaxology, which transposes paradox into a phenomenological key, can be read as a non-identical repetition of Chestertonian paradoxy.

The Metaxological Sense of Being

Desmond's metaxological sense of being can help us to come to terms with Chesterton's awareness of formal causality. Desmond posits metaxology as a metaphysical attunement to being itself while being mindful of a need to remain open to being even in our dialectical reasoning rather than having being submit entirely to thought. The grace of limitation keeps thought in check. This presumes an interplay of hermeneutics and phenomenology but remains rooted in metaphysics. To live in the world is to embody not only a horizontal mediation of being but also a vertical meeting of the heavenly and the earthly, the visible and the invisible, the conscious and the unconscious. Being is mediated but it is not mediated only by us. Being itself, as an agapeic community and manifestation of the love of God, is a co-mediator. It mediates itself with and to us.

Again, the dialectical reign of self-mediation, which tends towards immanentizing and immediatizing mediation, fails to account for being even while trying to be true. This does not mean, however, that we should resign ourselves again to unmediated univocity or unmediated equivocity. To do so would mean giving up the fight for a higher consciousness and resigning ourselves to unconsciousness. Instead, we can realize the vital presence of mediation apart from the egotism of self-mediation, and also without abdicating responsibility to the apparently unmediated. The metaxological sense of being restores a feeling for the dynamism of mediation. It especially makes room for participating in the transcendent. As this would suggest, the metaxological is impossible apart from a sense of Platonic form. Reality is not merely of the material realm but includes what shines through it from beyond it. "Everything has a halo," writes Chesterton. "Everything has a sort of atmosphere of what it signifies, which makes it sacred."[143]

The metaxological sense of being points to a "plurally intermediated relatedness between identity and difference."[144] It offers a hope that it is always possible to renew the openness of the between. This is particularly pertinent given a concern expressed by some about Chesterton's work being unsystematic. However, as I have already hinted, this should not be taken as a fair criticism of his work. He was unsystematic but not chaotic. Unsystematicity is no crime even if the word *unsystematicity* is one. As a journalist, Chesterton wanted to entertain his reader and not just make arguments. However, this is not the only reason that it is to his credit that he is not systematic. His attunement to being fits being as a "plurally intermediated

---

143. Chesterton, *Poet and the Lunatics*, 53.
144. Desmond, *Desire, Dialectic, and Otherness*, xix.

relatedness." While he does not attempt to delineate a focus along strictly disciplinary or methodological lines, for instance, this helps him to be attentive to the interweaving of figure and ground. Figure and ground are not separate univocal component parts but aspects of a single perception that is always in excess of our mediations. Figure and ground relate paradoxically to each other and to us as part of a whole and should therefore not be opposed to each other through any mental act of decontextualization.

By refusing constricted self-mediation, Chesterton remains open to the world presenting itself as it is. The world speaks to us in many voices but so many voices do not mean that the world is not one. Chesterton's approach to writing is a symbol of this. While a coherent horizon is discernible in his vast output, he does not stick to any single subject, and his pen often jumps from one topic to another within the same essay or paragraph. His journalistic essays form a mosaic built on a not-unreasonable trust that speaking the truth is sufficient for providing coherence. This is why he is so adept at perceiving pictures, patterns, and stories, and not just formulas. Truth is always of the whole. The ontological has a primacy over hermeneutics and epistemology. The world is imaginable as a non-identical, analogical repetition of a fuller reality not fully comprehended. The world we perceive calls us towards a deeper reality operating in, through, and beyond it.

Another result of this plurivocal metaxological sense pertains to the absence of a historicist method in Chesterton's writings. Such a method would risk dissolving tensions through self-mediation. It would therefore also risk destroying the tension between act and potency. This would have the unfortunate side-effect of rigging the game in favor of a particular and probably rather narrow conception of what historical progression ought to look like. It would involve an element of a certain judgment that Chesterton seems adverse to, where history itself, confined to ideological processes, would become the judge of the good and the bad, while people would be forced into passively observing what history has somehow, by its own apparent reasoning and logic, decided. Ironically, self-mediation creates the conditions according to which people are placed at the mercy of the world. Self-mediation, while seeming active, has a tendency to foster passivity. One of the consequences of this historicism is that it tends towards a determinism that regards as a mere appearance any sign of human will and action while claiming to perceive a reality of hidden forces with inevitable effects. Cause and effect remain, in this, strictly linear. Also in this, a sense of teleology is replaced by a commitment to watching events unfold along expected lines, detached from the fullness of a final cause.

Chesterton is aware that the unconscious is at work in the minds of people, just as he knows that it plays a significant role in shaping the world.[145] However, to him, it would be taking things too far to attribute all reality to some inscrutable aspect of human psychology while denying reality to those aspects of human thought and action that we do directly perceive. We make conscious decisions. Moreover, our sense that human actions are generally willful is no illusion. We also clearly, if only intuitively, perceive that things have ends; how things turn out ought to be shaped by their ends and not merely by the brute accumulation of events coalescing into emergent results. Effects can precede causes. The cause and effect sequence fits the self-mediation of modern dialectic with effects subsumed under the rule of the cause. But the metaxological allows effects to mediate themselves to causes as well. Potency places demands and limits on actuality. Effects are not just the results of efficient causality but are pervaded by final and formal causality.

Psychoanalytic readings of history may forget all of this as much as historicist readings do by committing to the cynical view that the irrational substructure of human consciousness, with its brute psychic events tumbling over each other in a mad rush, compels much of what happens in the human story, and that we must therefore try to interpret the nature of those psychic events. However, psychoanalysis would suggest we do this without having direct, experiential access to the unconscious.[146] While there are hidden meanings to be found in history, often they are forgotten meanings rather than just unconscious ones.[147] The more we look at such forgotten meanings, the more we are likely to realize that history does not move in only one direction at any given time.[148] The best kind of historicism, and I suspect Chesterton would agree with this, fully appreciates the complexity of history and the role of the historian as an interpreter of that complexity. The worst kind of historicism assumes that just by knowing a few things about a given time, we can be sure that we understand all of it.

Desmond's metaxological posture offers a way to see more clearly how paradox in Chesterton's work concerns not only a specific way of approaching verbal constructions but is a way of highlighting the tensions and clashes within being itself, as well as in our awareness of being. This is suggested by Kenner when he discusses Chestertonian paradox, which I take to be akin to metaxology; it is not merely, as Kenner argues, rhetorical or aesthetic but metaphysical.[149] What is crucial in Chestertonian paradox is

145. Chesterton, *Varied Types*, 3.
146. Chesterton, *Illustrated London News*, 21 December 1929.
147. Chesterton, *The Speaker*, 3 May 1902.
148. Chesterton, *Well and the Shallows*, 35.
149. See Kenner, *Paradox in Chesterton*.

not just that he juxtaposes words but that he is intent on recognizing actual juxtapositions—that is patterns and proportions and pictures—in being itself. Being cannot be reduced to either concreteness or transcendence; it cannot be reduced to things or thoughts. True universality and true intimacy are perfectly and harmoniously infused. Neither has to be in conflict with the other. This is another way of articulating the central paradox and miracle in Christian theology: the incarnation.

Incarnation, indicating the transcendent God of love fully present in Christ, means, among other things, a doubleness of *agape* and *eros*. Christ is both true God and true man, and there is no conflict or loss of unity in him. "There is an eros to perplexity," writes Desmond, and "there is also the promise of agapeic mind."[150] Eros suggests a dynamic and immanent exigency that opens us up to the true as surpassing pure immanence.[151] Reminding us of Plato's ladder, the intimacy of the between is recovered in this erotic desiring of an agapeic communion with the whole. This is always of the whole. It partakes of what transcends it while also desiring to transcend itself in its movement towards knowing the whole. But this intimate *eros* is also called from without by the *agape*. The bountiful otherness of *agape* is beyond the mind's erotic self-mediation.

Finitude and plenitude meet in the between, as do personality and immensity. Paradox implies that being is not merely an unfolding but a giving and a receiving in the given. Finitude, in its contingency and dependency, and even its poverty, is amply capable of accepting the wealth of God. In receiving divinity, in giving itself to God, finitude realizes its fullest potential. Even the apparent deficiency of the material order shows the divine in a special way. This is a principle for seeing paradoxes of other kinds in the world. To see things together, juxtaposed in their otherness, is to see things in the light of their self-giving and other-receiving. For example, to see that God makes man male and female does not mean seeing human beings as merely bifurcated into two separate and alienated quiddities; it means seeing them as paradoxically one. Ideally, Adam finds himself through Eve, as Eve finds herself through Adam, and the two find more than themselves through each other, and their children, and their children's children, all while they find themselves in God. Humanity's wholeness, its essential unity despite its manifest disunity, is rendered clearer through paradox, which is not static but generative.

We need to see the whole first, as Chesterton does, for instance, when noticing that the smallest essential unit of humanity is not the individual

---

150. Desmond, *Being and the Between*, 7.
151. Simpson, *Religion, Metaphysics, and the Postmodern*, 28.

but the family, and that proportions within the family are tampered with by certain social expectations and unnatural customs.[152] There are tensions and facets within this wholeness, and it is this that opens the way for a proper proportioning of the univocal, equivocal, and dialectical senses of being. To see the form of humanity is to see people and how they ought to relate to the world more clearly. This is arguably one of the strengths of Chesterton's Catholicism, which refuses to consider even Christ as entirely "individualistic" even in his earthly life. His life, as the revealed and embodied Word, is bound to the life of St. Mary and St. Joseph and to all those whom he came to save, serve, and call.

But what does all of this mean for understanding formal causality? Most obviously, it means that we should not attempt to understand the world from some artificial "view from nowhere," which becomes easier to do when the world is mediated by entirely artificial and largely context-free forms of communication. Our metaphysics does not have to be, and should not be, separated from the mundane. Chesterton is a helpful guide in this regard. He sees any conversation about the ordinary as a conversation about the sublime; he sees the intimate and the universal as companions; he finds that the strange and the familiar are friends. One example of this is in how Chesterton defends his faith. It is not possible, he says, "to evade the issue of God," even when we talk "about pigs or the binomial theory."[153] If Christianity were merely a bit of metaphysical nonsense invented by crooks, kooks, and ideologues, then defending it would simply mean "talking that metaphysical nonsense over and over again."[154] But if Christianity is true, defending it can mean discussing anything and everything, at any time. "Things can be irrelevant to the proposition that Christianity is false," he says, "but nothing can be irrelevant to the proposition that Christianity is true."[155] This is possibly one reason why Chesterton—unlike Carlyle or so many modern masters of suspicion like Marx, Nietzsche, and Freud—expends more energy trying to find and affirm what is true than trying to hunt out shams and falsehoods.[156] The endlessly suspicious will tear off branches to find a tree, but Chesterton would say that those very branches are proof that there is a tree and that we therefore do not need to be rid of them.

There is, in Chesterton's trust of being, a willingness to allow being to question and make demands of us. Adopting the metaxological sense of

---

152. See Chesterton, *What's Wrong with the World*.
153. Chesterton, *Daily News*, 12 December 1903.
154. Chesterton, *Daily News*, 12 December 1903.
155. Chesterton, *Daily News*, 12 December 1903.
156. Chesterton, *Collected Works, Volume 18*, 32.

being means attending to the relations between things and people. By doing this, Chesterton can notice especially where the tension is lost or the ratios between things are out of harmony. Paradoxical tension, in other words, is an essential aspect of formal causality. It is a means by which the interconnections of being can be discerned. Understandably, being clear on this particular aspect of form allows Chesterton to see something of the future. He does this, in part, by attending especially closely to the proportions between things in any relationship. Proportion is important to Chesterton.[157] He believes that "the preservation of proportion in the mind is the only thing that keeps a man from narrow-mindedness."[158] Proportion "is the principle of all reality."[159] It is the central principle guiding our engagement with reality.[160] When he perceives, for instance, the possibility of high heels getting severely out of proportion in the twenty-first century,[161] this is because he attends closely to the relationship between feet and walking and the world. Boots may take almost any shape. But when the essential proportion and function of boots is forgotten, as is a trend in unparadoxical modern thinking, it becomes quite reasonable to expect that people designing boots will take wrong turns and exceed reasonable limits.[162] We cannot attend to man-made boots rightly without being attentive to archetypal boots. Chesterton encourages us, therefore, to "keep the enormous proportions of a normal thing clear of various modifications and degrees and doubts."[163] We should focus on maintaining a sense of meaning with regard to how things relate to each other and to us, as well as how we relate to them. Chesterton cannot help but notice that this is an artistic metaphor. He notices, for example, how the artist will freeze a moment in time and "call a halt to progress in the name of proportion."[164] He does this because the proportion points beyond itself to an order; to the goodness or beauty that transcends all motion and becoming.

Notice Chesterton's attunement to the true drama of the world. He is wary of "the worst element in our anarchic world of to-day," which is that the world is set up as "one vast system of separation—an enormous philosophical Divorce Court."[165] He uses the frivolous example of bread and

---

157. Chesterton, *Illustrated London News*, 20 July 1918.
158. Chesterton, *Illustrated London News*, 12 November 1932.
159. Chesterton, *Everlasting Man*, 36.
160. Chesterton, *Everlasting Man*, 36.
161. Chesterton, *Everlasting Man*, 36.
162. Chesterton, *Illustrated London News*, 17 May 1930.
163. Chesterton, *Everlasting Man*, 53.
164. Chesterton, *Illustrated London News*, 31 May 1924.
165. Chesterton, *Daily News*, 31 March 1906.

cheese, which our taste buds experience not as two different elements of experience but as a single flavor. Only a profligate would insist that the two must not be allied on the assumption that bread is more breadish without cheese. A more culturally specific example of fragmenting the world is the idea of "art for art's sake," which is anarchy against the fact that art has a place within a world a meaning. Art for art's sake is a lie. We must be prepared to answer such unnecessary cleavages, the separation of bread from cheese and the separation of art from the world of meaning, "by insisting on the immemorial right of mankind to perpetuate such alliances."[166] We must also notice that things exist in a certain relation to each other that suggests the possibility of better and worse proportions. Bread and cheese go together well when the bread is not stale or soggy and when the cheese has not been left to mutate into something resembling a miniature forest of mold. The drama of meaning requires balance. A further example of this is that we need food but also periods of not eating, just as we may enjoy bread and cheese occasionally but might get tired of it if we were to attempt to live on bread and cheese alone. There is a rhythm to our eating and not eating, but notice that this rhythm does not necessarily create an entirely regular pattern. If anything, even something as regular as this ritual of eating and not eating is a non-identical repetition. It retrieves a form but modifies it to suit the conditions of a particular day.

Similarly, a drama of meaning is evident in the way that virtues guide the proportions of our actions. To perceive this drama rightly allows us to perceive clearly, for instance, when a "mountain has been made out of a molehill."[167] It means conceiving of things in a way that is attentive and faithful to the real, rather than setting up a simulation or mental projection to impose on the real.[168] Proportion seeks out a spiritual balance that keeps the intellectual hunger for truth in check. A unity arises in the interplay of meanings, and by attuning ourselves to this unity, we can more easily recognize distortions of its inner harmony, as well as when any methodical arrangement repeats itself for the sake of mere repetition. When people attend to proportions, disproportions in rigid schemas are more likely to be recognized. In this, we have an enormous insight into how Chesterton saw so much of the future. Being as attentive as he was, he noticed minor shifts of proportion in his own time and saw, as one would in seeing that the rudder of a ship is angled even just slightly too much to one side, certain likely long-term consequences. What starts as a minor error can, in the long run, spell doom.

166. Chesterton, *Daily News*, 31 March 1906.
167. Chesterton, *Illustrated London News*, 20 July 1918.
168. Chesterton, *Collected Works, Volume 5*, 74.

Chesterton applies something of the above principle of seeking to appreciate spiritual balance to interpreting history. He notices, quoting the book of Ecclesiastes, that in history there is "nothing new under the sun."[169] "This point is part of a general historical principle, about which we should be clearer than we are, and about which there is something more to be said."[170] Chesterton takes issue with the modern pursuit of novelty and the ever-present expectation that something radically different will appear in the world at any moment. In contrast, with regard to alleging declinism or what he calls "decay," for instance, it is good to notice that while societies have decayed before and while the possibility remains open for us to consider how our society may be in peril, both decay and the causes for decay are unlikely to be entirely novel.[171] What is vital here is the proportions between things. Chesterton is not ruling out progress or decline, or any signs of such things. He is ruling out any rule that renders them inevitable. Understanding something like decline, for example, "is a question of the proportion and not the existence of certain follies."[172] This, Chesterton acknowledges, is not easy to assess but it is worth making some attempt at assessing it if we want to understand the world. What makes this more difficult is that the question of proportion "is mostly overlooked by modern thought."[173] Modern thought replaces common sense with "uncommon nonsense."[174] It tends towards distortions, both subtle and dramatic. Most alarmingly, it tends to mechanize thinking, granting to the stiff pattern, largely negative,[175] a higher significance than the nuanced, dynamic, and overdeterminate drama of meaning.

While understanding the proportions of things in relation to each other is tricky, however, it is by no means impossible. Arguably, this is the central concern with attending to formal causality, which concerns noticing and maintaining the dynamic tensions that exist between things. It means noting not just that things relate to each other along the lines of tensions, correspondences, and negations; it also means being concerned with how things balance each other out or fail to do so. It is a concern with stabilities and instabilities in the relationships between things. It is a concern, as the metaphor of a picture might show, with composition and organization.

---

169. Chesterton, *Illustrated London News*, 9 July 1921; Ecclesiastes 1:9.
170. Chesterton, *Illustrated London News*, 9 July 1921.
171. Chesterton, *Illustrated London News*, 9 July 1921.
172. Chesterton, *Illustrated London News*, 9 July 1921.
173. Chesterton, *Illustrated London News*, 9 July 1921.
174. Chesterton, *Illustrated London News*, 9 July 1921.
175. Chesterton, *Collected Works, Volume 1*, 58.

When things are in proportion, they are alive. This, quite rightly, makes prediction slightly more difficult. Especially in the realm of human affairs, a balanced person or group of people will be free to choose in a way that an imbalanced person or group of people cannot. Thus, Chesterton, being mindful of the between, resists prophesying with too much certainty. He notices trends and possibilities but assumes, in keeping with the metaxological posture, that he does not and cannot see everything. What he does not see, in his view, may turn out to be of greater significance for how things turn out than what he does see.

We get a sense of this where Chesterton reflects on how Robert Blatchford, his "old friend and foe," denounces him "as a pessimist and a prophet of woe for suggesting that England might some day be a Servile State."[176] Chesterton is amused by this, given that Blatchford was once thought a pessimist and prophet of woe for declaring it conceivable that England would one day be at war with Germany. Dark prophets, Chesterton insists, are not always false prophets, as Blatchford himself can attest. Crucially, Chesterton's work is filled with many examples of how he denounces pessimism as a philosophy of life. He refuses to assert that pessimism, as a univocal or dialectical shadow cast on existence, is legitimate or true. With that in mind, it makes no sense to refer to anyone as an optimist or pessimist with regard to how things turn out, whether for good or ill. If a person were to be pessimistic about the possibility of rainfall on any given day, for example, his pessimism can do nothing to affect the result. If we wonder what is going to happen, it matters more how we discern the outcome than how we feel about life in general. Chesterton points out that, although "there is no comparison between natural laws and the human will, there are human wills that are almost as much beyond our private control as natural laws."[177] This, he continues, is what Blatchford perceived when he considered that England and Germany might end up fighting each other. "He did not think there was anything particularly agreeable or gratifying about saying that Prussia would attack. He simply doubted whether anybody could prevent Prussia from attacking."[178] He happened to be right, although Chesterton notes, "there is no reason to doubt that he would have been very much relieved if he had turned out to be wrong."[179] He sees the reasonable possibility of predicting something accurately, as well as the reasonable possibility of being wrong. He allows for self-mediation but expects reality to answer

---

176. Chesterton, *Illustrated London News*, 1 September 1923.
177. Chesterton, *Illustrated London News*, 1 September 1923.
178. Chesterton, *Illustrated London News*, 1 September 1923.
179. Chesterton, *Illustrated London News*, 1 September 1923.

back in a way that does not keep perfectly with that self-mediation. Sanity is to know our limits, beyond which we cannot claim mastery. We must, in the end, surrender to faith.[180]

Chesterton offers a similar approach to what Jean-Pierre Dupuy calls "enlightened doomsaying."[181] Dupuy means that often one is duty-bound to make predictions, especially about catastrophic possibilities, not because we must be proven right but rather because by sounding the alarm, we may help to better prepare ourselves and others for a difficult future or, better, may even help to prevent the very catastrophic outcome we are predicting. Dupuy writes, "Anyone who wishes to prevent a catastrophe must believe in its possibility before it occurs. If one succeeds in preventing it, its non-realization keeps it firmly within the realm of the impossible, and efforts at prevention appear in retrospect to have been useless: there was no need to get excited; the peril did not exist."[182] Chesterton puts the same idea forward in this way: "The prophet of woe, whenever he is really a true prophet, is always trying to be a false prophet. The prophet would not utter his prophecies except in order to falsify his prophecies."[183]

He has this in mind when he restates his expectation that England will turn into a servile state, a prediction that has proven prescient as that country has become caught up in surveilling its own people, controlling and policing what they say, and drowning the nation in all manner of laws, many of which fail the test of reason. Chesterton is clear that the English temperament has a lot to do with his concern, and especially the fact that its "valuable virtues are mixed" with "sleepy qualities."[184] He does not worry that the English will emulate the Bolsheviks. They lack the spirit and the context that would make such a revolutionary and violent consciousness possible. But he worries that there are forms of tyranny the English are prone to. The "peril of the English carelessness," he suggests, "is that all sorts of barbaric and heathen things will creep back into it, as moss and thorns creep back into a decaying place. And the first of these old heathen things is the easy, the slovenly, the very human habit of slavery."[185] We know today what Chesterton calls the *servile state* as the *nanny state* or *surveillance state*. We know, too, that England is not the only nation with this quality. A servile state has an overprotective government that interferes unduly in the lives

---

180. Chesterton, *Poet and the Lunatics*, 70.
181. Dupuy, *How to Think About Catastrophe*, xii.
182. Dupuy, *How to Think About Catastrophe*, xii.
183. Chesterton, *Illustrated London News*, 1 September 1923.
184. Chesterton, *Illustrated London News*, 1 September 1923.
185. Chesterton, *Illustrated London News*, 1 September 1923.

of its citizens. In some ways, as governmental overreach has become more evident in recent years in many countries, we might say that Chesterton's prophecy was not severe or pessimistic enough. This is debatable, and yet I mention it because inexact prophecies fit a metaxological perspective. Self-mediation is not the only philosophical game in town.

An example can clarify something of what this means. Take, for instance, the metaphor of the so-called historical pendulum. More particularly, consider the literal object that the metaphor invokes. The actual pendulum of a clock is simple enough to interpret because its movement is regular. It is an abstraction isolated from other elements. Its regularity is essentially out of proportion with almost anything else besides. One aspect of reality stands out; all others recede. A figure is selected at the expense of the ground. The point of the pendulum's existence is, like some scientific method or reductionist theory, to achieve a functional status involving as little interference as possible. We see the pendulum rise, fall, and rise again, and so on; and by this symmetry and uniformity, the constant ticking of a clock can be established and time can be kept. Metaxological time, with its vicissitudes, surprises, and kairology, is seemingly transformed into a stable and predictable chronology. Time loses its memory, scent, texture, and experiential depth; it becomes a mere measurement.

If history worked like a pendulum, we might say, "I see that we are now going through a decline. We know for sure it will not last, for soon enough progress will rise up once more." However, would this be true to history? Does it illuminate what history is about if we take every upturn as indicative of progress and every downturn as indicative of decline? Even if there are trends, can history be understood as following such a predictable pattern? On the one hand, it may be possible to discern an overall sense of decline or progress, depending on what we are measuring that decline or progress by. On the other hand, Chesterton sees this metaphorical stress on upward and downward movement as creating various interpretive problems. It suggests a decision by certain interpreters of history to solve how to interpret historical movements before grappling with and understanding them. It helps them to "so completely misunderstand that they think they understand."[186] As this shows, it matters how we frame our interpretations of history. We may begin, for example, with a "conservative clock" or a "progressive clock" and will therefore make the mistake of insisting that history must conform to an entirely mechanical sense of being.[187] What we see depends on what we

---

186. Chesterton, *Illustrated London News*, 21 February 1925.
187. Chesterton, *Illustrated London News*, 21 February 1925.

expect to see, as well as on how and where we happen to be looking.[188] The pendulum may simply ensure that we are never looking at the right thing.

"The other day," writes Chesterton, "I had an open discussion about what will happen next. As a matter of fact, I never have the wildest notion of what will happen next; least of all when I am speaking in public. My prophetic powers over the future go no further than a desperate guess about the nature of the next sentence."[189] To address the more dialectical-mechanical view of progress, Chesterton suggests that, "by the analogy of the past, it would appear that even progress never went in a straight line, but went in a sort of zig-zag."[190] By this he does not mean to invoke the idea of a pendulum at all, and his metaphor of a zig-zag is not intended to be thought regular like clockwork. He does not mean that history "is always rising and sinking on a perpetual see-saw."[191] The idea of a zig-zag suggests something of what it is like when a person, group, or nation, takes a journey on an uncharted course. Such a journey may involve mistakes, wrong turns, side steps, back-tracking, getting lost, walking on unsuitable paths, stopping to take in the view, many attempts at course correction, and more. Hopefully, in adventuring, people will generally find themselves heading in the right direction. But this is not guaranteed. Man wanders, Chesterton insists, and does not merely busy himself with "working out his destiny."[192]

Chesterton's metaxological awareness stops him from making the mistake of insisting upon dialectical predictability. In reality, as his own work shows us, the drama of being should not be reduced to any specific trend. The metaxological helps us to rethink unity in a more complex, less closed sense; it is mindful of the recalcitrances of the equivocal, as well as the limits of the dialectical. If we are to spot trends, we can remain open to the intrusion of what we have not considered possible. Further considering our propensity for zig-zagging, Chesterton writes, "What strikes me as curious is that this natural view of the soul straying hither and thither, like a living thing, is so unfamiliar to the modern mind that even when it is given as a description of a man it is received as a description of a machine; or that we cannot make a drawing of wings without it being copied as a diagram of wheels."[193] The temptation to reframe the given in terms we already ac-

---

188. Chesterton, *Illustrated London News*, 21 July 1923; 1 September 1923.
189. Chesterton, *Illustrated London News*, 21 February 1925.
190. Chesterton, *Illustrated London News*, 21 February 1925.
191. Chesterton, *Illustrated London News*, 21 February 1925.
192. Chesterton, *Illustrated London News*, 21 February 1925.
193. Chesterton, *Illustrated London News*, 21 February 1925.

cept is always there, waiting to render the metaxological subservient to the dialectical, or worse.

As the above implies, it is helpful to consider the importance of seeing our metaphors atmospherically; through a larger context or environment. An optimistic or pessimistic posture, for instance, affects how we reconcile ourselves to what is happening.[194] What we have in mind before we look at the facts we are given will shape how we make sense of the world, whether for good or ill. None of this is to say that we should not try to understand what sort of path people are taking or what path we ourselves are on. Some things are somewhat predictable. It is easy enough to predict, for instance, that the disproportionate amount of time a writer spends on his work predicts that he is likely to spend more time writing. Habits die hard. If, for example, he has been working on a book about Chesterton's remarkable prescience and formal causation, it is likely that when he sits down tomorrow or next week, he will continue to work on the same project until it is done. Nevertheless, given the dynamisms of life, which break the grooves of human habit, hurling into the drama different tensions to balance, counterbalance, and imbalance, it is unlikely to be predictable what he is going to write about once the project is done or even if he will manage to complete the project as intended. If he hopes to write more books in future, assuming he is of sound enough mind to think such a thing worthy of his or anyone else's time, there are no guarantees that this will be possible. Nevertheless, when individuals and societies are in a groove, we may have a better sense of where things are going. In all of this, "in both the singularity of beings and the mindful being," as well as always "*between* beings," as Desmond suggests, "there is a resistance to self-mediation."[195]

Still, Chesterton saw, in his time, and was honest enough to say so, many "modern groovings."[196] One example is that of a certain disproportionate "form of progress" that would have things "going quicker and quicker along a line in one direction."[197] Like the railway locomotive, "it has not the curiosity to stop, or the adventurous courage to go backwards."[198] From similar groovings, some sort of predictability is almost inevitable. But, as I have suggested above, we should be careful not to take this as a sign that we can therefore know precisely what will happen next in all cases and in all ways. Moreover, as I have argued above, we cannot interpret disproportions

---

194. Chesterton, *Illustrated London News*, 1 September 1923.
195. Desmond, *Being and the Between*, 194.
196. Chesterton, *Common Man*, 109.
197. Chesterton, *Common Man*, 109.
198. Chesterton, *Common Man*, 109.

without having a sense of proportion. We cannot understand anything apart from the *between*. This is an aspect of Chesterton's work, and especially of his awareness of the world, that Desmond helps us to notice. Still, to gain a clearer sense of how Chesterton attends to proportion requires a slightly different lens through which we can refract his work. That lens is provided by Platonism.

3

Being Formed

G. K. Chesterton Through Plato's Forms

WITH SOME ADJUSTMENTS, PLATO's contemplative philosophy is more than helpful for understanding Chesterton's attention to formal causality, although we should bear in mind that Plato's idea of form is not identical to the notion of the formal cause developed by his disciple Aristotle. Chesterton's echoes of Platonist thought are more playful than certain precisionists might appreciate. We ought to expect this given his vocation. Still, he makes fairly frequent, typically admiring, references to Plato,[1] and it is not difficult to pick up on his affinity with Platonist thought. He more than implies that his readers have a lot to learn from that philosophical pioneer, far more than I can hope to cover in this chapter. And yet, it may seem counter-intuitive to indicate Plato's understanding of cause as significant for understanding Chesterton's prescience. Would his understanding of sociology and history, together with his imaginative powers and the like, not better explain Chesterton's predictions of certain future happenings? To answer to this, I offer the counter-claim that we cannot understand how Chesterton understood anything, including sociology and history, without a sense of what he thought supreme.

I have in mind the fact that the Greek understanding of cause is broader and less univocal than what we typically take the idea to mean nowadays.

---

1. Chesterton, *The Speaker*, 3 May 1902; Chesterton, *Collected Works, Volume 1*, 79; Chesterton, *Saint Thomas Aquinas & Saint Francis of Assisi*, 29, 148–49; Chesterton, *Everlasting Man*, 125; Chesterton, *Illustrated London News*, 6 April 1907; 1 June 1935; 31 August 1935; 30 November 1935; 21 December 1935.

In the original language, it even implies notions of blame, responsibility, and petition, and indicates "a kind of dependence."[2] Form, in Plato's work, is not merely an explanation of how one thing leads to another; it suggests an account of the significance of things. It is not possible, in this perspective, to separate being from meaning and communication,[3] as Desmond's philosophy also reminds us. As Chesterton's many predictions show us, there is no way to tell what is going to happen without offering some judgment on its value, and especially on whether or not it conforms to God's original plan. Chesterton does not merely say that Socialism is likely to play a larger part in England's future, for example; he says that it is not a good thing and offers reasons why.[4] Chesterton has in mind a higher good than do the Socialists. When he suggests that satire is ending, he indicates that this is not pleasing.[5] He has in mind a clear idea of the good that all satire depends upon for its existence. He writes, "Satire may be mad and anarchic, but it presupposes an admitted superiority in certain things over others; it presupposes a standard."[6] By analogy, "When little boys in the street laugh at the fatness of some distinguished journalist, they are unconsciously assuming a standard of Greek sculpture. They are appealing to the marble Apollo. And the curious disappearance of satire from our literature is an instance of the fierce things fading for want of any principle to be fierce about."[7] In this, as in much else, he intimates the Platonist sense that the "Idea of the Good is the ultimate cause of all being," as well as the fact that "perfect causality cannot be anything but the communication of its own perfection."[8] The happening of being is impossible to separate from the good from which it is derived, if only imperfectly or even in degraded form.

With this in mind, I take up a selection of three Platonist themes most pertinent to the question of how Chesterton's attunement to formal causality informs his prescience. The first is what form means for Plato and why this matters for interpreting Chesterton. The second is how Chesterton takes up the idea of form as he points to the importance of having ideals. This second question, preempting the discussion in the next chapter, suggests the not yet differentiated interweaving of what Aristotle calls formal, final, and efficient causality. Finally, building on the discussion in the previous chapter on the

2. Schindler, *Catholicity of Reason*, 121.
3. Schindler, *Catholicity of Reason*, 122.
4. Chesterton, *Daily News*, 2 November 1907.
5. Chesterton, *Daily News*, 18 March 1911.
6. Chesterton, *Collected Works*, Volume 1, 245.
7. Chesterton, *Collected Works*, Volume 1, 245.
8. Chesterton, *Collected Works*, Volume 1, 123.

metaxological sense of being, I explore Chestertonian analogy as a vital way of attending to the world. This analogical mindfulness is part of Chesterton's intuition that the analogical play of thought is rooted in the analogical play of reality. Thought naturally wants to accord with being and only unnaturally and sinfully wants to evade it.

Reinstating the Form

To be true to being, although he never spells this out, it is safe to say that Chesterton remains faithful to a Christian-Platonist synthesis of a kind, like that of St. Ambrose and St. Augustine, which rejects some of the un-Christian or possibly pre-Christian tenets of Platonism. Since Christianity regards creation as a gratuitous gift and the result of God's freedom, for instance, it does not see creation as emanation, which it is for Plato. In Christianity, the created order remains a broken theophany that discloses something of God. Furthermore, in keeping with the doctrine of the incarnation, and informed by the slightly more Aristotelian Platonism of St. Thomas Aquinas, material reality is held in higher regard by Chesterton than it may have been by certain early Platonists, although we should bear in mind, better than Chesterton did,[9] that the denigration of concrete realities by certain Platonists has often been exaggerated. Moreover, the metaphysical hierarchy of Platonists, which includes a demiurge and daemons, is supplanted by a Christian trinitarian ontology, which includes its own cosmos of supernatural beings. The doctrine of the Trinity implies, among other things, that the paradox of the one and the many is not just in creation but at the heart of God.[10] With these modifications in mind, we can be sure that Chesterton remains true to the primary gift of Platonism to Christianity, which is the idea of *methexis* or participation. Intimacy is real by its participation in ultimacy—God, who is Goodness itself. The true is the mediation of God and God's goodness. Beauty binds all things together.[11]

Chesterton's realism adheres more closely to Plato than Aristotle in indicating an essential asymmetry in the structure of reality that favors the transcendent over the immanent and stresses intermediation over self-mediation. The immanent gains its reality by participating in the forms, just as we get closer to God in sacramental worship and faithful service. Universals *precede* things; they have an ontological priority over their

---

9. Chesterton, *Saint Thomas Aquinas & Saint Francis of Assisi*, 101.

10. Boersma, *Heavenly Participation*, 33–35.

11. Pickstock, *Aspects of Truth*, 235; See Schindler, *Love and the Postmodern Condition*.

expression in the mundane world. They grant a halo to the mundane world; they make the mundane magnificent. This does not mean, as Chesterton is aware, that existing things are unreal, only that their reality is "secondary and dependent."[12] The ordinary is best affirmed when its participation in the transcendent realm, within the finite limits of the given, is at a maximum. Transcendence does not take away from the immanent but grants it integrity and vibrancy. Differences are not dissolved by identity but all non-identical repetitions of form ought to be allowed to reveal their utmost attunement to the divine idea. Chesterton's attention to formal causality always has a singular aim: *contact with reality*.[13] This means knowing what is real as fully as possible; it means "knowledge by encounter" or "indirect encounter."[14] Knowledge is not foremost in replication, abstraction, or representation, but in participation. One can know, therefore, without being able to say what one knows. To encounter "things of this world" is to encounter the "things beyond this world in which they are rooted."[15]

One crucial aspect of all of this is that participation safeguards Chesterton's above-mentioned celebration of our need for adventure as balancing out our need for home. It nurtures the desire to love and know God and seek out his will. The phenomenal world cannot ever fully express everything contained in God. It always communicates an abundance to being that transcends human reasoning. It invites exploration. Also, this sense of being as a gift sustained apart from any mere appearance of autonomy points to the real value of things. They should not be reduced to the phenomenological given, which in its openness still risks a certain unhaloing of being. We should not want to have a "dreadful dry light shed on things" since this would only "wither up the moral mysteries as illusions" and turn "respect for age, respect for property" and any sense of the "sanctity of life" into mere "superstition."[16] To apprehend the halo on being and to be apprehended by it, in the tensions arising through paradox, is to admire the depth of reality and to refuse superficiality. It is to seek out wholeness and unity in the midst of multiplicity rather than to have multiplicity fragment our attention and lure us away from the God of unity whose love is the source of life.

Chesterton sides with Plato's delicate attention to integration in the dissimilarity of the transcendent and the immanent rather than to any other metaphysical proposition of monism or dualism. This is not an easy

---

12. Chesterton, *Saint Thomas Aquinas & Saint Francis of Assisi*, 158.
13. Chesterton, *Saint Thomas Aquinas & Saint Francis of Assisi*, 170.
14. Chesterton, *Daily News*, 25 February 1905; Pickstock, *Aspects of Truth*, 165.
15. Chesterton, *Daily* News, 25 February 1905; Pickstock, *Aspects of Truth*, 165.
16. Chesterton, *Poet and the Lunatics*, 54.

or obvious choice. All indications are that it is the more difficult form of metaphysical attunement because it demands of us a willingness to accept a degree of unknowing within our knowing. It demands the submission of understanding to faith. Chesterton is aware of how easy it would be to simply make a plan of life with a black background as pessimists do and then dismiss any speck of light as accidental, or to render the background plain white as some in the Christian Scientist movement do even while they explain smudges and dirt away with detached appeals to ready-made hope.[17] He knows how easy it would be to be a dualist who regards life as a chess board with good and evil as two equal but opposite forces. But all such pre-decided and often temperament-dependent patterns, while having a ring of truth to them, ultimately fail to account for and accord with what is real.

This is not to say that there are no fixed points of reference but rather that all fixity needs to be identified beyond heterogeneity. For instance, Chesterton agrees with Aquinas's contention that every existence, as such, is good.[18] Even where this phrase casts a shadow, it clarifies the place of rightness and also the fact that "wrong has no right to be wrong and therefore no right to be there."[19] For Chesterton, goodness is permanent and the created order partakes of this permanence. We are not merely looking for an impersonal or mathematical formula, in the end, but for the grounding ethos of the real that transcends any constructed ethos. Plato helps to account for this as we look at his theory of forms.

Plato's theory of forms, otherwise called his hypothesis of ideas, can be distilled beginning with the simple observation that existence is marked by consistency, unity, immutability, and timelessness, even while multiplicity and fragmentation are evident in experience. We perceive changes all the time, as light beyond light casts flickering shadows onto the wall of becoming. But for Plato such changes are fleeting and less real. Being, for Plato, is "identical to itself,"[20] although this identity retains a metaxological openness to non-identity. This is a testimony to the fact that "the ultimate lies beyond both change and unchanging, One and Many, being and non-being, and appearing and non-appearing."[21] The forms, as Catherine Pickstock notes, "both are and are not identical with the things that participate in them.

---

17. Chesterton, *Everlasting Man*, 245.
18. Chesterton, *Saint Thomas Aquinas & Saint Francis of Assisi*, 100.
19. Chesterton, *Everlasting Man*, 245.
20. Grondin, *Introduction to Metaphysics*, 24.
21. Pickstock, *Aspects of Truth*, 232.

Participation itself is contradictory because it shares in a transcendent reality without dividing it and imitates it without being separate from it."[22]

For Plato, being is *idea* or *form*. Both words translate his word *eidos*.[23] For the modern mind, the word *idea* is typically regarded as tenuous since it implies a merely subjective mental representation. For more materialistically minded moderns, an idea is not a reality but only the emergent result of subjective neurological processes. This is not what Plato believes. For him, *ideas* are real. While we carry subjective notions around with us, these notions are reflective, in better and worse ways, of our capacity to seek out the transcendent realm of ideas. Our understanding of the truth is derived from being in harmony with the ideas, which precede and outlast us. Ideas are fundamentally paradigmatic, in other words, and not propositional, and so they possess an autonomous and necessary existence apart from any evanescent imitations dependent on them. This appeal to necessity is no subversion of the metaxological posture that I have argued Chesterton exemplifies; it is its foundation.

Form, for Plato, implies the transcendent shape according to which we recognize and interpret reality. Form transcends us and mediates itself to us such that it gives intelligibility to things. This is true for Chesterton as well.[24] Form implies what things have in common, which we are remarkably capable of discerning in the intermediation of being. To use a Chestertonian example, I can identify an array of specific flowers as flowers, not because, as the nominalist might say, they happen to look similar but because they have enough in common that they appear to me to participate in one transcendent form. This appearance is not a mere appearance. The similarity is real and not merely representational. Difference in repetition emerges out of a prior unity. A greater proximity in likeness suggests a more direct sense of a particular form. One daisy looks more like another daisy than like a tulip or a rose because it shares in the form of the ideal *daisy*, even while all of these share in the form of *flower* and the unifying form of *beauty*.[25]

It would be a mistake to assume, as moderns do, that the similarity in daisies is simply because daisies grow from daisy seeds. This is no explanation at all since it only describes a starting point and does not account for the pattern of being that the daisy conforms to. It is true that "every great thing grows from a seed, or something smaller than itself." But, as Chesterton

---

22. Pickstock, *Aspects of Truth*, 232–33.
23. Grondin, *Introduction to Metaphysics*, 24.
24. Chesterton, *Illustrated London News*, 20 June 1936.
25. Chesterton, *Collected Works, Volume 1*, 39–46.

stresses, "every seed" originates in "something larger than itself."[26] As much as anyone may want to reduce this to a mechanical explanation, working only from parts towards a whole, such an explanation evades the issue of form and therefore evades the issue of formal causality. Even something as plain as a daisy, to be perceived as a daisy, must be recognized as meaningful according to the shape it takes and the form given to it by what transcends it. Its form, reflected and perceived in existence, is an echo of a higher form. We perceive a singular daisy because it is of the same species as other daisies. *Species* has a potentially reductive biological meaning, so it is helpful to recall that it comes from the Latin translation of the Greek *eidos*.

Because this example and explanation focuses on the general visual characteristics of a thing, there is a risk that we may adopt only a univocal or dialectical posture towards the being of daisies in particular and towards being in general. This would not fit with Plato or Chesterton. After all, the visual sense tends to prefer the linear to the environmental. It is therefore important to employ the full range of sensory and intellectual experience to properly appreciate how form is apprehended.[27] Metaxological attunement encourages transcending the false reduction of being to any entirely linear and individual understanding. We do not perceive things as participating in the same form only because of our private mental models. That we share in the perceptual worlds of others implies that we share in a form of mind that guides our receptivity to the same or similar patterns, just as we are intermediators of being with and for each other. What makes this miraculously universal receptivity possible, even if only potentially? No doubt, we should be mindful of how intermediation in the community of beings may corrupt our receptivity. We still inhabit a fallen world and are porous to distortions. But the sense we have of permanence beyond all variable permutations persists. Even the scientist atheist defaults to an assumed Christian morality to criticize Christians who fail to live up to their own moral standards. There are variations on the theme of every universal, from daisies to the minds that perceive them, and yet unity is what astonishes Plato and Chesterton, and we ought to welcome a similar astonishment as the spark of our philosophizing.

It is not unreasonable to deduce that if things share so much, and with such astounding regularity even in the presence of multiplicity and complexity, that it is because the forms are real and not just mental projections. To apprehend the idea or pattern of anything is to know it by participation. The milieu of mindfulness is capable of cooperating with the milieu of being

---

26. Chesterton, *Everlasting Man*, 87.
27. Chesterton, *Saint Thomas Aquinas & Saint Francis of Assisi*, 148.

as both part of it and as transcending it. This is a key aspect of formal causality for Chesterton, especially because of his basic trust in the intelligibility of reality. As in Plato's work, anticipating the doctrine of the analogy of being discussed below, it is vital to conceive of the relationship between the idea and what we experience in reality as being one of both separation and non-separation.[28] To be is to participate in the forms, and to participate means to imitate. Such imitation provides the basis of the existence of things.[29] This imitation should not be confused with mere cosmetic copying. It is a dynamic response to form and not an attempt to merely fuse the variations in being with the unity of form. To do so would mean to transform the metaxological into the univocal and thus also to transform metaphysics into ontotheology, meaning a instrumentalization of the idea of God and of other metaphysical categories as univocal foundations in the service of powermongering. Our knowing ought to be dynamic, as a certain intensification of our relationship with the world that furthers our participation in God.

If I see a flower and find it beautiful, it *is* beautiful; and its beauty expands in my noticing it and so does my mind expand as I attend to it. It is beautiful because it participates in the form of *beauty*, just as it is a flower by its participation in the form of *flower* and a daisy by its participation in the form of *daisy*. Beauty is both unified and separate here. I must be receptive to it to perceive it. For Chesterton, the world is charged with goodness, beauty, and truth. These forms are experienced in the immanent realm even while their source remains transcendent. As this implies, form refers to nature and structure as coherent and whole.[30] It means not only that any given thing is coherent in its identity but also that it conforms to a principle that allows it to endure beyond unfolding contingencies. In this, form is a principle of intelligibility. When we know something truly, we understand its form. Moreover, all forms are structured by and subservient to the form of goodness. Goodness is responsible for the knowability of all other individual types and governs all other forms.[31] However, the intelligibility of the forms can be harmed by our inattention to form. Virtue guides us to relate rightly to the ideal; vice corrupts us. Vice, in particular, is known not in itself but as privation, analogous to how we know a crooked line in comparison with a straight one.[32] Those most attentive to form are likely to be in some

---

28. Grondin, *Introduction to Metaphysics*, 29.
29. McLean, *Plenitude and Participation*, 49.
30. Whyte, *Aspects of Form*.
31. Plato, *Republic*, 507b–509c.
32. Plotinus, *Enneads*, 65; §1.8.9.

ways more aware of deviations and distortions of form, and Chesterton is an example of this. This informs his prescience, which, for reasons I get to below, tends to dwell on what is likely to go wrong. He does not predict the normal, which does not change, but the abnormal, which varies wildly.

Plato was aware of objections to his theory of forms but also equally aware that simply doing away with the forms would hardly be a solution to the conceptual difficulties that his theory raises.[33] If, for instance, we do not accept an "objective" realm of values, we are likely to reify both anarchy and tyranny, which demand consensus as a magical substitute for real ideas. Without form, it is impossible to hold fast to sustained meaning and intelligibility. As we know, however, Plato's hypothesis is adjusted in Christian tradition so that the forms are grounded in God. Philo of Alexandria is the first to regard the forms from an overtly monotheistic perspective. He takes the forms as equal to God's word or *logos*, and this contention is echoed in the Gospel of St. John.[34] To avoid the Platonist introduction of a demiurge and to better conform to biblical revelation, St. Augustine later draws a line between God and creation. For Augustine, the forms in their fixedness are reasons for and within being, always given by God as the ultimate reason for being.[35] After him, following thinkers like Pseudo-Dionysius and St. Maximus Confessor, Aquinas proposes that God knows himself perfectly, and in that single and simple act of self-knowledge, he knows everything about himself, including "all the ways in which he could be imitated, or participated in, by any creature he might create."[36] The ideas expressed in created beings, minus those transcendentals that are given as alternate names for God, exist within the mind of God; they are manifestations of God's mind without being equal to God.

As this suggests, God is recognized as the foundational formal cause or exemplary cause. All other causes or accounts of things find their meaning in God and in relation to God. There is therefore a doubleness within all causality. Everything is at once caused by God and separate from God. As Aristotle's four causes are discussed below, we should keep in mind that God remains the exemplary cause behind each cause; he remains the ultimate authority on form; the reason for the being of all things. There is a divine plan but also, because of the freedom God gives to created beings, the possibility that they can veer away from that plan. Chesterton is aware of this in seeking to know the essence of things. It is by knowing the essence and the

---

33. Kołakowski, *Why Is There Something Rather Than Nothing?*, 30.
34. Davison. *Participation in God*, 94.
35. Davison. *Participation in God*, 97.
36. Davison. *Participation in God*, 100.

tensions between actualities and potentialities that we can understand even how things fail to conform to their proper form.

The above is only a slice of a larger discussion but the key point of focus, the fact that reality is grounded in the intelligence and goodness of God and intelligible in its goodness because of this, is a key feature of Chesterton's philosophical theology. He therefore agrees with other Platonist ideas that have a bearing on his understanding of formal causality, and thus also on his ability to perceive rightly. These are as follows. Being, goodness, and intellection are intertwined. Reality is primarily a harmony of forms and not a random collection of arbitrary possibilities constructed by mental projection; by careful contemplation, the patterns of these forms are discernible in being, even while not being conflatable with being. In our worship of God, reality, as it is, is made most perceptible. Ethics is fundamentally a question of entering into a productive and wholesome dialogue with the real and not a detached system of nominalist markers for what is correct or incorrect, even if such markers, being dependent in many instances on real virtues, may prove instructive. Virtue is the chief guide for our conformity to reality, and Christ remains the archetype of the true human form. Human beings, as free beings, are nevertheless capable of choosing against the fundamental harmony of the real and are thus also capable of slipping away from reason. Even so, the coherence of reality, if understood, is sufficient for understanding where things go wrong. This last point is one I want to take up in particular below, as I begin to interpret how Chesterton adopts and applies something of this Platonist vision to understanding and interpreting the world.

Reclaiming the Ideal

To discover how Chesterton attends to form, I want to further consider something only briefly glanced at in the previous chapters, the fact that he did not ascribe to any particular theory of historical progression. He had no strict historicist method. Thankfully, this does not mean he had no method at all, otherwise my attempt here to offer an explanation for how he was able to be so prescient would be a rather lengthy evasion of its chief aim. His method was to attend to things through form and formal causality. In this, he stood at odds with a fashion in his own time that still holds significant sway today. The fashion in question was and is with a certain kind of progress. Today, we commonly find the idea of progress expressed less overtly than was once the case, in terms like *innovation, transformation,* and *change.* Many of the ideological aims implicit in the progressivism of today, found in words like *empowerment, inclusion,* and *diversity,* are substitutes for the older notion of *progress*. Progressives of various stripes are heard declaring those who have somehow failed to stay with the times to be dinosaurs. Any current year is taken as the supposed measure of how far we have apparently come, or perhaps it is the measure of how we have failed to progress. Even if progress is no longer as explicitly named as it was in Chesterton's time, there is ample evidence that the idea is still with us.

The sociologist Robert Nisbet claims, "No single idea has been more important than, perhaps [even] as important as, the idea of progress in Western civilization for nearly three thousand years."[37] Nisbet is not disparaging other important ideas in the West, including "liberty, justice, equality, community, and so forth," but he argues that such ideas, because they are typically taken up in the modern West, are rooted in "a philosophy of history that lends past, present, and future to their importance."[38] In other words, embedded in other prized ideas is the idea of sequential chronological advancement. Even if this makes sense on a clock or a calendar, however, this assumption that we should chop up time in this way is far from obvious. In reality, which includes our perceptions of reality, the past infiltrates the present in various ways, and so does the future. Our sense of time is more kairological than chronological, meaning that we feel some times to have different significances than other times. We experience time as folded in on itself, crumpled together rather messily, not as neatly strung up as clothes on a washing line to be read as one reads the words in a book.

Still, the general idea of progress suggests that people are in a continual state of improvement, having long ago departed from primitive or barbarous conditions while embracing developments as time moves on. This can only ever amount to being a fiction we tell ourselves and never a reality like formal causality. The mythical obsession with progression involves a concern only with figures but in the process it obscures the ground, which indicates that there can be not progress as such, only a complex interplay of trade-offs. J. B. Bury, gesturing towards the dialectical philosophy of Hegel, suggests that the idea of progress means the "synthesis of the past and a prophecy of the future. It is inseparable from a sense of time flowing in unilinear fashion."[39] Assuming this would imply the possibility of a science of stages that certain discerning minds, with the right method, would be able to figure out.

---

37. Nisbet, *History of the Idea of Progress*, 4.
38. Nisbet, *History of the Idea of Progress*, 4.
39. Nisbet, *History of the Idea of Progress*, 5.

One proposal of such a method is found in Marx's theory of historical prediction, which is rooted in a conception of history as developing according to economic and materialistic laws. As this example suggests, the idea of progress carries with it various assumptions of inexorability and inevitability. Even if there are occasional setbacks and accidents, history is taken by progressives—those who explicitly or implicitly accept this view of history—as something that complies with inevitable improvement as if it were equal to a law of nature. In other words, the concept of progress tends to view history as an aspect of nature, and culture is taken as only somewhat accidentally involved. Human beings, in this view, are passively carried along by progress like debris in the strong current of a river. This should not be taken to imply that reality is a solid thing for progressives who subscribe to such a view, though. Even nature seems to disappear under the spell of progress. The idea of progress excludes any sense that there are permanent conditions. All is becoming. Or, rather, because *what is* vanishes, all *becomes* becoming. As Chesterton points out with reference to Darwinian thought, which echoes this logic, because it erases the standard offered by unified being, this sort of thinking destroys our capacity to measure change.[40] Arguably, progressivism has found such wide acceptance in the West because of the Christian tradition. The Bible itself suggests the unfolding of history towards a glorious end, at which time all things will be reconciled and God's reign will be established forever and ever. But a more careful reading of the Scriptures and a more careful study of history suggests absolutely no clear movement from one step to the next, with things always incrementally improving. Another strong reason for progressivism's plausibility may simply be existential. We see children grow into adults, and we see technological developments of all kinds, and our inductive reasoning and pattern-seeking ability is quick to notice trends, one way or another. In this, however, we need to notice what must be left out for the myth of straightforward progress to remain in place.

The counterpart but not quite the opposite of the progressive, although still adhering to the idea that history operates predictably, is the declinist. The main difference between the progressive and the declinist is not in the principle that change is predictable but in the difference of the direction of change. Progressives think things are getting better while declinists think they are getting worse. History has a destiny for both groups, but that destiny is either pleasing or displeasing. It takes no trouble to see problems with the mere presence of these two different cases, just as it is not difficult to see that they are both prone to rigid historicism. The two positions, when taken

---

40. Chesterton, *Collected Works, Volume 1*, 237.

absolutely, are mutually exclusive. History cannot, in any rigid sense, be both improving and worsening, even if improvements in some things and deterioration in other things are detectable. Almost anyone can tell when surveying history with a touch of imagination that many things do seem to be getting better even while many other things are getting worse but it would be rather foolhardy to claim that we know exactly how things will look next Tuesday or next century. It may be foolhardy to claim we know what is going on right now, in the present. Take, for example, signs today that mental health is in decline. Even such signs are far from straightforward; they do not imply an incontestable interpretation. After all, the interest in measuring mental health has been on the rise for decades, along with therapeutic interventions. So many therapeutic perspectives do not agree with each other about what mental health even means. Moreover, and this is just for starters, it is not obvious that such measures are right, or even if the interventions themselves are without sometimes destructive consequences. The tool for measuring and the thing being measured are both haunted by equivocities. The mind studies itself but it is not transparent to itself.

"Human history," writes Chesterton, "is so rich and complicated that you can make out a case for any course of improvement or retrogression."[41] If we wanted to prove, for example, that the world has become "more democratic," we could easily find support for our claim, even if it is a dreadfully vague claim. Similarly, we might be able to support a case that aristocracy has gained power or that militarism has declined or even that the color green seems to be more popular today than it ever was. It turns out that progressives and declinists are somehow both wrong and right in their views. "The human race," Chesterton stresses, "has not been growing more and more anything from the beginning" and neither has it "been growing less and less anything from the beginning."[42] If there has been progress, he suggests, "there has been no progress which can be expressed simply in terms of one tendency or one thing."[43] The same applies to regression and decline. It matters how we interpret history, and the notion of progress makes for a poor interpretive lens. It assumes too much without acknowledging its assumptions.

One core problem with the modern idea of progress, Chesterton contends, is that it is "a comparative of which we have not settled the superlative."[44] Even today, people regard progress in somewhat evolutionary terms, not to mean that there is a clear measurement according to which we

---

41. Chesterton, *Illustrated London News*, 18 August 1906.
42. Chesterton, *Illustrated London News*, 10 February 1906.
43. Chesterton, *Illustrated London News*, 10 February 1906.
44. Chesterton, *Collected Works, Volume 1*, 52.

can insist that Thursday is better than Wednesday but to mean that a mere change has occurred. The judgment that the change has improved things is not determined according to a sound philosophy but rather by the passage of time and an insane compliance with happenstance fashions. This amounts, as exemplified especially in the art world influenced by the avant-garde, to mistaking novelty for improvement. A further problem is intertwined with this one. Progress means, more or less, getting away from whatever yesterday was. But this chronological snobbery, this arbitrary preference of the present over the past, is sure only of what we ought to avoid, rather than of what we ought to aim for. "A modern morality," for instance, "can only point with absolute conviction to the horrors that follow breaches of law; its only certainty is a certainty of ill. It can only point to imperfection. It has no perfection to point to."[45] In theological terms, Chesterton sees this as a further fall of man, after which only the knowledge of evil remains. As I have already noted, he aptly names this "certainty of ill" the "negative spirit."[46]

He tells a parable to show what he means by this idea. The story goes that there is a monk, representing the "spirit of the Middle Ages," who wants to discuss the value of light while standing beneath an illuminated lamppost at night. Just as he is about to get started, a commotion breaks out among his modern listeners who promptly knock him over and tear down the lamppost. They congratulate each other "on their unmedieval practicality."[47] But these moderns soon run into some difficulties, for each of them wanted to tear down the lamppost for an absurd array of different reasons: some because they preferred an electric light over gas, others because they wanted to repurpose the iron that kept the light in place, some because the light was too bright, others because it was too dull, some because they wanted darkness to hide their evil deeds, and others because they thought it would be fun to tear anything down—the lamp just happened to be a convenient target. "So, gradually and inevitably," writes Chesterton, "there comes back the conviction that the monk was right after all, and that all depends on what is the philosophy of Light."[48] Unfortunately, what could have been discussed under the glow of the gas lamp has now got to be discussed in darkness. What could once have been settled with reference to an ideal must be settled, somehow, in its absence. Elsewhere Chesterton argues that the essential insecurity of modern society is owed to its being "based on the notion that all men will do the same thing for different reasons. A virile and vigorous society should

---

45. Chesterton, *Collected Works*, Volume 1, 47.
46. Chesterton, *Collected Works*, Volume 1, 47.
47. Chesterton, *Collected Works*, Volume 1, 46.
48. Chesterton, *Collected Works*, Volume 1, 46.

rather be based on the notion that all men will do different things for the same reason."[49] Attunement to form by no means excludes creative possibilities; it secures them. Imagination thrives within limitations.

It is perhaps surprising to see that the allure of the idea of progress has survived so many reasonable and unanswerable criticisms.[50] As I have already suggested, this is probably the result of various biases, as well as many observable waxings and wanings. The idea of progress is evident in so much political sloganeering and posturing today, as well as in the conformist jargon of the managerial class, that it cannot be regarded as a mere fringe concern. And yet, again, the notion of progress remains "a comparative" term.[51] What, then, is the "superlative"?[52] It is no good to sleepwalk through the world without any sense of what we are aiming for. The Platonist can imagine what sort of toothpicks and toothbrushes we should have, but the progressive, who Chesterton also calls a "somnambulist," is a listless wanderer.[53] He "has no ideal standard; no goal which to him is what the Golden Age of Peace was to his grandfather or the Utopia of William Morris was to his father. He doesn't know whether he wants to be more individualistic or less, more communist or less."[54]

Form means having a teleological orientation guided by faith, hope, and love. But as Chesterton notices, the sleepwalking progressive sets a diminished hope against faith: "Hope is to us what faith was to our fathers; our ultimate hold is not on something we have got, but on something we are going to get. Only we have forgotten what it is."[55] When hope is untethered, ends become vague, and the task of inspiring warm feelings and rationalizations in people becomes more pressing. The modern focus is more on processes than on results. Consequently, there is no clarity about what it would mean to achieve what people are striving for. In speech and writing, for example, many are tempted to use secondary words as if they are primary words. *Happiness* is a primary word. You know when you are happy and you know when you are not. *Progress* is a secondary word. With respect to happiness, it would mean "the degree of one's approach to happiness."[56] You can tell if you are making progress toward happiness if you are feeling happier

---

49. Chesterton, *New Renascence*, 95.
50. See Slaboch, *Road to Nowhere*.
51. Chesterton, *Collected Works, Volume 1*, 52.
52. Chesterton, *Collected Works, Volume 1*, 52.
53. Chesterton, *New Renascence*, 64–65.
54. Chesterton, *New Renascence*, 64–65.
55. Chesterton, *New Renascence*, 62.
56. Chesterton, *Daily News*, 7 May 1910.

now than you were a few moments or days ago. However, this gets inverted when the idea of progress is regarded as primary. The question stops being one of how we are progressing toward happiness and starts being one of whether happiness helps progress in any way. To take another example, instead of asking what sort of education would be good for children or adults, education might be given such high rhetorical and political priority that school pupils and students at universities will spend hours of their precious time learning about things that may make their lives demonstrably more incoherent and miserable. Progressives may be thrilled that problems in education are being solved without pausing to reflect on whether the problems that are being solved have been understood. If everyone is being educated according to such logic, then perhaps education is the problem.

Here we find a decidedly Chestertonian response to a modern dialectical approach. One predominant expression of modern dialectic is that its opposition to a given is taken as a standard of sorts or as a point of departure. This is not necessarily a good or bad thing; it is less a matter of judgment than a matter of perception. In dialectic, a moment of instability or negation is given a certain perceptual priority. This negativity opposes a positive position, although it is perhaps not a well-articulated one. A negation functions, in a way, as a figure that seeks out the largely invisible and taken-for-granted ground, although it is possible for the negation, like Keats's notion of *negative capability*, to be more ground than figure. In this we find an echo of the posture of the boy mentioned in the first chapter who, without understanding, decides to attack the roots of the world. But this dialectical force still allows for otherness of a kind; it is not entirely closed to the equivocal or the metaxological. Resistance to the destabilizing force is granted some legitimacy by the boy. In the resulting interplay between identity and otherness here, between equivocity and univocity, a strange thing starts to happen. As the attacked positive and commonsensical position is increasingly informed and even transformed by the antithesis, the framing offered by the antithesis becomes the primary way that the normal position is known. It stops being an identity discovered through negation and becomes an identity formed, at least in the minds of people, by that negation. The new arising, which embraces both unmediated A and unmediated not-A within itself, is a synthesis of sorts.[57]

Notice how a negative and essentially formless posture towards a positive thing restructures the shape of that thing by sheer will. A concrete example of this would be that Christians everywhere have found themselves in the awkward position of explaining their beliefs in almost secular terms,

---

57. Fritzman, *Hegel*, 3–4.

as if Christianity has to appease the gods of the secular order. This may, however, have welcome side effects. For one thing, the believer may be able to explain what he thinks because of his confrontation with an opponent. As Chesterton observes, "Truths turn into dogmas the instant that they are disputed. Thus every man who utters a doubt defines a religion. And the scepticism of our time does not really destroy beliefs, rather it creates them; gives them their limits and their plain and defiant shape."[58] Nevertheless, one of the more detrimental effects of this could be that the real standard is, perhaps inadvertently, assumed to be substandard. The standard can become an addendum to, and relativized by, the substandard. In the end, the negation, which is flimsy and insubstantial at best, may be taken as having more authority and power than what it is attacking simply by being afforded a rhetorical position above what must now be defended. Chesterton wants to prevent this. An even more dramatic tendency to overrule the norm is found in the deconstructionist use of the marginal concern to tear away at what is central. Clarity about the ideal should be indispensable. Even if the ideal is attacked, we should not make the mistake of subordinating it to lesser things.

We can keep this in mind as we further consider how Chesterton opposes progress. When opposing progress, his Platonism becomes especially obvious. Even blasphemy, for instance, is threatened where no ideal is found since blasphemy depends on belief and can only fade where convictions have decayed to the point of formlessness.[59] The answer to this is not mere practicality, which Chesterton regards as one of the most misleading of modern materialist ideals. Arguably, keeping in mind what I have just said about modern dialectic, this is a standard in much modern morality, which has a tendency to invert the relationship between *vital* values (values and virtues in service of life) and *use* values (values in service of things), giving priority to the latter over the former.[60] This inversion is rendered likely with a forgetting of form since parts are more easily conceived of as separate from the whole. Practicality, for instance, compartmentalizes action and concerns itself with the realm of what is effective. Things are done quickly and efficiently. But *why* are they done and *to what end*? A guillotine is very efficient, for instance, but whether it is humane or moral is a different matter altogether. Mere practicality is equal to absolute relativity. To act quickly and effectively is by no means necessarily the same as acting according to the highest good. As Chesterton observes, there is nothing "so weak for

---

58. Chesterton, *Collected Works, Volume 1*, 206.
59. Chesterton, *Collected Works, Volume 1*, 44.
60. Scheler, *Ressentiment*, 106–8.

working purposes as this enormous importance attached to immediate victory. There is nothing that fails like success."[61]

Chesterton notes the absence of an aim or theory is likely to lead "nonconformists" to "persecute for a doctrine without stating it."[62] The absence of a form fosters an environment of terrible instability, in which mere novelty or shock value or tantrum-throwing can become standard ways of dealing with complex issues. The loss of formal depth becomes disturbingly apparent in this. But for Chesterton, the intelligibility of the world and the pursuit and achievement of justice are coextensive. He agrees with the essentialist stream of classical and medieval thought when regarding the marriage of thought and things meaningful; reality is, by its very nature, intellective. The structure of reality is intelligible because reality is made by the God who is the reason of being and the goodness of being. Without intelligibility and goodness, and without living in accordance with the intelligibility and goodness of being, we can only end up broken and living in a broken world. To pick a contest with the real in its intelligibility and goodness is to pick the losing side since it destroys the standard by which we might hope to achieve fullness.

We need to understand the "essence" of things, meaning their form. We need to know what things are before we understand how best to relate to them. We should ask about the essence of hammers[63] and fire pokers,[64] for instance, before we can know if, when, and how to use them, as well as if, when, and how not to use them. The same applies to people, who are ends in themselves and thus not to be abused. Chesterton especially explores this idea in *What's Wrong with the World* (1910). It is no good to reform society around men, women, and children without first answering questions about human dignity[65] and "the ultimate value of human life."[66] We should know the nature of men, women, and children before making any attempt to wreck their worlds with entirely theoretical systems. Without knowing the true meaning of anything, we are left with only our sentiments about them, together with our automatic and unquestioned cultural anti-metaphysics—our

---

61. Chesterton, *Collected Works, Volume 1*, 45.
62. Chesterton, *Collected Works, Volume 1*, 45.
63. Chesterton, *Collected Works, Volume 1*, 52.
64. Chesterton, *Collected Works, Volume 4*, 39–46.
65. Chesterton, *Autobiography*, 239; Chesterton, *Collected Works, Volume 1*, 94, 298; Chesterton, *Everlasting Man*, 52–53; Chesterton, *Saint Thomas Aquinas & Saint Francis of Assisi*, 36, 177; Chesterton, *What's Wrong with the World*, 15–24; Nichols, *Chesterton*, 121–59; Williams, *Mere Humanity*, 15–24; Maycock, "Introduction," 74.
66. Chesterton, *Collected Works, Volume 1*, 52.

"unconscious dogmas."[67] To be so disorientated by formlessness ensures the replication of an arbitrary awareness of being through corrupt human action.

Where others lose the ideal, Chesterton remains committed to it. His work shows his persistent ability to see where and how things can deviate from the ideal, as well as what is likely to happen if such deviations continue. Again, with regard to Plato's notion of form and with implications for Chesterton's intention to reclaim the ideal, note that efficient, final, and formal causality are undifferentiated. Although differentiating these can prove helpful, as I discuss in the following chapter, there are also two notable dangers in doing so. One is that we might fail to see that the causes are always interdependent. They are an agapeic community through which form retains its coherence and understandability. They rely on each other just as they rely on material causality. Another is that we may render formal causality subordinate to final causality, as Martin Heidegger does.[68] If we were to brazenly grant ontological and perceptual priority to any one of the causes, it would be best to regard formal causality as having the greatest weight, given that it unifies the other causes. Within the Platonist frame, however, all causes are essentially one. They represent the marriage of heaven and earth suggested in the Genesis account of creation.

It is not unimportant therefore that Chesterton equates his ideal with the Platonist notion of the idea. With a clear sense of the idea, he is mindful of how even unconscious dogmas can steer people. He claims that the mind grasps reality by either "a doctrine or a prejudice."[69] "A doctrine is a definite point," he writes, whereas a prejudice only provides "a direction."[70] An example of a doctrine would be the idea that "a man should not be eaten" even if eating meat might generally be fine. A prejudice, however, would be that "as little as possible of anything should be eaten."[71] The prejudice is enough to cause people to get lost in a conceptual fog because it amounts to little more than a vague promise to see how things will take shape. It cannot be relied upon, and Chesterton knows this. But this does not mean that prejudices are completely indeterminate. They reveal possibilities within a somewhat expected range.

Another salient component of understanding the essence of things, a vital dimension of Platonism in Chesterton's philosophy worth highlighting, is the importance of answering the question of what is good. "Every one

---

67. Chesterton, *Illustrated London News*, 15 March 1919.
68. Heidegger, *Question Concerning Technology*.
69. Chesterton, *What's Wrong with the World*, 23.
70. Chesterton, *What's Wrong with the World*, 23.
71. Chesterton, *What's Wrong with the World*, 23.

of the popular modern phrases and ideals," Chesterton writes, "is a dodge in order to shirk the problem of what is good."[72] *Progress, education*, and *liberty* can be far too glibly discussed without any reference to the question of what sort of good they are aiming for, especially with respect to human dignity. In noting the absence of a virtuous aim in progressive ideology, Chesterton gestures towards one of the distinct marks of modernity, namely the inversion of what the old metaphysicians called *act* and *potency*. This is more of an Aristotelian or Thomistic idea, perhaps, but it is already hinted at in the work of Plato, who notes the importance of aligning our lives with the highest ideal. *Act* refers to what possesses reality, and *potency* refers to potential or potentiality. The former leans towards being and the latter leans towards becoming. Potentiality remains tied to actuality. What is possible must be latent within reality and limited by actuality.

In the metaphysical philosophy of St. Thomas, only God is pure actuality. He is true reality without potency. In contrast, God's creation involves a mixture of act and potency, the suggestion being that potency is reliant upon actuality even as it makes certain demands on actuality. All true potentials are potentials of being. Even potency has to possess actuality first in order *to be* potency. The myth of progress that Chesterton so consistently attacks commits only to potency while forgetting this. Since he attends as closely as he can to actuality, in its intelligibility and its goodness, he notices potencies with reference to actuality even where others fail to do so. As a writer of fiction, he is especially skilled at noticing the rules of the world he is working with, as well as how things can and cannot play out given those rules. If, for example, in the courtroom drama *Manalive* (1912), his one character Innocent Smith has not committed any crimes *and* witnesses have seen him commit crimes, there must be an explanation that accounts for both his apparent innocence and his apparent guilt.[73] He could not have committed those crimes—and yet he did. In that particular story, the resolution is captured in the idea that Smith has broken with convention without contravening the law. His crimes were not crimes after all. What *seemed* (a question of potentiality) was not identical with what *was* (a question of actuality). Innocent Smith can therefore be proven innocent. This is a parable that involves a basic trust in the real. There is a proportion between actuality and potentiality, as well as a range of gradations (act, and act-potency mixtures, together with tensions between active potency and passive potency); from logical necessity (God as pure act), to mixed act (all things that are a mixture of act and potency), to real potency (potential existing in being and not

---

72. Chesterton, *Collected Works, Volume 1*, 51.
73. See Chesterton, *Manalive*.

just in thought), to logical possibility (such as unicorns, which exist only in theory and not in actuality). It is our job to attend to these, even if we do not yet fully understand them. Knowledge intertwines with wisdom, belief intertwines with truth, and reality intertwines with being. The mind can come into contact with reality because both have been given to the other by God.

For Chesterton, we should care more for truth than for consistency. This is possible for him because he does not equate participating in the forms of the real with mechanical replication. If we find two apparently contradictory truths, we should accept the two truths and the contradiction along with them.[74] Chesterton focuses on how reality is made manifest, and he knows that it cannot be intelligible only as a vague instability moving from becoming to becoming. He criticizes progress, that principle of pure potency, not because it is an illegitimate word or a useless idea. It is not intrinsically wrong to notice potentials. It is simply wrong to divorce potential from the actualizing power of form. You cannot be truly progressive, Chesterton reminds us, "without being doctrinal."[75] It would be a mistake, however, to regard Chesterton's focus on doctrines as absolutist in a dialectical sense. At the heart of his Christian Platonism is an intuitive play with being far more attuned to participation than to some narrow modernist concern with correctness. A clearer view of this is achievable when we consider the role played in Chesterton's thinking by the Catholic doctrine of the analogy of being.

Restoring Analogy

The recovery of a true idealism that focuses on the intelligibility of the forms accords beautifully with the *analogia entis* or analogy of being. At its simplest, the analogy of being means that there is an analogy between God and creation. We find "infinite plenitude refracted through finite multiplicity" in a participatory likeness, as Andrew Davison writes.[76] This is not to be taken only as an imaginative diversion because it claims to describe the actual relationship between God and creatures with echoes in the realm of reason. Being *is* analogical.[77] Intellection, which grasps the truth in the mediation of being, is also analogical. This implies a refusal of two equal but opposite metaphysical errors. The first is the error of pure identity, which refers to the univocal sense of being discussed above. The second error is that of

---

74. Chesterton, *Collected Works, Volume 1*, 230.
75. Chesterton, *Collected Works, Volume 1*, 53.
76. Davison, *Participation in God*, 105.
77. Kenner, *Paradox in Chesterton*, 27.

dissolute dialectic. Both errors try to resolve the difference between God and creatures into an equivalence that is somehow supposed to be more fundamental and comprehensive than any metaxological opening, and therefore also more foundational and comprehensive than God himself.[78] Both errors want to dissolve the difference between the hidden and the manifest, and between mind and being. However, to do such a thing would be to deny the truth, the mediation of being, a place. The conformation of mind and being gives rise to truth, whereas, in an immediate identity between them, truth becomes redundant. Truth itself is participatory, which is the real meaning of Aquinas's *adequatio*, and cannot be reduced to a game of exact duplication or conflation. If we forget this, we will tragically deny our participation, which exists in the between.

The analogy of being rests on the idea that God created the world *ex nihilo*, out of nothing.[79] God, the ultimate good and aim of created being,[80] is no dependent entity composed of parts like we are. God is being itself. As I have already said, Plato's forms live in the mind of God. Creation, unlike God, is not self-grounding but is radically contingent, although not so contingent as to have no foundation whatsoever. Creation comes from a gratuitous act of creative love, not some bizarre divine need, as if God were supposed to depend on his work for the meaning of his own existence. The contingency of creation relies on the Utmost Actualizer. All creatures, at every moment, are granted being by what transcends them. Whereas God's essence and his existence are identical, this does not apply to creatures. Our being, this mixture of act and potency, always given as a gift, and enmeshed in contingent becoming, never settles down into a calm self-supporting identity. At no point, in other words, can any created thing exist apart from God. God is being as such, while creatures are beings only by participation.

God and creatures do not therefore fit into some larger category of being. *Being* does not refer to or apply univocally to both God and creation; it is an analogy. There is, as this implies, a fundamental and unbridgeable dissimilarity between God and his creatures. However, on this point we should be careful not to assume that God is merely a sort of inaccessible other who merely negates the immanent realm the way a tiled floor negates the fallen porcelain plate that shatters against it. "Absolute otherness," as David Bentley Hart points out, "is not transcendence, but merely a kind of 'negative

---

78. Hart, *Hidden and the Manifest*, 97–112.

79. Chesterton, *Collected Works, Volume 1*, 57.

80. Chesterton, *Saint Thomas Aquinas & Saint Francis of Assisi*, 98; Chesterton, *Collected Works, Volume 1*, 347, 389.

immanence.'"[81] After all, true transcendence must transcend all negation. Crucial to the distinction between God and creation is the idea that there is no rivalry or competition between God and his creatures. Creation is not different from God in the way that an iguana is different from butternut soup. It is therefore no addition to God either. To assume such a difference would require some sort of mediating third, perhaps a demiurge, to assist with the communion of God and creation. This is why there is no competition between our fulfillment and God's glory. Arguably, it is a feature of the fall of man to regard God as a rival. Redemption, in contrast, means union with God; and union does not mean, in this case, the dissolving of one sort of being into another.

Our ideals, our striving for unity, goodness, truth, and beauty, ultimately gain their fullness by participating in God. This does not mean that there is a neat ontological continuum between God and creation. In radical discontinuity or ontological difference, which is another way of highlighting creation's analogous relationship with God, creation is given its being and identity. Creation is at every moment freed to be itself, sustained in being by the God of love, and prevented by God from disintegrating into the nothingness out of which he calls it. To reach the ideal or achieve the wholeness that is our end coincides perfectly with returning to God. Our fullness does not and cannot take anything away from God but is his desire for us.

Importantly, when Aquinas discusses analogy, his concern is not with abstracting or judging reason but with the intuitive intellect. Analogy does not merely split the world up into its constituent parts. It supports a holistic and harmonious perception within which being can be encountered as a whole. The analogy of being is not meant to render everything remote but the opposite; it reminds us of an intimacy in being. When I experience unity in the world, that unity is real. It is not conjured within my subjective experience but exists in a dynamic communion between me and the world. It is also not simply replicated by my mind, although the mind is moved in response to it. Analogy accounts for both the complexity of reality and the limits of language with respect to communicating what is real.[82] It is an agreement between similarity and difference; between, as Chesterton says, "agreement and disagreement."[83]

The prevalence of analogy in Chesterton's work is significant in that it stands in opposition to the dichotomous logic that dominates modern

---

81. Hart, *Hidden and the Manifest*, 99–100.
82. Kenner, *Paradox in Chesterton*, 27.
83. Chesterton, *Autobiography*, 332.

Western thought.[84] Against proposals of obvious univocal oppositions, equivocal differences, and dialectical relations, analogy sustains difference even in its articulations of commonality. It "intervenes in the dichotomies of logic" that dominate modern thought—dichotomies of particularity versus universality, form versus content, lawfulness versus exemplarity, and so on—not by resolving them by a higher synthesis but by confirming their identities as essentially relational and not as separate.[85] This principle has implications for all of life and, in his wisdom, Chesterton sees this. He wants us to notice that *to be* is *to be in relation*. To name just two examples, this is why, for him, the smallest human unit is not the individual but the family. This is also why it is impossible to solve political matters apart from solving the question of how we relate to property. To exist means to be in relation to people, the world, and God. In adhering to the primacy of analogy, Chesterton affirms the independence of dependent things while he confirms the dependence of independent things.[86]

One of the implications of this, especially for how we understand Chesterton's attunement to formal causality, is in how we enter into a speaking of the between. The analogy of being gives us a way of speaking of God and so articulates the real relation between the mind and reality in general. Analogy is as much a part of the logic of the incarnation as it is about the logic of our participation in being itself. In analogy we find that every concept is an approximate, malleable hermeneutical forcefield; and we should be careful not to treat any concept as a univocally exact, rigid hermeneutical fortress or even as an impenetrable cloud of equivocal bewilderment. We can notice this even in the most ordinary words we use. Take that word *ordinary*, for example. The word has several possible meanings that are by no means univocal. However, in using it, I would hope that, as an echo of my participation in the world, some sense of its meaning would be accessible. It implies the usual, normal, standard, typical, common, customary, habitual, expected, everyday, regular, routine, settled, set, fixed, traditional, quotidian, and prevailing, for starters. It also suggests the colorlessness, the mundane, the humdrum, and the mediocre. But it could imply more positive meanings, such as the homely, the humble, and the unpretentious. To be ordinary means to conform to an order. Even within those terms, we find almost endless complexities and nuances in the play of meaning. And yet, we have a *feel* for what *ordinary* means. Meaning, as meaning, is relational; it is also, for this reason, not removed from our experience of the world. It

---

84. Agamben, *Signature of All Things*, 7.
85. Agamben, *Signature of All Things*, 8.
86. Chesterton, *Saint Thomas Aquinas & Saint Francis of Assisi*, 36.

is not as rigid as literalists would have it be, nor is it as vague or unwieldy as some deconstructionists might suggest. We understand the concept, as we understand all concepts, by analogy.[87]

To define anything means to see it through another thing. This does not imply that we are left only with an infinite regress of discrete meanings, forever alienated from each other. All meanings are intertwined because they all share in being. Meanings influence each other because they are always of the whole. This applies not only to how words inform our understanding of other words but how real experiences and our responses to those experiences inform our perceptions. To perceive clearly means being open to the whole because the whole has its foundation in God and in God's ideas. It means allowing meanings to generate resonances and dissonances in all truth seeking and truth speaking. There is a freedom in this to escape the dominance of literalness in speech, which corrodes meaning. What is essential, again, is the real relations and proportions between things. At one point, Chesterton even suggests that the most important components of any utterance are the conjunctions.[88] How things relate to each other is of utmost importance for interpreting them rightly.[89] There is a world of difference, for example, between the sentence, "She is your mother, but she is trying to poison you" and "She is trying to poison you, but she is your mother."[90] The different structure indicates a shift in proportion. Moreover, the proportion, as I have already suggested in my discussion of the metaxological sense of being, invites us to perceive the shape of the formal cause—or, in this case, its distortion. This allows the further possibility of noticing how the formal cause evident in past or present circumstances may be echoed in future circumstances as well.

In a little book published in 1940, Chesterton's friend Hilaire Belloc reflects on Chesterton's place in English letters. Belloc discusses several key facets of Chesterton's work that stand out. He names the following as especially important: Chesterton wrote in and for a clear national context; consistently demonstrated an "extreme precision of thought"; was uniquely brilliant at using parallelism; was mindful of history; consistently demonstrated charity in his work; and, finally, he favorably received the Catholic faith.[91] Each of these facets has a bearing on Chesterton's attention to formal causality. However, with respect to Chesterton's intuition of the analogy of

---

87. See Hofstadter and Sander, *Surfaces and Essences*.
88. Chesterton, *Illustrated London News*, 3 August 1907.
89. Reyburn, *Seeing Things as They Are*, 262.
90. Chesterton, *Illustrated London News*, 3 August 1907.
91. Belloc, *On the Place of Gilbert Chesterton in English Letters*, 14–16.

being, as well as the analogical structure of consciousness, Chesterton's gift for parallelism is especially worth reflecting on. It is also, as I show below, significant for understanding his prescience. Here, at long last, and not a moment too soon, we can get a more concrete sense of how Chesterton saw the future.

At first, parallelism may seem only to be a fairly casual rhetorical feature of his work, but attention to Chestertonian parallelism reveals something more. "I have said," writes Belloc, "that parallelism was the weapon peculiar to Chesterton's genius."[92] Belloc clarifies his meaning by noting Chesterton's "unique, his capital, genius for illustration by parallel, by example" as "his peculiar mark."[93] Significantly, parallel to Chesterton's image of a poet as the symbol of sanity,[94] Gerard Manley Hopkins suggests that all poetry ultimately "reduces itself to the principle of parallelism."[95] By definition, parallelism refers to successive verbal constructions that connect meaning through an echo of form. This may involve an echo of grammatical structure, sound, or meter. However, Chestertonian parallelism is concerned with meaning itself in its analogical form. Belloc therefore defines his unique brand of parallelism as "the illustration of some unperceived truth by its exact consonance with the reflection of a truth already known and perceived."[96] For Belloc, no one comes close to Chesterton "in the whole course of English letters" to "his amazing" and even "superhuman . . . capacity for parallelism."[97] Parallelism is a non-identical repetition of analogy. It is a literary device that rests on a theological truth. No doubt it can be abused but, under Chesterton's pen, the aim is to use it to express the truth.

Belloc explains how easy it is to miss overly familiar truths that have sunk into the unconscious through habituation, as well as how we miss truths simply because they are unfamiliar to us. Similarly, we may miss truths when they are imperfectly expressed and articulated, as we are reminded in daily life. In other words, when "imperfect forms" are used to convey important things, we are likely to fail to recognize their importance. Parallelism, when used well, becomes a way to surprise the mind of the reader or hearer by ensuring the possibility of a genuine encounter.[98] As Bel-

---

92. Belloc, *On the Place of Gilbert Chesterton in English Letters*, 36.
93. Belloc, *On the Place of Gilbert Chesterton in English Letters*, 36.
94. Chesterton, *Collected Works, Volume 1*, 220, 230–31.
95. Jakobson, *Language in Literature*, 82; I owe Michael Hurley thanks for pointing this out to me.
96. Belloc, *On the Place of Gilbert Chesterton in English Letters*, 37.
97. Belloc, *On the Place of Gilbert Chesterton in English Letters*, 36.
98. Belloc, *On the Place of Gilbert Chesterton in English Letters*, 37.

loc also notices, the most "invaluable instrument of exposition, parallelism" is often found in "metaphor; and in metaphor (or in its parent, simile) Chesterton also excelled."[99]

Metaphor, a subcategory of analogy, means giving priority to resonant meaning over merely defining things. In the West, which seems to have suffered a severe decline in metaphorical thinking in recent decades, the tendency has been to define a thing by a movement away from that thing. If asked what is *red*, the Westerner will typically say it is a *color*. When asked what a *color* is, he will say it is a particular vibration of reflected light particles working in concert with the eye and the brain. When asked what a *vibration* is, he will define it with words like *frequency* and *energy*. But against this movement away from experience and perceptual openness, which is a nominalist tendency, metaphor seeks to root understanding in what is known—not in a movement away from the known. Red is a rose, the darkest part of a fire, the anger we feel at injustice, or the blood that pours from a wound.[100] Metaphor, which is extended through parallelism and granted a more definite shape in the process, carries one form across by another. It affirms the analogical structure of being.

This furthers the earlier discussion regarding a metaxological attunement to real relations. Chesterton advises us to know the distinction between a "real relation" and a "theoretical relation."[101] He offers the example of evolutionists, which suggests a relationship between man and ape. While we can see that there is insight to be gained from this parallel, Chesterton notices that it tends to be too abstract and therefore too removed from human experience. But there is, he says, a real and historic relation between man and his dog. It implies a tradition and not just a fad. The theoretical relation, which is removed from life and experience, sets up the distinct possibility of misunderstanding the formal cause, as when all nations are treated the same because they are all nations. Chesterton mentions this very example as a parallel to the scientific comparison of people to chimpanzees. But the real relation brings us closer to the formal cause, as when each nation is recognized for its own unique patterns and character traits. Chesterton mentions this as a parallel to the poetic image of a man and his dog. "Now," he writes, "according to whether men feel that difference between an experience and a notion, he will or will not understand the good and evil of a nation; for a nation is not a notion."[102] The implication is this: we perceive

---

99. Belloc, *On the Place of Gilbert Chesterton in English Letters*, 38.
100. McLuhan and McLuhan, *Media and Formal Cause*, 47.
101. Chesterton, *Illustrated London News*, 1 July 1933.
102. Chesterton, *Illustrated London News*, 1 July 1933.

more clearly when we factor in the concrete particulars of our own poetic lives, as well as the poetic lives of others.

Belloc makes some attempt to clue the reader into how Chesterton uses parallelism.[103] However, there does not seem to be only one method up Chesterton's philosophical sleeve. You will find parallelism everywhere, whether in metaphors, parables, illustrations, comparisons, or allusions. These things, myriad expressions of the deep truth of the analogy of being, are subtle variations on a general perceptual theme. Chesterton uses parallelism "to perfection and in abundance," whether in writing or in conversation.[104] He seems to be somewhat perplexed that others do not use it in as prodigal a fashion as he does, given just how powerful it is.[105] Still, it should be used well and not just merely in great quantities. Chesterton happens on most occasions, I believe, to get the balance between quality and quantity right. He does this because analogy is not only a verbal construction for him but suggests a participation in reality. It is central to how he views the world.

As noted above, analogy describes our natural capacity for pattern recognition. We might describe people fighting like cats and dogs or say that an explanation we have heard is as clear as mud, for instance. And yet to focus on such simple comparisons may cause us to miss the genius of Chesterton's intuition. For Chesterton, intuition is not just concerned with simple parallels but with more complex patterns as well, as well as with how such patterns reveal the nature of reality, which is granted permission to surprise us. I'll take Chesterton's criticism of the prohibitionist laws against alcohol in America as one instructive example, especially since he uses it as the foundation for a prediction or two. This was a contentious issue both before and during his day. Between 1920 and 1933, there was a constitutional ban in America on producing, importing, transporting, and selling alcoholic beverages. This was argued to be a response to terrible social problems that Chesterton was definitely sensitive to. However, crucial to his perspective was his awareness that alcohol was a figure and not the ground. It was an indicator of a formal cause, or perhaps of a forgetting of the formal cause. However, it was not the formal cause itself. To deal with social and political problems such as family violence and general intemperance by removing alcohol would therefore have been, as he saw it, to begin at the wrong end, with a poor understanding of formal causality. Even to notice this is not necessarily to claim that the formal cause has been properly understood but

---

103. Belloc, *On the Place of Gilbert Chesterton in English Letters*, 39.
104. Belloc, *On the Place of Gilbert Chesterton in English Letters*, 40.
105. Belloc, *On the Place of Gilbert Chesterton in English Letters*, 41.

it suggests that we need more than the blatantly obvious if we are to figure out what is going on.

In a series of articles published in *Vanity Fair* between 1920 and 1921, Chesterton analyzes certain social issues, including the issue of prohibition. There he also proposes a way forward for what he calls "a new renascence."[106] The series, published around the time Chesterton completed *The Superstition of Divorce* (1920), *The Uses of Diversity* (1920), *Eugenics and Other Evils* (1922), and *What I Saw in America* (1922), was written shortly after the Great War, when Chesterton was concerned with the consequences of some societal issues for the future. He had personally felt the cost of the Great War during which his brother had died, for one thing, and he noticed that it spoke of certain trends in the West that were more than a little disconcerting. In *The Superstition of Divorce* (1920), he restates the importance of returning to first principles and attending to formal causality; he notes, "It is futile to talk of reform without reference to form."[107] What is being "done" is entangled in what is being "undone."[108]

What makes the collection of articles in *Vanity Fair* especially noteworthy is Chesterton's self-conscious attention to prophecy. The subtitle of the series is, *Thoughts on the Structure of the Future*. I do not know whether this title was chosen by Chesterton, the commissioning editor, or someone else, but the title is apt given what is contained in the series. The series is, in my view, a remarkable collection because it exemplifies Chesterton's attunement to formal causality in general. There, echoing my argument above suggesting Chesterton's metaxological awareness, he even warns against an excess of pattern recognition where "parallels of intellectual architecture elongate themselves into the endless perspectives of a nightmare."[109] It is important to recognize patterns, he suggests, but it is also vital to notice the possibility that what one has seen does not account for everything. We need more than pattern recognition because pattern recognition means only observing what is happening on the surface. Inductive reasoning should not replace abductive reasoning. We need to know the formal cause. We must

---

106. Chesterton, *New Renascence*.

107. Chesterton, *Collected Works, Volume 4*, 229. There is a typographic error in some editions of *The Superstition of Divorce*, including the edition I am referencing, that indicates the exact opposite of this meaning, namely, "It is futile to talk of reform *with* reference to form." This is clearly nonsense, not only in the context of the discussion towards the beginning of that book which focuses directly on *form* but also in the context of Chesterton's work as a whole. Here, for instance, Chesterton talks about people who "want divorce, without asking themselves whether they want marriage." The former is the bothersome *reform*; the latter is the *form*.

108. Chesterton, *Collected Works, Volume 4*, 229.

109. Chesterton, *New Renascence*, 44.

remain open to the world enough to pick up where there are deviations from our narrow conceptions of things. Nevertheless, there are patterns and they are discernible.

This is evident in how Chesterton addresses prohibition. He wrote a lot about this controversy at that time, and I am by no means aiming to discuss his arguments against prohibition in full. But I want to illustrate his use of parallelism in connection with his awareness of form. He situates this issue within a larger perceptible pattern. He considers a mosaic of other aspects of society, including the seriousness with which games are played,[110] how sports are treated religiously,[111] how "progress" often means a "stiffening of formalities,"[112] how tools are used versus how toys are used, and how "scientific appliances" affect human creativity.[113] These are just a few examples but they all build towards the sense of the formal cause that Chesterton has in mind. He sees similar distortions of form at play in plumbing, cinema, carpentry, and train-driving. After building up one parallel after another of seemingly disconnected matters, he distills them into a single principle or law of the situation: "Something has come between the man and his materials, of which the effect here involved is this; that the same materials used for a serious purpose cannot be moulded to a more frivolous purpose."[114] This is a notably negative statement. But it implies a positive idea. *Nothing* should come between the man and his materials in this way. It is important, by implication, to be allowed an appropriate frivolity when the time is right. There is a deeper implication to this. The correct form ensures a right relationship between people and the world, and especially their tools, as well as with culture.

As this suggests, a specific way of mediating the world, connected with scientific thought and a largely univocal or perhaps dialectical sense of being, has substituted "being amused" for "amusing oneself."[115] Chesterton sees a dramatic shift, evident in something as seemingly frivolous as the invention of modern cinema, toward rendering people largely passive and so also at the mercy of the world; people are having their perceptions numbed. Already in this observation, which is echoed today, certain implications become clearer. Chesterton worries about how people get too quickly squeezed into a mechanical mold, such that their dignity is threatened.

110. Chesterton, *New Renascence*, 9.
111. Chesterton, *New Renascence*, 11–13.
112. Chesterton, *New Renascence*, 14.
113. Chesterton, *New Renascence*, 9, 18.
114. Chesterton, *New Renascence*, 19.
115. Chesterton, *New Renascence*, 20.

Indicating heavy drinking as a cause for the loss of dignity thus means mistakenly treating heavy drinking as that which *accounts* for a loss of dignity. This is backwards, however. It is more likely that heavy drinking makes an already-evident loss of dignity both worse and more apparent. This is to say heavy drinking is *caused* by a loss of dignity. If dignity is the formal cause, a loss of dignity elevated to the status of an ideal is its counterfeit double. The causal relation is, by implication, the opposite of what prohibitionists claim. Even sitting in a cinema to be entertained, Chesterton suggests, may leave us feeling degraded, but such degradation already precedes the creation of cinematic entertainment.

In the above, I have implied that the term *formal cause* is equivocal. On the one hand, it refers to the ideal form that any given thing ought to conform to. In an ultimate sense, this sense of formal causality is what shapes and accounts for the meaning of anything perceived. And, in an ideal world, this would be the only meaning of formal cause that would have any real significance. But we do not inhabit an ideal world. For this reason, the formal cause must necessarily also imply those violations and disproportions of form that account for the meaning of any given thing in the present, as well as its possible meaning in the future. The above example was this: "Something," by which Chesterton implies sin, "has come between the man and his materials, of which the effect here involved is this; that the same materials used for a serious purpose cannot be moulded to a more frivolous purpose."[116] In one sense, this is the formal cause. This is, in other words, the *account* or pattern of what has gone wrong. However, we should keep in mind that this *formal cause* is the deformation of a deeper form. This deformity is intelligible only according to a sense, even a vague sense, of actual form. To consider formal cause in general must therefore mean having a sense of this equivocation. We must know what is right before we can grasp how things have gone and might go wrong.

With this in mind, Chesterton writes, "The most startling and rending revolution in our politics would be the introduction of self-government. We are perhaps further from it than any human beings in history."[117] Prohibition, in his view, follows the same pattern as the other things. It is a movement towards removing responsibility from people. This removal of responsibility is likely causing people to drink without restraint. It assumes that people ought not to be responsible and therefore rests in a misapprehension of the human being. It takes a drift towards something negative and extends it. It deepens an already worryingly deep groove. "Governing

---

116. Chesterton, *New Renascence*, 19.
117. Chesterton, *New Renascence*, 23.

ourselves," Chesterton says, "would mean governing our own furniture, architecture and landscape; and what we eat and drink and wear."[118]

Once he has noticed the abandonment of principled form in favor of its degraded materialist manifestation, he can turn his attention to the future. What will happen if this form of transferring agency away from people towards the state becomes even more predominant in any society? Here, Chesterton's use of parallelism takes on a speculative shape but it is astounding what this shape reveals. It allows him, for instance, to see a connection between prohibitionism in America and the possibility of limitations being placed on speech itself, as well as the possibility of more surveillance. If governments cannot trust people to determine what to put into their bodies, why would they trust them to say the right thing or do the right thing? Such parallels would ordinarily seem unconnected, and yet Chesterton's identification of the formal cause, distilled into an articulated law of the situation, shows the opposite.

Even if the issue of prohibition ceases to be taken seriously in American society, as has indeed happened, the underlying cause identified by Chesterton might almost effortlessly lead to other abominable consequences. If the root of the deformity isn't uprooted, the deformity will continue, only it will take on a variety of shapes. As people begin to be more dependent and more powerless, they become increasingly more manipulable. What other terrible addictions could be fostered within such an environment? What about the possibility of mandatory ideological conformity training or the possibility of state-mandated medical and therapeutic interventions? On this, Chesterton's thinking is remarkable. The presence of one trend in society does not have to necessarily lead to its intensification, as many shoddy modern prophets might assume. Keeping metaxology in play, Chesterton recognizes that there may even be a radical discontinuity between one thing and another while the formal cause remains identical. This is why he can say on a different matter, for instance, that he has "not the slightest difficulty in imagining the world of the future taking a turn which would bring back the fact, if not the form, of witch-hunting and slavery and the persecution of heresies."[119] If the form is conceivable in one era it is replicable in another.

At one point, Chesterton asks the reader to "picture the horrible pantomime that life would be, if we made a public rule" on a very "private matter."[120] He continues, "Suppose the State interfered with speech as it now interferes with drink, with diet and details of hygiene. Suppose there were a

---

118. Chesterton, *New Renascence*, 23.
119. Chesterton, *Illustrated London News*, 9 June 1934.
120. Chesterton, *New Renascence*, 25–26.

Conversation Ministry as there is a Health Ministry in England to-day. Suppose the State sent out armies of eavesdroppers to hide behind doors and under tables; as it now sends out armies of inspectors to measure windows or analyse water."[121] Such speculations probably appeared outlandish to his readers, and yet, in our time, speech is frequently censored, especially when it is truthful, and surveillance is an ordinary part of everyday life, albeit in a more technological form than what Chesterton had in mind. To question a consensus these days can be a dangerous thing. His concept here of a Conversation Ministry is mirrored in Orwell's Ministry of Truth in the novel *1984* (1949), and even this speculation has parallels in our time. Increasingly, as such contemporary phenomena as Ministers of Loneliness show, governmental "interference" in private affairs has become fairly normal. We have something of a clue in all of this into the importance of analogy in Chesterton's work, especially in relation to parallelism. It shows that deformations of form, as distorted or misconceived ideals, still operate according to analogy and non-identical repetition. Speculations may be inexact but they still serve the purpose of warning people about where they might be going wrong, as well as how they might gain a better sense of what is right.

As is already evident, after noticing the formal cause, parallelism allows Chesterton to look into the future and consider certain possibilities. It would not be difficult to emulate him in this respect. If we notice a disproportion between state power and individual responsibility, as he does, we may begin to wonder how this may affect all kinds of things and what this would mean for our future. We may pick something outrageous, something like a law that forces parents to subject their children to certain untested, life-risking medical procedures. Such things are not inevitable but understanding them as a possibility may help us to ask again: What is the ideal here? What would a government hope to achieve by monstrous decrees? What proportion between governments and citizens would be best? Sadly, as I hardly need to make explicit, such speculation is by no means unrealistic. We have already seen evidence of a turn in this direction in some nations around the globe. The servile state is as much a reality as the surveillance state nowadays.

We might similarly notice the increasing codependence between people and their tools, and so also speculate about the subservience of people to electronic media. To see the pattern is to begin to see what is possible. As with the rise of the surveillance state and the curbing of speech, Chesterton seems to have seen this more technological matter already more than a

---

121. Chesterton, *New Renascence*, 26.

century ago.¹²² It runs parallel to the trend of rendering people passive. Nevertheless, history does not merely repeat itself even if it is given to rhyming and similitude. History speaks using analogies and parallelisms.¹²³ We should therefore once again be cautious when declaring inevitability even where we have spotted a groove. And yet, what the recovery of analogy means for us is the possibility of clearly perceiving those pictures and patterns and intelligibilities that are there.

What should be clear from the above is that Chesterton's attention to formal causality, implying reclaiming the ideals of an analogical intuition, also involves an exuberant and often playful use of imagination. It is as if he is not merely predicting the future but, in a certain sense, creating it. He is brainstorming. One of his ongoing concerns is with how "modern mechanical society" negatively affects our love and capacity for imaginative thought.¹²⁴ To think of things mechanically, especially through a univocal or dialectical sense of being, amounts to confusing invention (and inventions) with improvement.¹²⁵ One of the most alarming aspects of modern mechanical society is its tendency to reduce the world to a static image, a picture that fails to say a thousand or even just a few words. One example of this is found in any photograph, which "professes to be realistic" even while it omits so much of what is real.¹²⁶ A photographic image petrifies the world like Medusa's gaze. It may not be lying but it can still mislead because of how it makes reality seem flat.¹²⁷ It confirms the Platonic fear that art may imitate not the forms but only imitations of the forms. It precipitates the forgetting of being together with forgetting the process that gives rise to its existence.¹²⁸ The image, removed from its world and so also from the world of meaning, almost suggests insanity. It represents but simultaneously removes genuine presence. It insists on transparency at the expense of mystery. We look at a photograph but too easily forget the photographic negative, which suggests to us, as every decent photographer knows, that things may have turned out differently. In our time, the fact that photography no longer requires a photographic negative has tremendous symbolic significance. A sense of mediation is oddly foreign in our time, despite it being the most over-mediated age in human history. Incidentally, this is also

---

122. Chesterton, *Collected Works, Volume 5*, 151–58.
123. Chesterton, *Illustrated London News*, 11 September 1923.
124. Chesterton, *Collected Works, Volume 5*, 154.
125. Chesterton, *Collected Works, Volume 5*, 154.
126. Chesterton, *Illustrated London News*, 9 February 1907.
127. Chesterton, *Illustrated London News*, 17 June 1913.
128. Chesterton, *Illustrated London News*, 16 June 1934.

something Chesterton foresaw, together with his prediction that American culture would become dominant not just in America but across the whole world. "The American never wants to hide," he writes, even if he perhaps underestimates the degree of this dominance.[129]

The overly mechanical photographic mind, which in its unreflective desire for immediacy removes imagination from the sphere of truth and meaning, is, unfortunately, evident in so much modern and contemporary thought. Chesterton jokes that it would perhaps be better, when searching for a lost poet, to find a decent caricature of him instead of relying on a photograph. As silly as the suggestion might seem, Chesterton contends that the caricature is "far more likely" to help us to "find the man."[130] The suggestion for intervening into a world saturated with flat, scientific thinking, in other words, is to involve imagination, which inspires us to think in a way that the flatness of a photograph does not.

As the organ of meaning, the imagination helps us to recognize the part played by mediation in our perceptions. In its proportional awareness of act and potency, imagination is metaxological. Chesterton is aware that modern inventiveness is owed to imagination, and especially its "vivid calculation of remote events."[131] The very best civilization, he writes, "merely means the full authority of the human spirit over all externals. Barbarism means the worship of those externals in their crude and unconquered state."[132] In other words, to be civilized, to be mutually cultivating the world even as we ourselves are nurtured by it, we need to be able to imagine the world before us as co-participants in creation rather than accepting it on the basis of unconscious and possibly flawed metaphysical assumptions. The truth of being is in being first, before it is in the mind and before our theoretical reason can direct practical action towards making the world better.

We are not supposed to be passive observers, although we must remain receptive. We must allow higher actualities to activate mental potentialities. Chesterton's stance against historicism is arguably part of a refusal to be subservient to the movements of history, which would depersonalize the person and render the question of a standard or ideal shaky at best. We need, against this, to regard the world as we are, as creatures endowed with creative power. Just as we are receptive to the world, we are able to perceive the good and to prudently act in the world to bring it about. Imagination itself is not primarily, therefore, a means by which we can escape reality. It

---

129. Chesterton, *Illustrated London News*, 2 February 1924.
130. Chesterton, *Miscellany of Men*, 199.
131. Chesterton, *Illustrated London News*, 18 August 1906.
132. Chesterton, *Illustrated London News*, 18 August 1906.

is the means by which we can recover a clear sense of what is real. To quote Chesterton, "We must invoke the most wild and soaring sort of imagination; the imagination that can see what is there."[133] As this shows, there is plenty of room to play. In speculating about the future, we may even risk a few generalizations, although not at the expense of principles and particulars. We can explore meanings and surplus meanings using language as a way to see form. As we avoid being too certain about our speculations, we should also resist being too ready to doubt or too willing to let doubt have the last word.

From what I have presented in this chapter, a further facet of Chesterton's predictions becomes clear, namely that he tackles future possibilities primarily as ideas, and especially commonly as ideas to be opposed because they do not live up to an ideal. This is made most explicit in his 1907 article, "The Fallacies of the Future."[134] There, Chesterton proposes that the mind of a genuinely free thinker—if it is free and not just possessed by notions of a seemingly free sort—should have no trouble at all imagining "all the mental mistakes that men may make in the future, and brand them beforehand; it might prophesy future heresies as it prophesies future social systems."[135] Answering an argument that your enemies are not yet "clever enough to invent" is a way to prepare for a battle that is surely on its way.[136] "Whatever be the form of the next fancy that attacks human equality and justice, we should be prepared for it, and not permit it to throw us off our balance."[137] It is better, Chesterton believes, that the arrival of new falsehoods should be met in a world already "placarded with their refutation."[138]

Here is one future fallacy predicted by Chesterton. Just as Swinburne "practically praised lust as an expression of the love of life," cowardice might be "praised as a sign of the love of life."[139] Indeed, one does not have to look far to notice that this prediction has come true in the form of the so-called coddling of the American Mind—also called the ideology of safteyism.[140] The current obsession with safetyism suggested by this fallacy, which is unfortunately now a fallacy of the present and not of the future, has been opposed by some resilience psychologists. But Chesterton argued against it

---

133. Chesterton, *Everlasting Man*, 14.
134. Chesterton, *Daily News*, 2 March 1907.
135. Chesterton, *Daily News*, 2 March 1907.
136. Chesterton, *Daily News*, 2 March 1907.
137. Chesterton, *Daily News*, 2 March 1907.
138. Chesterton, *Daily News*, 2 March 1907.
139. Chesterton, *Daily News*, 2 March 1907.
140. See Haidt and Lukianoff, *Coddling of the American Mind*.

over a century ago by noting something that today is typically forgotten. The failure of virtue, more than bad psychology, is at the root of the problem. Another fallacy predicted by Chesterton is also of a psychological nature but with a moral root. He notices that "people enjoy most the unexpected pleasure, the edges and the beginnings of things. In two words, we know that joy depends on wonder; and we know that wonder partly depends on rarity."[141] This simple truth, Chesterton predicts, might plausibly be taken to such extremes that people would treat others and themselves badly with the express aim of allowing them to "enjoy their occasional joys."[142] He notes the fact "that abstinence intensifies pleasure may go to as wild lengths as Hedonism has gone."[143] Recently, psychologists have discovered that delaying gratification too severely can prove not only harmful but dangerous. Enjoyment itself may be the cost of this fallacy of the future—and the present.

When Chesterton warns the world of dooms and diseases, he does so always, ultimately, because of his deep love of people. When he warns against unruly legal fictions, against nominalist distortions of real things, against the forgetting of virtue, and so on, he is trying to redirect our attention to what is good. "If you want a white house," he reminds us, "you must continually be painting it white, beginning all over again and re-creating your ideal. In other words, if you want your old white house you must have a new white house. You must have a revolution."[144] It helps, as this analogy suggests, to know where repainting is most needed. A good example of this is found, again, in Chesterton's *Vanity Fair* articles.[145] There he spots certain negative trends; he perceives where things are likely to be headed. He notes, for instance, that we go wrong in our hopes for progress especially when we fail to heed the doctrine of the fall of man.[146] But he also suggests a different way. He imagines a world and a future in which wholeness is possible. He shows us, again and again, that we can only properly interpret where we and others might be going wrong when we have a good sense of what is right. We need a picture of the form before we can understand both conformity and deformity. We need a clear view of the form to understand our present and to have any idea of what sort of future we might be—and should be—moving towards.

---

141. Chesterton, *Daily News*, 2 March 1907.
142. Chesterton, *Daily News*, 2 March 1907.
143. Chesterton, *Daily News*, 2 March 1907.
144. Chesterton, *Daily News*, 24 August 1907.
145. Chesterton, *New Renascence*.
146. Chesterton, *New Renascence*, 87.

4

Being Informed

G. K. Chesterton Through Aristotle's Fourfold

CHESTERTON KNOWS THAT AN overly otherworldly Platonism, a Platonism that is not Platonist enough, can negate rather than inform the importance of materiality. He knows that we must participate in the ideal with our whole lives; that the word must become flesh. He credits Aquinas for sparing us the necessity of conforming to a hyperbolic Platonism by bringing Plato into closer dialogue with Aristotle and Christian theology.[147] Crucial to this, as far as he is concerned, is the centrality of the incarnation and how the doctrine of the incarnation redeems the importance of the witness of the senses in the between. The incarnation is a paradox that requires a metaxological posture to be perceived and articulated. It reinterprets the interplay between the intimate and the universal as central to gaining a proper perspective on all things.

Aristotle, who we should not forget was himself a Platonist,[148] reframes Plato's concern with form through his notion of formal causality. Form remains the essence of anything; it grants definition to things and therefore allows us to appreciate their limits. It makes sense for this reason to continue this discussion of causality with Aristotle, whom Chesterton calls "perhaps the wisest and most wide-minded man that ever lived."[149] Chesterton often speaks in superlatives, aware that comparatives may lead

---

147. Chesterton, *Saint Thomas Aquinas & Saint Francis of Assisi*, 148.
148. Gerson, *Aristotle and Other Platonists*.
149. Chesterton, *Everlasting Man*, 194.

us to realize that the superlative is not quite right.[1] Perhaps that is the case here. However, an Aristotelian lens reveals how to further understand Chesterton's appreciation of formal causality through his fourfold of causality. To consider Aristotelian causality is to correct the still prevalent modern preoccupation with causality as a concern with linear, mechanical, or dialectical processes, which stem from methodological reductionism. Unfortunately, mechanical cause and effect can be mistaken as what counts most when proposing an explanation of why things are the way they are, as well as where things might be going given the way they are. It is not uncommon today, for instance, to find journalists in mainstream news media explaining extremely complex events using only facile cause-and-effect explanations, which are so often merely correlations that have been mistaken for causes. This indicates just how normal it is these days for people to think without even the slightest awareness not only of how causation is enmeshed in the moral order but also of how complex causality is. Aristotle undoubtedly provides us with a much richer perspective on nature and reality than what the modern perspective on causality can.

However, this remains a study of Chesterton and not of any other thinker, Aristotle included. My aim here is to elucidate causality as it relates to the thought of the former more than the latter, even if the latter offers one way to do this. We can be certain that Chesterton read Aristotle, although direct references to him are few and far between.[2] We also know that Chesterton encountered Aristotle's fourfold, although, despite some obviously perceptive comments on Aristotle, we cannot be sure of the extent and depth of his engagement with his work. The most direct mention of Aristotle's fourfold is in his biography on *St. Thomas Aquinas* (1933), a book published late in his career and life. There he refers to "Form" and "Matter," and names efficient causality as "Effective Causality" in keeping with the convention of certain sources of his time.[3] But did Chesterton have this same fourfold in mind earlier in his career? While he does not explicitly mention it, his earlier writings indicate a more than passing awareness of that ancient analytic of being.

In *Heretics* (1905), for instance, his penetrating analysis of the ideas and moods of some of his contemporaries frequently involves pointing out their deficits along Aristotelian lines, echoing the fourfold analytic. He shows where people like Rudyard Kipling, Henrik Ibsen, George Bernard

1. Chesterton, *The Speaker*, 3 May 1902.
2. Chesterton, *Daily News*, 25 September 1902; 28 January 1903; Chesterton, *Illustrated London News*, 20 April 1935; 21 September 1935; 2 November 1935; 23 November 1935; 30 November 1935.
3. Chesterton, *St. Thomas Aquinas, St. Francis of Assisi*, 120.

Shaw, and H. G. Wells, among others, seem especially oblivious to final and formal causality. Supporting my contention that Chesterton was not accidentally aware of Aristotle's analytic, Aidan Nichols remarks on the importance of this emphasis on final and formal causality in Chesterton's work.[4] Note again the parable mentioned earlier about the monk and the moderns under the lamppost.[5] The story stresses how modern efficiency and materialism, to the neglect of formal and final causality, destroys understanding. The moderns see the intelligibility of the lamppost through a narrow lens, removed from purpose and pattern, extracted from the primal ethos. Chesterton, at the end of that parable, then points to the importance of knowing the value of light, and therefore indicates both the final and formal causes that are absent from the minds of his parabolic moderns.

I contend that there is a strong link between Chesterton's and Aristotle's analytic of causality; it pervades Chesterton's work as a whole. It is not difficult to reconcile Aristotle to Chesterton by establishing a sense of how the latter's attention to causality is closer to the former's model than to the modern obsession with cause and effect as "newly-tabulated"[6] dimensions of a procedural chain. There is evidence of his alertness to how modern conceptions of cause and effect had to be "carefully constructed by the old materialists" even as newer materialists have found ways to deconstruct it.[7] While he frequently refers to the dialectic of cause and effect, and regards it as important,[8] he does not think of it as sufficient for understanding anything.[9] On the contrary, his implicit regard of causality involves seeing that it is caught up in systems, patterns, providence, and meaning, and not just in sequential material events.[10] "Everyone knows that there are such things as physical causes and results," he writes, just as everyone knows "there are such things as mental causes and results. How far either of them goes nobody knows."[11] In stating this, he casually introduces a way to complicate the modern preoccupation with cause and effect.

By implication, causality cannot be separated in Chesterton's work from perception itself and its orientation towards making sense of the world.

4. Nichols, *Chesterton*, 171.
5. Chesterton, *Collected Works*, Volume 1, 46.
6. Chesterton, *Collected Works*, Volume 18, 33–36.
7. Chesterton, *Illustrated London News*, 16 May 1925.
8. Chesterton, *Defendant*, 122.
9. Chesterton, *Collected Works*, Volume 1, 249–68.
10. Chesterton, *Illustrated London News*, 4 April 1914; 16 May 1925; Chesterton, *Collected Works*, Volume 4, 239.
11. Chesterton, *Illustrated London News*, 9 December 1905.

"For the mind moves by instincts, associations, premonitions and not by fixed dates or completed processes," he writes.[12] "Action and reaction" can "occur simultaneously" in the mind and "the cause" can "be found after the effect. Errors will be resisted before they have been properly promulgated: notions will be first defined long after they are dead."[13] While he does not directly engage with Aristotle on causality or an obviously systematic analytic of causality, he nevertheless has an approximately Aristotelian awareness of causality that transcends the usual modern framework. Like Aristotle, he regards the mind as capable of delving into the structures of reality. Reality is not some merely objective phenomenon set against subjectivity. Mind and being exist in a permanent relational openness to each other. "The human spirit is not . . . bounded like a circle by one black line," Chesterton writes. "Its relation with its spiritual environment is a relation of degree. The soul of man is, so to speak, vignetted."[14]

As already noted and as I explain more fully towards the end of this chapter, to consider Chesterton's concern with formal causality does not imply excluding Aristotle's other causes. Final, formal, and efficient causality can be reduced, as Aquinas suggests, to formal causality.[15] However, material causality seems always already to be caught up in formal causality as well. Arguably, Plato's notion of form is differentiated and modified by Aristotle. The Platonist meaning of form is retained while Aristotle transforms it into formal causality, which considers the intelligible whole even if that whole is not always wholly intelligible to or dialectically reducible by any individual. While elucidating Aristotle's philosophy, my intention is to explain each of his causes without exaggerating their separateness; my aim is to stress each cause's inseparability from the others.

Aristotle's *Metaphysics* begins with this famous idea: "All men by nature desire to know."[16] "The deepest of all desires for knowledge," writes Chesterton, "is the desire to know what the world is for and what we are for."[17] This claim is controversial only to those who have been corrupted into accepting their ignorance, a sign of unrealized potential, as a natural and desirable state. Although Aristotle discusses causality in various places in his work, we should keep in mind this desire for knowledge as a guiding idea. To understand causality is to discover the intelligibility of nature and

---

12. Chesterton, *Victorian Age in Literature*, 25.
13. Chesterton, *Victorian Age in Literature*, 25.
14. Chesterton, *The Speaker*, 31 May 1902.
15. Liñán, *Formal Cause in Marshall McLuhan's Thinking*, 35.
16. Aristotle, *Metaphysics*, 980a.
17. Quoted in Lauer, *Chesterton*, 12.

therefore of reality. Causality is a matter of *why*; it is a matter of *because*.[18] Another way of describing formal causality, albeit awkwardly, is as *formal becausality*. To know means to know why, and to know why means understanding principles and causes. Put differently, the most important science has to do with the "most known things," namely the "causes."[19] After all, "it is through [the causes] and from them that the other things are known."[20]

Aristotle regarded his own theory of causes as his most important contribution to first philosophy. The theory allows him to debate his predecessors, especially Plato, and also to justify his science of physics through rigorous conceptual analysis.[21] More particularly, Aristotle stresses that the essential business of any science is to "discern for what end each thing must be done."[22] Above all, this means knowing the good of all things—a very Platonist contention. This good is not some arbitrary imposition cobbled together by people out of preferred fictions but is inherent to the being of things. On this last point especially, Aristotle echoes Plato even as he prepares to duel with him. In seeking a more careful analysis, he contends that Plato fails especially to discern two things, namely the varied meanings of being, and also the meanings of the plurivocal concern that is causality. As important as it is to know the form of things, as in Plato, for Aristotle this simply does not explain enough. Just as being can be said in many ways, so cause should also be said in many ways.

While Chesterton does not present us with a science of being, he still offers reflections born out of a desire to make sense of the world and to clarify what it means to live well in it. In this, as with Aristotle, he prioritizes knowing the good of things over understanding them along the lines of their materiality and efficiency. Things go wrong when there is no ideal to point to; when there is no conceivable goodness towards which we ought to act. As stressed above, Chesterton notices that effort is made "to shirk the problem" of understanding "what is good."[23] Various notions can be too easily flung about with little to no concrete sense provided for how they might shape the minds of people or create good outcomes for them. They become rhetorical incantations, capable of evoking a feeling but incapable of articulating anything beyond sophistry. They show that something is up or that things are being done but the precise idea of what the aim of

18. Aristotle, *Metaphysics*, 981a.
19. Aristotle, *Metaphysics*, 981a.
20. Aristotle, *Metaphysics*, 982b.
21. Grondin, *Introduction to Metaphysics*, 49.
22. Aristotle, *Metaphysics*, 982b.
23. Chesterton, *Collected Works, Volume 1*, 51.

such happenings would be is anyone's guess. A sufficiently complex understanding of implications becomes nearly impossible within a context that suppresses or denies any proper consideration of formal causality. We find ourselves with more fashionable efficiency but less goodness.

This is to say that the reduction of causality to cause and effect has serious social and ethical consequences. By implicitly removing teleology from being, as well as denying an awareness of patterns in being, every path might be seen to break off into innumerable different directions as potentiality metastasizes. Often, the moral burden is placed, if inadvertently, on every individual to make countless minuscule choices, without any reference to virtue, in the hope that each choice will, somehow (we do not know how), be the right one. The result of this experimental or vivisectional moral guesswork is often, paradoxically, a kind of excessive puritanism or micro-managerial bureaucratic system.[24] And yet, the modern world simultaneously removes any sense of agency and freedom from people by, to use Chesterton's metaphor, creating passengers instead of train drivers.[25] Christianity presents a different view: there are only two ways, one of life and one of death, and we do have the ability to choose which road to walk on.[26] Our future holiness, our true end to be found in union with God, is always both with us and ahead of us, pulling us forward. Final causality is implicit in the form of life suggested by the two ways. This may explain why so many of Chesterton's predictions appear in an exaggerated form. He is drawing our attention to the fact that any veering from our true aim is to be well off the path we need to be on. Any slight deviation is already a catastrophe. But the good news is that salvation is not thereby rendered inaccessible. For, as St. Paul writes, "When we were yet without strength, in due time Christ died for the ungodly."[27] Even in our weakness, grace abounds.[28]

With this in mind and with the stage set in Aristotle's declaration that we can claim each person has knowledge when we think he knows the primary causes, Aristotle explains that the causes are spoken of in four ways. The chief focus of his understanding of these four ways is movement or change. Within every being, as actual, there is potential existence; there are potentials. As Aquinas writes, "A thing's power or potential is its openness to some act or actuality, either the primary act of having form, or the

---

24. Chesterton, *Illustrated London News*, 11 March 1932.
25. Chesterton, *Collected Works, Volume 5*, 159–64.
26. See Stewart-Sykes, *On The Two Ways*.
27. Romans 5:6.
28. 2 Corinthians 12:9.

secondary act of action."[29] Change suggests that potentials must be actualized and so the question naturally arises: What does the actualizing? The assumption here is that whatever is contingent has a cause. In theological terms, God is the actuality that causes all contingent beings to have being. He is the life beyond life that grants life. Moreover, God sets creation up such that things with greater actuality can impart that actuality to contingent things and so can transform potentiality into actuality. Actual heat is required, for example, to transform cool water into boiling water, just as actual goodness is required to transform an imperfect human being into a virtuous one. Nothing contingent is its own cause. It is, in its very essence, dependent. This is not to say that *everything* has a cause, only that *contingent* being is always caused.

What this means for joining formal causality to prescience should already be implicit but some key ideas are worth noting. For one thing, contemplating act and potency allows us to consider what changes, what about it is changing, and in what way it is changing. Chesterton does this when considering the possibility of altering human nature, which is a perennial concern but which has also taken on absurd qualities in recent years. Chesterton quickly notes, "In strict logic and philosophy, if you could actually alter the nature of human beings, they would cease to be human beings. So you could not really point to them as human beings whose nature had altered."[30] It would be better, he notes, to ask what elements in human nature are changeable or unchangeable.[31] For example, modern medicine has ways to change the appearance of a man so that he looks like a woman. But can modern medicine change the biology of a man so that he becomes a woman? The answer is, quite simply, no. Can people be mistaken about the former fact or the latter or both? Of course. People can be mistaken about all kinds of things. Understanding what is changeable is thus essential for seeing how things might turn out.

While contemplating what is changing, we may also consider what might bring about the change, as well as whether the interaction between two or more beings is proportional enough to allow change. Water can put out a fire, for example. But if a blaze is too large and we have only a small cup full of water at our disposal, the active potency of water to put the fire out is likely to mean nothing. Our prediction about what the water will do depends on our understanding of the elements of the situation. Then, in addition to considering what is changed and what might bring about that

---

29. Aquinas, *Selected Philosophical Writings*, 65.
30. Chesterton, *Illustrated London News*, 9 June 1934.
31. Chesterton, *Illustrated London News*, 9 June 1934.

change, we may also be mindful of what kind of change is occurring or might occur.[32] If I pour coffee into a cup, I witness a change in *quantity* as my cup fills up. If I spill my coffee, I witness a change in its *location*. If my coffee cools down, I sense a *qualitative* change. *Substantial* change is also possible, such as the change that had to take place for a coffee berry to be capable of yielding that coffee, or, more dramatically, when a live thing becomes a dead thing. Such considerations are not inessential when considering future possibilities. Having some idea of how these things operate in concert with their environments is sufficient to suggest possibilities and likelihoods, as well as impossibilities and unlikelihoods. Also, while I have used physicalist metaphors here, the principles suggested—to consider what changes, what is instigating those changes and in what proportion, as well as in what way change is taking place—apply even to the psychological, moral, and societal concerns that preoccupy Chesterton. In all such considerations, act precedes potency. Even potency must have actuality to allow actualization.

In some of what I have said, I have already exited the Aristotelian room and entered the Thomistic room. Still, already in Aristotle is the recognition of a real dynamism in nature. Things give of themselves to other things. Tautologically put, no conditional being is self-caused. We perceive stability, as we must, if we are to make sense of anything. But stability is not the only dimension of reality worth contemplating. Stability yields to change and change makes way for stability. And even stability in the created order is not permanently stable; it rests in God. Reality is less an object or system of properties than it is a happening, always calling out for the human being to understand it. Aristotle recognizes that things cannot be properly comprehended in isolation, especially apart from guiding principles. Knowing *what* happens can never replace the importance of knowing *how* it happens and knowing *why* it happens. D. C. Schindler notes, "In Aristotle's sense, a cause is not an event that produces a subsequent event, but is rather anything that accounts for a thing—what, how, or why it is."[33] This interwoven *what-how-why* of being is a matter of the interconnectedness of all things in the drama of creation. Things do not exist in atomic isolation but in an order of self-giving and receiving, always dependent, even in rebellion, on the love of God.

To return to the Aristotelian stress on movement, Aristotle says that nature contains the principle of movement and rest. This means the universe is alive and far from being without regularity and purpose. However, while the aim of things remains important, their purpose is not the only thing shaping

---

32. Feser, *Five Proofs of the Existence of God*, 17.
33. Schindler, *Catholicity of Reason*, 140.

our interpretations. We interpret things, generally speaking, as answering questions of what they consist of, what instigates their transformation, how it does this, why it does this, as well as what the pattern of their transformation is or in what way they fit within a larger economy of interactions. This reminds us again of how Aristotle finds *cause* to mean explanation, ground, sense, or logical description. It does not refer only to material or efficient phenomena or conditions that result in certain things happening.

Martin Heidegger is right to point out, challenging modern assumptions that we may accidentally import into the notion of cause, that the doctrine of the four causes did not fall from heaven fully formed and self-evident.[34] Causality should not be taken as a synonym for instrumentality. There is a hint of the idea of responsibility in this, which is central to Chesterton's awareness of formal causality. Always beneath his search for the reasons of things, he assumes that responsibility must be attributed. Typically, that responsibility is ours and does not only belong to what we are questioning. By interpreting unities as the intertwining of four causes, Aristotle is looking at the rational relations in being. David Bentley Hart points out in this regard, "The older fourfold nexus of causality was not . . . a defective attempt at modern physical science, but was instead chiefly a grammar of predication, describing the inherent logical structure of anything that exists insofar as it exists, and reflecting a world in which things and events are at once discretely identifiable and yet part of the larger dynamic continuum of the whole."[35] For ancients like Plato and Aristotle, ontology and semiology were not so easy to tell apart.

The four causes are not separable. They are co-responsible. To separate them would destroy the intelligibility they serve. It is telling that modern science dissolved this fourfold relation and thus set up the very possibility of rendering existence less intelligible even while trying to proclaim its superiority in explaining existence. Historically speaking, this could only be the result of a misconstrual of the meaning of the causes as referring to the mechanics of reality. More particularly, final and formal causality were mistaken for being extraneous to matter; and so matter was transformed, interpretively speaking, from being imbued with meaning and potentiality to being inert, impersonal, and unarticulated. Chesterton knew about this redefinition of reality, and much of his work concerns reestablishing and recapitulating the logical relations between things, and thus also concerns recovering a sense that reality is intrinsically meaningful, with truth as intrinsically personal.[36]

---

34. Heidegger, *Question Concerning Technology*, 6.
35. See Hart, *Tradition and Apocalypse*.
36. Chesterton, *Collected Works*, Volume 1, 238.

As I take each of Aristotle's causes in turn below, I elucidate more fully how Chesterton insists on a world of meaningful causal relations.

The Material Cause

Aristotle begins by claiming that cause means *matter*. This echoes Plato, who saw being as composed of matter and form. Matter, as the so-called material cause, is the substrate of physical things and registers predominantly as potentiality. Matter, in other words, tends to be equivocal.ABstractly speaking, prime matter is pure potentiality or pure equivocity. This is to say that matter would be a kind of non-being without form. Matter only has being because it has form. This suggests that Aristotle does not see existence as having any meaning without intelligibility. The meaning of this is simple enough. If it were possible for me to look at something utterly amorphous and radically indeterminate without being able to make any sense of it, it would be as good as non-existent to me. Of course, something must be there to be formed. Form must make use of something to render it meaningful.

Matter answers the question of *what a thing is made of*. This designation of matter as matter, while seeming so simple to us now, was an exceptional philosophical achievement when first introduced to the world.[37] Before Aristotle, the term *hylè* that we translate as *matter* meant only *lumber*, connoting the stuff out of which furniture is made. This etymological origin is important since it suggests that, for Aristotle, although matter is indeterminate in its openness to actualization, it does not ever exist in a completely raw form. To consider matter, even primal matter, which is pure potentiality by definition, is already to interpret it in relation to form.

Matter, although not having any meaningful being as such, is easily interpreted as potentially purposeful and realizable. This is true even if the purpose of any material may not yet be fully spelt out. In the awareness of latent potentiality, matter is logically related to the other causes as co-responsible. This is to say that the other causes are indebted to the material cause, just as they are indebted to each other. Something must be moved by something else; it must fit a form and serve a purpose. Any tendency to reduce matter to being a dead fact should be resisted. Matter is not lifeless and meaningless because it calls out to form. It cannot exist on its own and apart from the world of meaning. To regard it as necessarily meaningless would be to deny the inescapable relation between mind and matter, and also between matter's actuality and its potentiality.

---

37. Grondin, *Introduction to Metaphysics*, 50.

Such relations are essential for Chesterton. For him, as already suggested, there are no mere facts. There is ultimately no inert, meaning-free, or meaningless stuff, if only because we so naturally perceive things as meaningful or potentially meaningful. For this reason, Chesterton frequently takes aim at materialists, who tend to want to relinquish higher forms for the sake of lower ones. They have "the fewest vistas and the fewest doubts."[38] They make the awful mistake of trying to keep mind from interfering with matter, although this is to demand the impossible. They trade a larger awareness of the world for a smaller one. Materialists function more like "one small and particular sect" than like a collective of reasonable thinkers.[39] They want the story of the world to be told from a very particular point of view that is anything but objective, even when they assume it to be the *most* objective perspective.[40] They skewer and reshape matter through their obsession with modern efficient causality and so forget that matter is inseparable from form. They approach matter with too many shrunken presuppositions, which reduce the potentialities of meaning to their own self-mediation. In this, we find the importance of reframing the material cause as representing potentiality; it means not just material potentiality but meaningful potentiality. Matter calls out for realization and intelligibility.

We must not look at things and only concern ourselves with their uses. We must consider their significance within a world of meaning; as contributing to our participation in the truth. We must therefore also consider ourselves and our attitudes and motivations with regard to materiality and its meaning. Chesterton has a lot to say on this. He is aware, for example, that we cannot improve anything without loving it first.[41] Our intentions toward things influence how we understand them. What we feel about them must be taken into account because everything is an attitude of mind.[42] Moreover, our attitudes and doctrines are interwoven. Understanding well, in Chesterton's view, depends on our awareness. One's "ultimate attitudes" are the "soils for the seeds of doctrine."[43] This is why he pays so much attention not only to things but also to atmospheres, moods, and attitudes. He is aware that how we look at things affects the sense we make of them; our intentions affect what we see and do. This illuminates his attunement to formal causality. Formal causality is not "out there" while consciousness is "in

---

38. Chesterton, *Illustrated London News*, 22 December 1906.
39. Chesterton, *Illustrated London News*, 22 December 1906.
40. Chesterton, *Illustrated London News*, 22 December 1906.
41. Chesterton, *Defendant*, xii; Chesterton, *Collected Works, Volume 1*, 274.
42. Chesterton, *Daily News*, 7 June 1901.
43. Chesterton, *Collected Works, Volume 1*, 268.

here." Formal causality is already bound up in the interplay of the perceiver and the perceived, as well as the form that unifies the two.

In one essay, Chesterton draws the reader's attention to an issue of *The Illustrated London News* published on the 1st of December 1906. In that issue, he finds "a picture of a modern Belgian miracle, or, as some call it," using inverted commas, "'miracle,' a fungus formation on a door at Borgerhout," which appears to have the "form of the traditional Virgin of Christian art."[44] His reference to how some call it a "miracle," in inverted commas, together with his pointing out twice that the "literary authorities of the *Illustrated London News* . . . cannot err" offers us a lovely case of him playfully mocking the establishment for failing to question their materialist assumptions.[45] He echoes the original caption under the photograph of the fungus in question, which points out that many have gone on to view it "growing on some rotten planks" and have believed it to be a miracle.[46] But then, as the caption also states, there are "politicians" who regard the whole event as having been sparked by little more than a superstition.[47] Those "politicians are utilising the event and its result as an argument in favor of some obligatory form of instruction to fight superstition."[48] Material causation is thus reduced by the modernists to instrumental reason, at the expense of what Aquinas says are the twin components of reason: theoretical and practical reason.

For Chesterton, the distinction between ordinary people and politicians is significant, although we should be careful not to take it too far. The way that politicians want to instruct ordinary people is important for understanding a stance on materiality and material causality that is diametrically opposed to the one he takes. There is a distinction between people caught up in the business of living an ordinary life and those who hold some pretense to be above the business of living such a life and so also above the authority of the senses.[49] In this, Chesterton expresses a concern that appears throughout his work in favor of the common man—not the construct, the human being as imagined by elites, but the ordinary person leading an ordinary life with ordinary cares. Everyone is, in a sense, the common man, until he pridefully stops regarding himself as one. The politician, as an example of such a prideful person, who has not realized that he is among his fellow men, represents someone whose theory of being is at odds with being;

---

44. Chesterton, *Illustrated London News*, 22 December 1906.
45. Chesterton, *Illustrated London News*, 22 December 1906.
46. Chesterton, *Illustrated London News*, 22 December 1906.
47. Chesterton, *Illustrated London News*, 22 December 1906.
48. Chesterton, *Illustrated London News*, 1 December 1906.
49. Chesterton, *Saint Thomas Aquinas & Saint Francis of Assisi*, 29.

the politician symbolizes someone "separated" by his own misperceptions from everyday concerns, and who at first may "represent" the concerns of the common man only to later "misrepresent" them.[50] There is a transition here from being caught up in everyday concerns to being detached from them, a movement from being enveloped in a meaningful world—in the *between*—to being concerned only with a certain conception of meaning removed from being itself. Actuality and potentiality have been separated.

Chesterton notes how the apparent concern for doing away with superstition is less a matter of regarding matter (or *the* matter) as neutral than of exerting power over matter, and therefore over the world and over people. The politician is a personified version of a shrunken efficient causality, separated from the other causes. The politician represents anyone with power who "persuades the people that they really want what he wants."[51] But "what is really intolerable, what is really atrocious, is . . . that politicians should venture not only to deceive the people about the things that the people do care about, but should insolently attempt to oppress the people in the things that the people do care about."[52] What appears at first to be a concern for facts becomes a means to "persecute" people.[53] The apparently neutral stance of the powerful person is anything but neutral. His apparently objective posture is ideologically loaded and deceitful. Here is a lesson on prescience: there is no prediction about the future that is unconnected to the ethos. Vatication is not just about getting the facts right but is also about discerning what virtues and values are in play and ought to be in play.

To separate mind from being, meaning from materiality, and actuality from potentiality, is to set up a relationship with being that is one of power over truth. Some "obligatory form of instruction to fight superstition"[54] symbolizes "the whole unfairness of so much modern education."[55] The "rich," the "politicians," the "professors"—all of whom stand in for Chesterton as symbolic of a destructive dualism—"want not only to have a mood; they want to persecute for a mood. They want to persecute swiftly and fiercely for a mood, before the mood shall have time to disappear."[56] The rich and powerful, having rallied many to believe and accommodate their cause, may want to insist on "vaccination" against "baptism" or on "science" rather than

50. Chesterton, *Illustrated London News*, 22 December 1906.
51. Chesterton, *Illustrated London News*, 22 December 1906.
52. Chesterton, *Illustrated London News*, 22 December 1906.
53. Chesterton, *Illustrated London News*, 22 December 1906.
54. Chesterton, *Illustrated London News*, 1 December 1906.
55. Chesterton, *Illustrated London News*, 22 December 1906.
56. Chesterton, *Illustrated London News*, 22 December 1906.

on reading fairy tales to children.[57] The "educating class," believing only in dead materiality, becomes a "persecuting class."[58] If truth is not in the world and in our relationship to it, truth becomes a matter of fashion only, and of various attempts to take hold of power.

Does all of this mean that the fungus mentioned above definitely is the image of the Blessed Virgin? Well, the photograph in the *Illustrated London News* that Chesterton refers to of that strange fungus does look like Our Lady. Is this a miracle? Chesterton offers that he does not pin his faith on those rotten planks, although the fungus does look like "a startling replica of the typical reliefs of the Virgin."[59] But "such correspondences are common enough."[60] In the flowers that surround that strange fungus in the photograph, Chesterton jokingly admits seeing an impression of "Edna May dancing in a big hat."[61] Is that a miracle? Whether it is one or not, the man of faith can take the meaning lightly just as he can take the miracle lightly. But taking it lightly is not something the man of science can do since it is his entire worldview that is tested by the appearance of the miracle and by those who affirm it. The man of science can only accept one miracle, the impossible emergence of everything, but no more. To the man of faith, however, the world is all miracles. Perhaps we should be surprised when we don't see a miracle a minute.

The man of faith expects the world, even in something as seemingly formless as a fungus growing on decaying wood, to be meaningful. We will find the truth because the truth wants to be found. If the world is made of meaning, it should not surprise us to find meaning manifest everywhere in various ways, including in science. There can be no doubt that meaning is inescapably entangled in being itself and in our participation with being. It is already there, just as the potential is already there for us to find of it. Chesterton, being mindful of the ground and not just of the figure, wants to remain open to considering other possibilities than the one handed to him. Something of what has been predecided may already be there. But there is also more to discover and understand than what we have already discovered and understood. He jokes that scientists, although not just scientists, should be careful to assume that their discoveries will have only the consequences and meanings they expect: "The great Science of Fingerprints, discovered by a brilliant French criminologist, has produced its principal or ultimate effect

57. Chesterton, *Illustrated London News*, 22 December 1906.
58. Chesterton, *Illustrated London News*, 22 December 1906.
59. Chesterton, *Illustrated London News*, 22 December 1906.
60. Chesterton, *Illustrated London News*, 22 December 1906.
61. Chesterton, *Illustrated London News*, 22 December 1906.

on the world, which is this: that whereas a gentleman was expected to put on gloves to dance with a lady, he may now be expected to put on gloves in order to strangle her."[62]

Chesterton considers something of the mutual openness of mind and matter by setting up a distinction between what is "said" and what is "meant."[63] "When a man says something to us in the street, we hear what he means: we do not hear what he says. When we read some sentence in a book, we read what it means: we cannot see what it says."[64] This may seem an overstatement of the point but Chesterton is being more than a little circumspect. "It is impossible," he writes, "for the human intellect (which is divine) to hear a fact as a fact. It always hears a fact as a *truth*, which is an entirely different thing. A truth is a fact with a meaning."[65] Just as you cannot look at these typographic marks on this page in front of you without perceiving words, so we cannot see facts without perceiving meaning; we cannot perceive matter without registering form. Someone who cannot read English will still assume that there is meaning in these words, even if the meaning is not readily accessible to him. No one can perceive "saidness" apart from "meantness." "Saidness" is something arrived at, perhaps guessed at, after "meantness" has already been planted in our minds. Being precedes understanding just as metaxology precedes all other ways of being attuned to being.

Our inability to totally strip the world of meaning down to some apparently neutral, univocal component part of being suggests a natural capacity within any person: "the moment we have the fact we cannot help feeling as if it is something more than a fact."[66] Matter still calls out to form just as univocity calls out to the other senses of being. We do not only intellectualize meaning, and thus reduce it to some dialectical articulation, but feel it. We do not theorize being but participate in it. Chesterton makes use of this distinction between the said and the meant while looking at the example of statistics, which mimic the modern's concern with inert materiality; with materiality that must have actuality imposed upon it rather than drawn out of it.[67] But thought is not just calculation. Truth is no procedure. Chesterton points out, quite rightly, that the supposed neutrality of statistics is illusory because, as mere facts, they are without reasons and principles. In the presentation of statistics, reasons are not given and principles are not

---

62. Chesterton, *Illustrated London News*, 15 April 1933.
63. Chesterton, *Illustrated London News*, 18 November 1905.
64. Chesterton, *Illustrated London News*, 18 November 1905.
65. Chesterton, *Illustrated London News*, 18 November 1905.
66. Chesterton, *Illustrated London News*, 18 November 1905.
67. Chesterton, *Illustrated London News*, 18 November 1905.

explicitly named. And yet, the mind cannot help but have reasons, even if such reasons are supplied or read into the so-called facts from without. The modern conception of neutral or neutralized being is not neutral.

It would be a mistake to assume, however, that an Aristotelian view on material causality is taken as gospel by Chesterton. Remember, Chesterton conceives of being as good. Matter is not evil in itself even when it is nondescript. It is innocent or more than innocent. It is a manifestation of God's creative love. Our task, therefore, is not to just manipulate matter or bend it to suit our own ends but to seek out the ways in which matter manifests goodness and can manifest greater goodness. We ought to remain open to how form reveals itself to us in things. While a technological frame of mind in particular might restrict how being is allowed to manifest goodness and may even overtly seek to destroy any manifest goodness, a grateful, contemplative awareness allows being to show itself in its fullness. If the technologically oriented mind would render being as a mere stockpile reserve, waiting to be called upon to suit a predecided idea, it is our job to let go and to let be. Being is not meant to be equated with having.

There is always more going on in things than the reduction of things to univocal facts would suggest. For one thing, matter is not the cause of things, in the sense of making itself change. Lumber does not magically turn itself of its own accord into a chair and paper does not turn of its own accord into a *papier-mâché* sculpture or a book. Something or someone, using whatever tools he has at his disposal, must instigate the change in matter. Something or someone must perceive that actualizing a certain potential, or reducing act and potency in a certain way, is possible to disclose new meanings. Nevertheless, something must be there to be changeable. Some form of determinacy must be present to us even if it presences a range of manifest indeterminacies. What instigates change and thus intervenes against any pandemonium of indeterminacies is the second principle of causality, another co-responsible cause that Aristotle calls the efficient cause.

The Efficient Cause

The efficient cause answers the question of what instigates change in matter or what transforms it from one state into another. The efficient cause is the assisting agency, the chief principle of movement. It gets things going or makes them stop. It uses its own actuality to realize the potentiality of another being. Efficient cause does not belong to the being itself; the being is changed externally by what it is not. As already noted, this type of cause is probably the most familiar to us today. However, this claim must be carefully qualified if we are to resist importing modern assumptions into a pre-modern idea. With efficient causality, we are not just looking at something like a series of chemical reactions but are instead considering the most salient explanatory factor for any transformation in matter. We are still looking more at reason than at mechanics, although mechanics are often involved. Nevertheless, with the modern denial of formal cause and formal patterns, as well as the tendency to reject final ends, the efficient cause has become "*the* cause par excellence."[68] Intelligibility tends to be reduced to "relations between antecedents and consequents."[69] Things, human beings included, "become units of effective power."[70]

This has the perhaps inadvertent consequence of translating everything, often by dialectical intervention, into a possible subject of effective power. People are included in this as merely useful and manipulable. Where being manifests as too equivocal, for instance, the chief purpose of effective power is to "homogenize and determine."[71] The human being, when he has a certain status or level of wealth, is reconceived as the chief agent of this effective power, a carver and splitter of all meaning to be consumed in bite-sized portions. A certain kind of man is therefore reconceived as a self-determining law unto himself, an autonomous being with profound dialectical powers. All others become projects to be exploited. And yet man can turn himself into a project as well. By allowing himself to be given over to this faulty conception, this fallacy about the present and the future, he would tend to place himself under the general pragmatic heuristic of *controlling* rather than *understanding*, and *having* rather than *being*. And yet this remains a modified, shrunken sense of what Aristotle intends by efficient cause.

Thankfully, Chesterton sees through the modern chatter about efficient causality exceptionally well. He notices that, in the modern era, efficient causality is typically reduced to a simple sequence of cause and effect, with depth sacrificed in the name of dull linearity. The result of such a sacrifice is the tendency to notice figures and not the ground. We should be careful to avoid this trap if we want to more clearly see the formal cause. In contrast with the typical modern understanding of efficient causality, Aristotle provides examples of efficient causes that may be surprising, especially because they do not conform to modern univocity. A seed, for instance, is the efficient cause of a plant. And while an artist is involved in making an

---

68. Desmond, *William Desmond Reader*, 67.
69. Desmond, *William Desmond Reader*, 67.
70. Desmond, *William Desmond Reader*, 67.
71. Desmond, *William Desmond Reader*, 67.

artwork and while a doctor implements what is necessary to heal a patient, Aristotle elects to name *artistry* and *medicine* as the primary efficient causes or explanations for what instigates the change at work through artists and doctors as mediators of efficient causation. Such examples reveal the primacy of efficient causality as a mode of intelligibility over efficient causality as a way of catalyzing a process. In this we find that efficient cause is more expansive than is likely to be obvious.

This last idea seems to encroach on formal causality. Perhaps it does, although efficient causality does not grant a thing its essence and definition as formal causality does. It remains true that each cause necessarily gives itself to the other causes and takes from the other causes. Causality remains dynamic and interwoven. That said, some clarification regarding efficient causality, as granting but not originating form, may be helpful. If a patient is healed by the doctor's expertise, for instance, it is obvious that the doctor in question possesses the know-how to heal the patient. That knowledge is in him and he remains a secondary agent, even while his mediatory agency initiates his role in formal causality. However, Aristotle argues that the relevant medical knowledge is the primary agent that heals, rather than the doctor. The doctor's chief function, as one whose position as a doctor is owed to a higher reality, is therefore to understand, recognize, and manifest that knowledge, as well as apply it correctly without overruling being's mediation of itself to him. Aristotle prioritizes the practice over the practitioner to suggest that what matters most here is not the beliefs, desires, and intentions of the individual but the precise factors at play in a specific happening of being. Without the knowledge of medicine, there would be no cure; without the practice of medicine, there would be no healing. The doctor is far from irrelevant. His specific expertise and wisdom are important and he remains the embodiment of medical knowledge and medical practice. His intelligence and actions channel that knowledge into bringing about change. Aristotle emphasizes general principles as well as specific applications of those principles.

This is one way to avoid the modern reduction of efficient causality to mere agent- or will-driven cause and effect. As this example shows, the doctor works on material causes according to specific knowledge and certain anticipations of outcomes. His actions, if we take the ideal case, are (or should be) anything but arbitrary. This knowledge is a complex interweaving of diagnostic methodologies, treatment procedures, and medical technologies, but against the modern reduction of a person to a body or even to flesh, this knowledge may also include such practices as praying for and anointing the sick, in recognition of God's invisible involvement in the manifest.[72] In our minds, the efficient cause should remain, as should the other causes, true to metaxology. Goodness remains the ultimate cause of healing. Any change is owed to a complex pattern but must be channeled in some way. The way, here, is the efficient cause. It is not, given the analogical relation to the real, entirely captured by dialectical intellection. We can therefore say that efficient causality is porous to formal causality. Such an interweaving of components and proportions suggests, in other words, what Aristotle calls the formal cause of medicine. The efficient cause as the locus of agency is a mediator between the material cause and the formal cause, although arguably the efficient cause leans less on a sense of the future than does the formal cause. With regard to a doctor, he brings the skills he has learned into contact with the specific embodied matter, the patient and the illness he is treating. But he does not thereby transform the patient into a mere object or corpse. From a certain perspective the patient and the patient's potential or future health is the formal cause of his specific treatment, in which various material components are necessarily involved, needing to be actualized in specific ways.

Why the doctor bothers to do what he does suggests the final cause, about which some provisional comments need to be offered here before the fuller discussion below. The final cause indicates the *goal* of the other causes. The preceding causes, in other words, come together to serve some function, purpose, or end. Aristotle uses the example of health as the cause of exercising. Health is also the final cause in the example of the doctor's treatment of a patient. Importantly, Aristotle finds teleology everywhere in nature. Why do plants have leaves? To protect their fruit. Why do plant roots grow so deep into the ground? To find nourishment in the soil. It is perhaps surprising but also funny that atheistic evolutionists struggle in vain, even after having bracketed God out of the question—God being, for Aristotle, the ultimate final cause—to completely evade teleology in their explanations of natural phenomena. This is not proof for the existence of God, even if it does gesture towards an ultimacy that transcends immediate happenings. It shows that it is human, and I would say God-given, to seek ends. Human ways of interpreting are inescapable, even if we may attempt, for whatever reasons, to suppress or distort them. As Chesterton reminds us, "The truth is that everything that ever came out of a human mouth had a human meaning."[73] We cannot help but see everything as meant for something, even if we might interpret this meaning wrongly.

---

72. Davison, *Participation in God*, 33.
73. Chesterton, *Collected Works, Volume 4*, 378.

Chesterton notices a skepticism in his age, which is still with us today, that joins forces with nominalism and voluntarism, as well as the denial of the analogy of being that supports these heretical distortions, to ensure the radical contraction of efficient causality. And this, he knows, is certain to have consequences in the real world. People he describes as "will worshippers"[74] start to take over. They worship *mere choice*, the mere power to choose. Ironically, though, worshiping will negates will; "admiring mere choice is to refuse to choose."[75] Deterministic historicism conforms to this pattern. While trying to discern the inner meaning of history, there is a forgetting of what freedom means. Those who worship the will are fond of discussing things by expansion and breaking out.[76] But, in reality, self-limitation is built into any act of will. "To desire action is to desire limitation," even if only inadvertently.[77] As Chesterton's analysis suggests, those who worship will may be denying final and formal causality. However, this does not mean that final and formal causality are not at work. They cannot ultimately be avoided. Reality works along the lines described by Aristotle whether we want it to or not. Every act of will must, because it is an act of will, select and exclude; it must desire an end and conform to a form, even if it does not want to. Thus, the aim and form of any decision is likely to be evident to those, like Chesterton, who are aware of the shape of the real, even if those who make the decision remain in the dark. Willing often inadvertently exposes the indispensability of formal causality even if will-worshipers deny this.

This is especially evident in any scientific sphere. In one essay, Chesterton reflects on certain possible technological developments. He wonders about the possibility of decline, saying that "it is not impossible that our own hustling industrialism may be simplified in spite of itself, as the cabs might turn into cottages. It may become stable by becoming what it would call a stick-in-the-mud."[78] Chesterton suggests that communications might break down and "bureaucracy and big business" might give way to "a simpler life."[79] "Our cities may be deserted and our palaces in ruins; and there may be a chance yet for humanity to become human."[80] But Chesterton also perceives the accelerationist tendencies of modern science, which conditions constant

---

74. Chesterton, *Collected Works, Volume I*, 242.
75. Chesterton, *Collected Works, Volume I*, 242.
76. Chesterton, *Collected Works, Volume I*, 242.
77. Chesterton, *Collected Works, Volume I*, 242.
78. Chesterton, *Illustrated London News*, 11 October 1924.
79. Chesterton, *Illustrated London News*, 11 October 1924.
80. Chesterton, *Illustrated London News*, 11 October 1924.

and increasingly rapid improvements to fit the logic of rationalization and perfectibility. Those who worship the will might consider this a victory, and yet, Chesterton suggests, we would still feel that something fundamental has been lost if science gets to call all the shots. We will be alienated from being and uprooted. What if some kind of decline is not to be mourned but hoped for?

Chesterton is aware that virtue, the call for the full realization of our human potentials, structures human character and awareness in such a way as to allow reality to reveal itself in its reality. This is true even at the level of the material and efficient causes. What we perceive through the uses and enjoyment of matter depends not just on instrumental logic but on our attunement to the good. Immoralists are blind to the real because being and goodness are coextensive. But to idolize willpower is to forget how easy it is to want things that are not good; things that do not serve human flourishing. This is a subject I return to below with respect to the question of how human rights, as a morality divorced from natural law and the obligations of virtue, distort perception. Whatever efficient causality means, however, it cannot mean that we can want whatever we want or call things whatever we want. Interpretation remains central to understanding and we can allow degrees of relativity, but never absolute relativism. As the example above shows how medical knowledge is mediated by a doctor, it is clear that bad mediations and misunderstandings may also shape the future. But sanity requires us to know the essences of things; to know their forms as Plato does. Sanity requires us to seek out the right shape by understanding both what things are and what they could be.[81] This implies having a sense of what they are *for*.

The Final Cause

The intelligibility of things, as the above already suggests, is entangled not only in means but also in ends. Aristotle's final cause seeks to question and address what any given thing is for.[82] As noted above, the modern sense of efficient causality as cause and effect sacrifices this aspect of causality, and this means sacrificing intelligibility as well. Still, final causality has a habit of showing up everywhere. Why exercise? For the sake of the enjoyment of exercising or for the sake of health. Why write or read books about Chesterton and formal causality? Arguably, if only partly, for the sake of making better sense of the world we live in. While treating nature as being indifferent to

---

81. Chesterton, *Collected Works, Volume I*, 78–79.
82. Grondin, *Introduction to Metaphysics*, 52.

ends, even Darwinists seem to constantly find themselves on the side of survival and of life, of things that are perceived to have value. There seems to be a point to things, after all, and intelligibility suffers when we refuse to accept this. Care is built into being, as atheists like Nietzsche and Heidegger have insisted. We want to flourish, even when our understanding of what it means to flourish may be distorted.

I have already discussed, in the light of Plato, Chesterton's awareness of how moderns like to suspend any attempt to answer the question "of what is good."[83] It is as if, according to a voluntarist and nominalist tendency, moderns want to remove teleology from being to legitimate doing whatever they please. This cannot be without consequences, however, even where moderns want to silence consequences. Where the form of the family is denied, for instance, people in society suffer pain and society itself is left worse off. Where the form of marriage is denied, as has happened in the wake of the sexual revolution that Chesterton himself foresaw, human flourishing has been severely curtailed. Where vows decay into contracts, with the result that human bonds become tenuous, human happiness becomes impossible. Where the goal of human life, namely union with God, is denied, human beings become subject to idols, which are cruel and exacting. The principle of worship remains the same: we become what we behold.[84] Without a sense of what things and people are for, and especially what good they aim to achieve, we can be sure that misery will be multiplied. The grace of a true aim transforms into judgment and punishment when that aim is missed or avoided.

The sense of ends is nowhere more evident than in Chesterton's Catholicism, the doctrines of which always keep in mind the archetypal final cause, and the rituals and sacraments that guide Christians towards the good life. Chesterton jokes that he developed his own thinking as an attempt to generate his very own heresy but found, after various intellectual twists and turns, that his heresy was identical with orthodoxy as summarized by the Apostle's Creed.[85] Human life and human flourishing ought to always be directed towards God. The same is true for all the causes, perhaps exempting material causality. God remains the chief archetype, the one *from whom* (efficient cause, symbolized by the Father), *to whom* (final cause, symbolized by the Son), and *through whom* (formal cause, symbolized by the Holy Spirit) all things have their being.[86] I want to focus on how

---

83. Chesterton, *Collected Works, Volume I*, 51.
84. Psalm 115:4–8.
85. Chesterton, *Collected Works, Volume I*, 215.
86. Davison, *Participation in God*, 44.

Catholicism points to a "definite ideal," which turns out to be an "urgent and practical matter."[87] I want to consider especially how the notion of the "modern project" parodies the Catholic sense of final causality. This offers further clues into why Chesterton so clearly understood so much of what was happening around him and where it was more than likely to lead.

Remi Brague points out that, for Chesterton, the modern world is "living on Catholic capital."[88] The modern world, Chesterton writes, "is using, and using up, the truths that remain to it out of the old treasury of Christendom, including of course many truths known to pagan antiquity but crystalised in Christendom."[89] This pronouncement offers a way not only to understand a trend in his time but also his work in general. "When the world goes wrong," it shows us where "the Church is right."[90] The trend he spots is still evident now. He sees the modern world as having no new enthusiasms of its own, although many people make up for its lack of novelties by resorting to generating new names and labels following the manner of the advertising industry. "For these are the two marks of modern moral ideals," Chesterton writes, gesturing to the modern denigration of final causality: "First, that they were borrowed or snatched out of ancient or medieval hands" and "second, that they whither very quickly in modern hands."[91] The modern world is parasitic in a specific way. It tries to pick up what has been handed to it but it cannot carry it well. It corrupts what is given by shrinking it to a more manageable size. Large ideas, embedded in a complex world of meaning, atrophy. They are still at work, certainly, but their work is hampered by a contagion of ignorance, discarnate abstractions, false absolutes, and deformed forms. Chesterton often reflects on how forgetting one's heritage does not mean that it goes away or that the truths known by our forebears cease to be true. Truth persists. But like the boy in the story of the roots of the world cited in the first chapter, we hurt ourselves against it, and hurt others and the world by failing to recognize its meaning for the present.

Consider, for instance, some specific insights into what a breakdown in Catholicism has meant for the modern world in the form of the now commonplace notion at the heart of human rights ethics that the individual human being is intrinsically valuable. In the first article of the Universal Declaration of Human Rights, we find this asserted: "All human beings are

---

87. Chesterton, *Collected Works, Volume 4*, 44.
88. Brague, *Curing Mad Truths*, 3.
89. Chesterton, *Thing*, 16–17.
90. Chesterton, *Everlasting Man*, 10.
91. Chesterton, *Thing*, 16–17.

born free and equal in dignity and rights."[92] Much can be said about the notion of equality, and how it shifts from being about fairness, with every person treated as equal before the law (this is Chesterton's understanding of the idea), to being about a highly abstract equation of one person with the next. That said, I focus here, respectively, on the notions of *dignity* and *rights*. At first, the idea of human dignity sounds decidedly Christian, a wonderful declaration of a *telos*. Chesterton often uses the word dignity to urge its urgent defense.[93] But he is clear that dignity is a divine gift to man, just as he is clear that human beings can be undignified. This incongruity between the ideal and our failures commonly spurs us to laugh.[94] The trouble is, as Ryszard Legutko has shown, that the concept of dignity is used very strangely in that famous Declaration.[95] It implies, or so we are led to believe, a strong view of human nature and human freedom. However, such an interpretation is undermined by an adherence to what Roger Scruton calls the "born free fallacy," which, in its blank-slatism, denies any inherent and clear end for human beings.[96] The term *dignity* now implies no noble, immortal soul, and no innate desire for the good. The notion has been emptied of both moral content and teleology. The human being does not need to live in a certain way to be dignified, apparently, but *is* dignified, just because—in nominalist-voluntarist fashion—we say so. Somehow, a man has dignity even when he acts like a brute. Higher duties and obligations have been subtly stripped, starved, and flogged; they have given way to smaller duties guided by shrunken teleologies conforming to the bureaucratic expectations of states and businesses. Man is dignified now for no reason, and yet he is often made to feel he is owed the whole world. He may gain the world, but it is a much shallower, less meaningful world. If he gains this world, it is at the cost of his soul.

As Christianity would have it, and as I have noted, human value is found in its being ultimately *for God*. In modernity, though, man has dignity not because it is given but because it is taken. Man has rights, supposedly. This conclusion is not inevitable. If subtler and more sensible ways of thinking about rights are available, the uprooting of the notion of dignity from its metaphysical basis means that it becomes fairly inevitable to have an

---

92. Nolde, *Freedom's Charter*, 56.

93. Maycock, "Introduction," 74; Chesterton, *Autobiography*, 239; Chesterton, *Collected Works, Volume 1*, 94, 298; Chesterton, *Everlasting Man*, 52–53; Chesterton, *Saint Thomas Aquinas & Saint Francis of Assisi*, 36, 177; Chesterton, *What's Wrong with the World*, 15–24; Nichols, *Chesterton*, 121–59; Williams, *Mere Humanity*, 15–24.

94. Chesterton, *All Things Considered*, 153–54.

95. See Legutko, *Demon in Democracy*.

96. Scruton, *Uses of Pessimism*, 42–61.

intelligible final cause transformed into a merely efficient one of will without considering proper ends. A rhetorical sleight of hand, separating dignity from its grounding in Christianity, results in a legitimation for entitlements and demands without reciprocity and with almost no moral effort. Human rights are apparently universal, and all cultures and ways of life are equal, including those that refuse to accept human equality.[97] This is contradictory in a way that cannot be resolved without restoring the Catholic sense of human dignity. After all, at the center of the general ethos of human rights is the thoroughly modern and ultimately fallacious idea of the autonomous and supposedly good individual. Humanism, and therefore human rights ethics, remains an exercise in self-predication divorced from any transcendental ground or meaning.

Already in perceiving the contrast between the original Catholic idea of the good and the modern notion of rights, we might begin to sense, as Chesterton does, what might happen if the former were replaced by the latter. Even at the level of pure abstraction, we would be able to tell that fracturing the moral landscape is fairly inevitable.[98] What is also striking is that the so-called right that forms the apparent basis of all other rights in much modern thought, although by no means an absolute in the current climate, is the right to life. This life is bare life, however; it is life without form and no higher *telos*. A weak notion of human dignity supports this appeal to formless life, rendering people vulnerable to the abuse of sovereign political power, including whatever state power would encourage and mandate something as abhorrent as euthanasia. What starts to matter most is not human flourishing, in the ethical sense, but conformity to the given political and ideological regime.

Consider another example, highlighted especially in the work of René Girard, who admired Chesterton but developed his own way of grappling with the meaning of formal causality in his mimetic theory. For Girard, we understand the formal cause by observing the consequences of mimetic desire, the contention that our desire for being is essentially mediated. The example Girard homes in on is the contemporary consciousness around victimhood, and especially the trend to victimize in the name of the victim. This "rise in victimhood culture"[99] is linked with a larger "rise and triumph of the modern [identitarian, psychological] self."[100] But as Girard stresses, the deep roots of this phenomenon are found in misunderstanding how

---

97. Manent, *Human Rights and Natural Law*, 3.
98. Chesterton, *Collected Works, Volume 1*, 233.
99. Campbell and Manning, *Rise of Victimhood Culture*.
100. Trueman, *Rise and Triumph of the Modern Self*.

Christianity has always valued personhood, as well as the special charity distributed to the marginalized—the widow, the orphan, and the stranger. Girard's own prediction of a gloomy future looks eerily accurate in some places now: "You can foresee the shape of what the Antichrist is going to be in the future: a super-victimary machine that will keep on sacrificing in the name of the victim."[101] What appears as anti-Christian is nevertheless reliant on a Christian foundation; it tries to "outchristianize Christianity" by being an "ultra-Christian caricature."[102] It imitates Christianity but in a spirit of rivalry foreign to Christianity. The turn towards idolizing the victim, even rendering the victim as a totem, turns the victim into an uncritiqueable subject. The victim becomes a sign that can undermine any other form of meaning. Of course, there are real victims and Christianity demands that mercy be extended to them. But the point here is that the transformation of a terrible reminder of human fallenness and the need for healing and redemption into an admirable thing-in-itself is a sign of how far the original Christian idea has deteriorated throughout Christendom. Although he did not articulate himself in these Girardian terms, Chesterton nevertheless saw in his own time what would happen if a small group of people were to be in charge: "This is the age of minorities; of groups that rule rather than represent."[103] It would perhaps not have been that surprising to Chesterton to see that one minority might be a special class of self-proclaimed victims and that their status as victims would become a way to rise to the top of the liberal social hierarchy.

As the above highlights, Catholic capital is spent despite being divorced from the larger scheme of Catholicism. Much done in the name of justice is thus often little more than *ressentiment*, which is a concealed and more socially acceptable form of revenge.[104] A cheap imitation *logos* replaces the universal, divine *logos*. Chesterton is proved right for having perceived all of this in his own way. Whether he was warning medical scientists of the inhumanity of eugenics[105] or warning Americans of the potential harms of certain social policies, he has often been correct. He has been right because he knew that bad ideas have always been plagiarisms of better ideas. Evil is always and without exception a parasite that relies upon the good even as it corrupts it. It rests on a solid foundation even as it tears up and destroys that very foundation by opposing the good as a whole by lesser goods.

101. Girard, *Evolution and Conversion*, 168–69.
102. Girard, *Evolution and Conversion*, 168–69.
103. Chesterton, *Irish Impressions*, 148.
104. See Scheler, *Ressentiment*.
105. Chesterton, *Collected Works, Volume 4*, 297–418.

Regarding the above sketch of modern adjustments to the ethical landscape, Chesterton suggests that "the modern world is not evil; in some ways the modern world is far too good."[106] The trouble is, it "is full of wild and wasted virtues. When a religious scheme is shattered (as Christianity was shattered at the Reformation), it is not merely the vices that are let loose. The vices are, indeed, let loose, and they wander and do damage. But the virtues are let loose also; and the virtues wander more wildly, and the virtues do more terrible damage."[107] As virtues get "isolated from each other," they go "mad."[108] Unfortunately, this is not where the process stops. The part, severed from the whole, soon begins to tyrannize the whole. The ideological fragment begins to destabilize the world to which it owes its existence. "Thus some scientists care for truth," Chesterton notes, and yet "their truth is pitiless." Moreover, there are "humanitarians" that "only care for pity" and the result is that "their pity . . . is often untruthful."[109] In separation and fragmentation, and especially in the gradual or sometimes dramatic erasure of final causality, the ethical realm loses all form. But these fragmentations may well ossify into ironclad social rules; the perpetuation of the parasitic may become a standardized social expectation.

Chesterton begins to suggest that the essential character of modernity is heretical—an idea taken up by his friend Hillaire Belloc in his book *The Great Heresies* (1938), published two years after Chesterton's death.[110] To recognize heresy, one must have a clear idea of what orthodoxy looks like. To understand madness, a clear view of sanity is required. More specifically, modernity is idolatrous, meaning that it constantly and almost predictably grants an absolute status to relative values. We cannot help but worship,[111] after all, although the orientation and attitude of our worship informs the shape of our lives and also the shape of what we can perceive.[112] To have an attentional foundation in reality, as Chesterton does, results in being able to perceive not only when things are in their right place but also means perceiving what is going on when things are out of place, as well as what is to be done to put things back where they are supposed to be. To fail to see things in their right place is to be at risk of criticizing what is real by what

---

106. Chesterton, *Collected Works, Volume 1*, 233.
107. Chesterton, *Collected Works, Volume 1*, 233.
108. Chesterton, *Collected Works, Volume 1*, 233.
109. Chesterton, *Collected Works, Volume 1*, 233.
110. See Belloc, *Great Heresies*.
111. Chesterton, *Everlasting Man*, 112.
112. McGilchrist, *Matter with Things, Volume 1*, 26.

is make-believe.[113] One will always be failing to see things as they are even while one is convinced that one is in the right.

Nevertheless, idolatry is funny in a way, Chesterton contends, "because it is not only an incongruity but an inversion."[114] The loss of final causality brings about a tendency to, mentally at least, turn the world upside-down. The idea of idolatry is summed up perfectly "in the one unanswerable formula: 'They worship the work of their own hands.'"[115] This formula means that "the fetish-worshipper" can take a lump of clay and make something out of it but, "instead of thanking God that he has made it, he worships it as the God that has made him.[116] The moment after the masterpiece is completed, the relations between the master and the masterpiece are mystically reversed. The last and newest thing in the world becomes the first and oldest."[117] It becomes "the maker of his own maker."[118] Chesterton is clear that while this sounds and is ridiculous, "*this* is exactly what all the most advanced modern philosophers are doing now."[119] Unlike the ancient fetish worshiper who tries to make his idol "as unlike himself as possible," the "professor of sociology and ethics so often makes his ideal exactly like himself."[120]

Chesterton frequently points at professors, scientists, and politicians as symbols, not to be taken literally, for modern degradation; this shows how modernity institutes the likelihood of its own suicide. As Brague intimates, modernity is set up as a *project* rather than as a *task*. This idea is captured in Daniel Defoe's designation of his time as the "Projecting Age" and Jonathan Swift's brilliant parody of professors in his Academy of Projectors in *Gulliver's Travels* (1726).[121] "A project," Brague writes, "is what we decide to undertake, whereas a task is entrusted to us by some higher power."[122] The emphasis of the task is on the givenness and gift of being, whereas the project, at the mercy of self-mediation, transforms givenness into the taken-for-granted. Even paganism would see things along the lines of a task, since nature or the gods would entrust human beings with something to do. Christianity acknowledges God as the Task-Giver. God gives the world to

---

113. Chesterton, *Collected Works, Volume 1*, 68.
114. Chesterton, *Illustrated London News*, 14 April 1934.
115. Chesterton, *Illustrated London News*, 14 April 1934; Isaiah 2:8; Jeremiah 1:16.
116. Chesterton, *Illustrated London News*, 14 April 1934.
117. Chesterton, *Illustrated London News*, 14 April 1934.
118. Chesterton, *Illustrated London News*, 14 April 1934.
119. Chesterton, *Illustrated London News*, 14 April 1934.
120. Chesterton, *Illustrated London News*, 14 April 1934.
121. Brague, *Curing Mad Truths*, 3.
122. Brague, *Curing Mad Truths*, 3.

man. He places creation under man's dominion and care. But the modern project, resting on the experimental mind, transforms creation into largely dead and impersonal matter, and so even the idea of dominion is perverted to mean not care but control. Dominion is replaced by domination. This shift from task to project is therefore by no means a merely semantic issue; the words designate a shift in focus and attitude. Because of this, perhaps, the consequences of this shift are not too perceptible to moderns, while Chesterton can see perfectly clearly what sort of mess we will end up in and what sort of mess we *have* ended up in as a result.

Essentially, the task is set up to understand any part within and for a given whole. The task is enworlded and can therefore only be carried out within a given context of meanings and relationships. By contrast, the project, understood primarily if not only under the heuristic of efficiency, is unworlded. The atomized man, the person Hannah Arendt calls world-alienated, establishes the limits of his project. In this, the nineteenth century in particular could be distinguished not by the triumph of science but by the triumph of method over science. However, fairly obviously, we cannot assume that this triumph of method was contained within the nineteenth century and abandoned after it. Even if much has changed, the twenty-first century remains haunted by the ghosts of modern projectors. Arguably, with the rise of biopolitics, technocracies, and data mining, the projectors of our time put the former projectors to shame for being too timid in their antagonism towards reality. The projectors of an earlier age were cowardly by comparison, even, to use Swift's images, in trying to extract sunbeams from cucumbers or attempting to transform excrement back into food. Our projectors are more and not less object-oriented and more project-oriented than in Chesterton's time. In many ways, with so much added artificiality guiding our thoughts and actions, the world has become even more impersonal, not less.[123]

Taking the etymology of the word *project* seriously as referring to the throwing (*jacere*) forth (*pro*) of a body, as is the case of a missile that "loses contact with the mover,"[124] Brague suggests three ways that the modern project reinterprets time—and thus everything else temporal along with it. First is the idea of moving away from the past towards an ever newer beginning. Second is the idea of moving towards the present and becoming a self-determined individual. Third is the idea of moving towards the future in a way that maintains the ideal of progress, whether implicitly or explicitly.[125]

---

123. Chesterton, *Collected Works, Volume 4*, 378–84.
124. Brague, *Curing Mad Truths*, 11.
125. Brague, *Curing Mad Truths*, 12.

Chesterton sees a joke in this tiresome preoccupation with the new, the now, and the next: "It is incomprehensible to me that any thinker can calmly call himself a modernist; he might as well call himself a Thursdayite."[126] Without seeking and articulating a final cause, modernity has no way to measure the new, the now, and the next. It can declare that such things are better but cannot prove this.

However, modernity does not purport to be comprehensible. It is a prejudice alone and not a dogma and so it offers direction without any directive apart from insisting merely that we get away from here—wherever here happens to be. In this we find especially starkly how the project stands in opposition to providence. The gift of being is devalued right from the outset. If providence provides an aim, the modern project wants to determine its own aims and therefore its own content. Nevertheless, this opposition between providence and project does not mean altering the essential content but instead means opting for a less robust and thus narrower and smaller version of that content. I return to an example already mentioned above in passing, the idea that dominion over nature is providential.[127] Nature is a gift to be nurtured, guided, and guarded. But in modernity, dominion over nature is distorted when the project takes over. Nature is plundered, mined, and manipulated. To mention another example, the idea of progress is fundamental to the biblical narrative, especially as a desired movement towards fullness, wholeness, redemption, restoration, and glory. But the project takes this providential idea, and especially the idea that a *telos* beyond the human sets limits on the meaning of progress, and reshapes it to suit whatever aims have been set by human actors. What is desirable, but not inevitable given human fallibility, is replaced with a sort of blind inevitability, especially embodied in Whig and Communist historiography, both of which famously straightjacket the complexities of real events within a rigid interpretive schema that is entirely theoretical and not incarnational.

The modern project refracts reality, especially through the voluntarist question of power, and therefore suppresses the question of goodness. As a consequence, as modern projectors would have it, the main way to arrive at truth is not through seeking and finding; by attending to and allowing the given. Truth is arrived at through testing and confirming; through self-mediation. Providential seeking and finding, reframed in the discovery that one has already been sought and found like Adam in the garden, sees existence as a gift. However, as Brague contends, "Wherever the idea of a project plays the lead, the very figure of Truth changes. Truth becomes the result of

---

126. Chesterton, *All Things Considered*, 9.
127. Genesis 1:28.

an experiment."¹²⁸ As Chesterton's friend and part-time intellectual sparring partner H. G. Wells put it, quoted in a letter on Chesterton's work in the *Daily News*: "Individuality" becomes "an experiment."¹²⁹ Phenomena can be removed from their situated givenness and so can be, in a sense, "produced" by being subjected to experimentation. Put more strongly, the projector's trend is to disregard the disclosures of being that gently emerge through contemplation and persuasion and relationality in favor of those exposures acquired through technique and technological force. Reality is tortured to reveal its truths. Being is revealed, as this idolatry would have it, only when subjected to private demands.

However, to arrive at truth by experiment alone is ultimately to lose the meaning even of that discovered truth. By analogy, the machinery of miners may seek out the "truth" of the gold buried in a landscape but with the tragic result of leaving the landscape devoured and destroyed. Truth becomes not something located in being itself, as it is in the work of St. Augustine or St. Thomas, but gets regarded as something of an epistemological side-effect, the result of the interference of too much dialectical self-mediation. This sets up a shift towards a kind of technological gnosticism, without the implied religious meaning. Truth becomes less a matter of participation in reality than a matter of what we currently know, want to know, and perhaps can possibly know, but only by experiment. There may be positive and productive yields to this. For example, it is through evidence-based medicine that we have been able to learn crucial things to help the sick and ease suffering. Through other scientific and technological research, we have many examples of significant discoveries. However, such projecting is often dangerously decontextualized. To continue with medicine as an example, various forms of iatrogenesis and cultural iatrogenesis are often overlooked or dismissed as so-called side effects. A tragic response to suffering has arisen, for instance, in the form of an opioid crisis.¹³⁰ Problems are also evident in the social sciences. Unguided by wisdom, many so-called discoveries in the social sciences inform how social systems are designed, often to the detriment of many people affected by those systems. An overly dialectical posture comes to view discoveries as objective and thus as irrefutable even though they remain little more than confirmations of the axioms that sparked their discovery.

The trouble is this. Projects tend to discover only what they are looking for. As a consequence, they find less than what they are looking for. The

---

128. Brague, *Curing Mad Truths*, 15.
129. Chesterton, *Daily News*, 10 October 1906.
130. See Illich, *Limits to Medicine*; Han, *Palliative Society*.

results of mere projects can therefore be used to reshape and distort contexts in favor of those results. Systems tilt in favor of constructed biases. Negative results can be mitigated somewhat if the modern equivalent of the academy of projectors is carefully attuned to contexts. But the paradigm of the project itself threatens such an environmental awareness. We now live in a world in which it is possible to employ the mindset of the projector without any careful attunement to reality as a whole. Specialization contributes to this. Evidence-based medicine, for instance, can be and often has been hijacked by corporate and political interests that tamper with the procedures that would yield relevant acumen.[131]

Science cannot be theory-neutral, in the end, and so it is no wonder that ideological interests in favor of cosmetics, commerciality, and military advancements have often overtaken any desire to allow science to serve the common good of common people. You can commonly find people arguing in favor of abortion or euthanasia, not on moral grounds, but rather because of a commitment to specific financial and personal gains that have nothing to do with ethics. Efficiency, of which so-called rights ethics is often an example, usurps real virtue.[132] Chesterton sees this in his own time and place and says that efficiency is ultimately futile because "it only deals with actions after they have been performed. It has no philosophy for incidents before they happen; therefore it has no power of choice. An act can only be successful or unsuccessful when it is over; if it is to begin, it must be, in the abstract, right or wrong."[133] The logic of efficiency, which is a kind of unreason, fails to see that there "is no such thing as backing a winner; for he cannot be a winner when he is backed. There is no such thing as fighting on the winning side; one fights to find out which is the winning side."[134]

Efficiency drives confirmation bias or a collection of biases; it drives the manipulation of reality rather than the discovery of truth. All of the above reflects the essential character of liberalism, discussed in more detail below, which inverts the relationship between the metaphysical categories of act and potency. Liberalism, one of the dominant ideological forms produced by modernity, rejects pure act, namely God, and then mistakenly gives priority to potency over act in everything else. Potentials, as possibilities present within concrete givens, are swept aside as unbridled possibility takes the reins, even to the point of upending the given. This is something that concerned Chesterton, as I explore more later. Chesterton saw all of

131. Jureidini and McHenry, "Illusion of Evidence Based Medicine."
132. Chesterton, *Collected Works, Volume 4*, 44.
133. Chesterton, *Collected Works, Volume 4*, 44.
134. Chesterton, *Collected Works, Volume 4*, 44.

this, and he saw what would arise as a result. He perceived that the modern project did not appreciate limits, the interplay of act and potency, as he did.

As the philosopher Byung-Chul Han notes, in recent years, the subject who was once subject to higher laws becomes *a* project, if not *the* project, in modern liberalism.[135] Quite easily in our time, people start to view others and themselves not through the grateful lens of the gift or the given but rather through the lens of the modern project itself. Perhaps unexpectedly, this further reinforces the already pervasive conception, noticed by Chesterton long ago, of the human being as a passive entity. Inwardness and human agency are no longer valued because they are difficult to experiment with to determine their presence, quality, and value. As a consequence, the modern project deals almost exclusively by objectifying personhood. Mystery gives way to an insistence that everything should be transparent in an age of hyper-communication. The truth is considered not as apparent in his or her given being, in the complexity that yields to identity and form, but rather as something yielded to understanding in and through experiment and its concomitant nominalist terminologies, whether self-imposed or imposed from without by various things, like laws, bureaucratic procedures, medical procedures, psychological theories, as well as political and social pressures.

The result is not a deep understanding of human existence but a shallow, theoretical notion of personhood. An image poorly reasoned through can be superimposed onto people. This is perhaps nowhere more vividly articulated than in the work of Jean Baudrillard who argues that reality no longer holds as a principle.[136] Baudrillard is careful to point out that real things do happen. Events are not merely imagined. He does not deny the existence of the real, as a solipsist would, even if he tends towards nihilism. However, he contends that, in the hypermediated world, the principle of reality as a metaphysical anchor no longer holds. The construct or simulacrum, the conception of reality filtered through the univocal gaze of electric immediacy, is all that matters. Media, which have all been built according to the logic of the modern project, start to block out the windows of the five senses with theoretical reconstructions of imaginary objects. Truth becomes a matter not of agreement with reality but of univocal consensus. We find that the post-truth age within which we now live begins with the modern project itself. Again, there is much in Chesterton's work that suggests that this result is not so far from the picture he imagined in his own time. Towards the end of *Heretics* (1905), he foresees a time is coming, the very time that is upon us, in which believing what is real will become an act

---

135. See Han, *In the Swarm*.
136. Baudrillard, *Perfect Crime*, 1–8.

of faith.[137] It is striking that those who know the truth find it confirmed by the contradictions of maniacs. Unarticulated truths transform into dogmas when they are disputed.[138] "Thus every man who utters a doubt defines a religion," says Chesterton, and "the scepticism of our time does not really destroy the beliefs, rather it creates them; gives them their limits and their plain and defiant shape."[139]

In our world now, skepticism has taken on some very strange shapes. A person will be widely applauded by politicians and corporations and those duped by them for deciding to self-identify as almost anything he envisions, except as what he is. He can self-identify as a woman, for one thing, but extreme examples have been proliferating in our time of people even self-identifying as animals or food. Given limits are despised and unbridled desire can take on almost any form, including that of body modification and mutilation, as well as including indulging various forms of depravity. What Philip Rieff has called the triumph of the therapeutic,[140] the progeny of a history of alienation and Freudian-style attacks on repression, makes room for a person's (entirely negative) freedom from providential calling.[141] Scientific falsification, which has dominated the modern era, takes on a cultural form. The so-called individual's life is his own to make of it what he wants—although this supposed ownership of his life must be strictly in keeping with the demands of the market and the predominating liberal-democratic order.

It is not surprising that the removal of constraints does not leave room for freedom.[142] As Han writes, "The freedom of *Can* generates even more coercion than the disciplinarian *Should*, which issues commandments and prohibitions. *Should* has a limit. In contrast, *Can* has none. Thus, the compulsion entailed by *Can* is unlimited."[143] One irony of the modern project, discussed at length by so many thinkers now, is that the quest for freedom in modernity—this projection into endless possibilities that substitutes potentiality for actuality—has produced only slavery.[144] This is also predicted in Chesterton's work.[145] The still present trend in the wake of modernity is to

---

137. Chesterton, *Collected Works, Volume 1*, 207.
138. Chesterton, *Collected Works, Volume 1*, 207.
139. Chesterton, *Collected Works, Volume 1*, 207.
140. Rieff, *Triumph of the Therapeutic*.
141. Rieff, *Triumph of the Therapeutic*.
142. See Philips, *Obedience Is Freedom*.
143. Han, *Psychopolitics*, 1–2.
144. See Schindler, *Freedom from Reality*.
145. Chesterton, *Illustrated London News*, 9 June 9 1934.

concentrate efforts on an ever-shrinking circle around individual subjects. Those individual subjects are placed entirely at the mercy of interests that do not work in their favor. In the name of so-called autonomy, that well-worn Cartesian fiction, choice disappears.

Thinking like a projector can easily turn a living being into a corpse, if only through a specific mode of conceptualization. What is most worrying is a trend in our time towards radical exteriorization, which I noted above with regard to rendering everything external, transparent, and therefore, supposedly, objective. This trend should not be so surprising since it continues the trajectory of the modern project. What is inward is projected outward, and thus helps to sustain the overreach of government surveillance and control. The Confessional has been abandoned as a place where the person can meet with God and receive absolution, only to be replaced by confessional cultures that will have people announce their failures to everyone, only to receive condemnation upon condemnation, heaped upon the guilt they feel for not conforming to the madness of crowds. There is, in this, a terrible confusion between the personal and the political. The isolated, atomized individual tries to reach out to reclaim what is lost. But the logic of the project, divorced as it is from teleology, ensures that he will end up, even in his earnest seeking, more lost than before.

The Formal Cause

By now, a partial sense of Aristotelian formal causality should already be in place. However, I want to take a moment to briefly clarify some less-than-obvious ways to understand formal causality as it relates to Chesterton's work and especially to his prescience. Commonly, the formal cause is regarded as the shape of any given object. If, for example, the *causa materialis* of a silver chalice is silver, the "*causa formalis*" of the chalice is then likely to be understood as "the form, shape into which the material enters."[146] This, however, is not only too narrow a way of considering the formal cause but also a misleading way of considering formal causation, if we want to understand how Chesterton looks at the world. The trouble is that formal causality is constricted here to being considered a dimension of the figure rather than the ground. Perhaps, given that efficient causality tends to be more easily perceptible as a figure, it was this mistake that lead to the formal cause being not just subservient to but reducible to the efficient cause.

To correct this mistake, it is helpful to remember that, in theological terms, the formal cause echoes the life and work of the Holy Spirit, the third

---

146. Heidegger, *Question Concerning Technology*, 6.

person of the Trinity, who is the love between God the Father and God the Son and the mediator of reality present in the mystical body that is the church. Formal cause concerns the ground as the "seedbed" of all being, action, and teleology.[147] This is to say that the formal cause "is also the conformal cause," simultaneously causing and providing intelligibility to both the figure and the ground. It accounts for both formation and counterformation, both environment and anti-environment. This idea moves us away from a sense of the merely chronological order of cause and effect, something I say more about in the following chapter. Formal causality is even somewhat irrational, although the word *nonrational* is probably better.[148] That form is more indistinct is echoed in Chesterton's sense that identity should be regarded as an "atmosphere" or "primary condition" rather than an exact image.[149] Determinacy and indeterminacy collaborate here. What we are after in the formal cause is an approximation and not a mechanical reproduction. Even the idea of a design or blueprint is too solid to capture the sense of the formal cause that fits Chesterton's work. It is not possible to force the formal cause to fit instrumental logic without sacrificing the formal cause. As Eric McLuhan suggests, the "modality of formal cause is that of abrasive interface, an exchange of pressures and textures between situations."[150] It involves the whole of being, including the senses of touch, movement, and proprioception, and not merely the highly linear sense of vision. It is synesthetic.

While efficient and final causes tend to suggest a strong sense of temporality, a *before* and an *after*, formal causality, like material causality, tends to be atemporal. This is significant for considering Chestertonian prescience. By attuning himself to formal causality, Chesterton sees patterns that could be evident at any point in history. He can predict, as I have already indicated, what has already happened. Material conditions and forms of social organization, and efficiency can change but the formal cause transcends such things. Formal causality transcends while including the other causes. When understood in this way, it presents a logical structure even in its speculations. That structure can be stated as follows: if conditions follow the pattern I perceive, given how they conform and/or fail to conform to a discernible form, then certain nameable consequences, or something analogically like them, is not inconceivable. This is not the same as declaring with absolute certainty or dialectical inevitability, along the lines of a strict progression, if

---

147. McLuhan and McLuhan, *Media and Formal Cause*, 126.
148. McLuhan and McLuhan, *Media and Formal Cause*, 127.
149. Chesterton, *Illustrated London News*, 15 March 1924.
150. McLuhan and McLuhan, *Media and Formal Cause*, 128.

a then *b*. There is a hesitancy in Chesterton's prescience, even an imaginative space for diversions and differences. But his basic trust in the structure of reality makes it possible for him to consider the structure of the future without straight-jacketing anything he says into chronological determinism.

Formal causality, for Chesterton, retains an imaginative, dialogical playfulness between figure and ground. Such playfulness is metaxological. It refuses to conflate any of the causes to any of the others, even while it acknowledges that they intertwine and even recognizes how they intertwine. Bad art and bad articles, for instance, result from a confusion of formal causality with any of the other causes, usually final causality.[151] Often, this amounts to denying the presence of formal causality or suggesting that it can be explained only with reference to one of the other causes. Bad reasoning in general tends to neglect or obsolesce the so-called irrational formal cause and substitute for it one of the other causes. Efficient causality is often popular because it is the most supposedly rational, meaning the most univocal, of the causes. Given that the neglect of formal causality has become typical in our time, how do we recover a renewed sense of its importance? The best shot we have is through what McLuhan calls a "counter-environment" or "anti-environment."[152] An anti-environment is anything that sufficiently contradicts the overly familiar environment such that the nature of the primary environment becomes startlingly clear. As already discussed, Chesterton uses defamiliarization especially to serve this function. He uses his vivid and poetic imagination to allow his reader to see the world as if for the first time, as a series of "stratified revolutions."[153] That said, to draw too much of a distinction between an environment and its anti-environment would be a mistake. It would mean failing to be true to the analogical structure of consciousness, which is mindful of both similarities and dissimilarities and also notices how things are vignetted in the mind and not always so neat or discrete. Nevertheless, the friction of an anti-environment, which often precedes the friction offered by the formal cause, is a powerful aid to perception.

Chesterton is aware of our need for a way to recover a renewed perception of things. He speaks, for instance, about St. Francis of Assisi and St. Thomas Aquinas as saints who converted the people of their age by contradicting it, by being counter-environmental.[154] Arguably, their contradiction of the age in which they lived indicates that they were offering a true form as a remedy to false form. This counter-environmentality is very different from

---

151. McLuhan and McLuhan, *Media and Formal Cause*, 130.
152. McLuhan and McLuhan, *Media and Formal Cause*, 138.
153. Chesterton, *Defendant*, 84.
154. Chesterton, *St. Thomas Aquinas & St. Francis of Assisi*, 22.

the idol of the negative spirit that possesses the boy who tugs at the roots of the world.[155] It does not merely mean to oppose or erase but wants to define. Definition can be subtle rather than uncompromising; it should be clear while offering an invitation to seek interpretive depth. One reason for Chesterton's adherence to Catholicism, echoed by Marshall McLuhan and William Desmond, was because of a recognition that without clear lines and dogmas, we can have little hope of perceiving the world we live in rightly. To be dogmatic is to be free. To see the world and criticize it while wanting to improve it, we need to not be too worldly. We need to have a form by which we can be informed and to which we can be conformed, even as we learn to notice the deformed or malformed patterns of this world.

---

155. Chesterton, *Daily News*, 17 August 1907.

5

Being Conformed

G. K. Chesterton Through Marshall McLuhan's Tetrad

IN HIS ESSAY, "FORMAL Causality in Chesterton," Marshall McLuhan's main aim is to "illustrate" Chesterton's "concern with formal causality."[1] McLuhan notices that philosophers and scholars in the West have tended to shirk any consideration of the formal cause in the arts and sciences.[2] He suggests that this is owed to what he designates as the "visual bias of Western man."[3] This idea is echoed in the designation of our age as "ocularcentric," meaning that it is "dominated" by vision, although there are many signs around us indicating the abandonment of the West's visual emphasis.[4] Still, among other things, this ocularcentrism implies a concern with the linear over the spatial, as well as a focus on figures over the ground.[5] This insight is echoed and deepened in Iain McGilchrist's analysis of the West as having adopted a left-hemispheric bias; he means a bias that favors the strengths of the brain's left hemisphere while downplaying and even ignoring the strengths of the brain's right hemisphere.[6] This extends and amplifies the concern of phenomenologists like Martin Heidegger, Max Scheler, and

---

1. McLuhan and McLuhan, *Media and Formal Cause*, 73.
2. McLuhan and McLuhan, *Media and Formal Cause*, 76.
3. McLuhan and McLuhan, *Media and Formal Cause*, 76.
4. Jay, *Downcast Eyes*, 3.
5. McLuhan and McLuhan, *Media and Formal Cause*, 76.
6. McGilchrist, *Master and His Emissary*; McGilchrist, *Matter with Things*; McLuhan and Powers, *Global Village*, 72.

Maurice Merleau-Ponty, who note a trend in modernity that favors abstract theories more than historically situated existence. This is exaggerated later, as Jean Baudrillard notes in his work, when language becomes so dramatically divorced from reality that reality, overwhelmed by mediations composed of so many falsehoods, cannot be perceived at all.[7] In other words, we adopt representations, often circulating as a hurricane of sign exchanges, but without any solid ontological support. This results often in the construction of a false image of formal causation out of fragments, the way Dr. Frankenstein constructs the body of a monster out of components in Mary Shelly's famous story.

McGilchrist summarizes the left-hemispheric bias of our age, which I take to echo the general neglect of formal causality, as having to do with, among other things: prioritizing manipulation over understanding, electing sharp focus over peripheral vision, focusing on local rather than global attention, a tendency to narrow things down to familiar formulas rather than to embrace them in their complexity and otherness, a preoccupation with sameness over difference, the triumph of fragmentation over unity, the preference for stasis and fixity over flow, the tendency to decontextualize things rather than to understand them in context, the tendency to impersonalize things and denarrativize meaning, the tendency to prioritize disembodied notions over embodied experience, and the favoring of uncritical or unscrupulous hope over realistic pessimism.[8] Jacques Ellul's research on the so-called humiliation of the word supports McGilchrist's thesis, albeit without reference to the brain's hemispheric differences. He observes a priority of imperatives over understanding, irreversibility over complementarity, invariability over flux, pointillist reasoning over continuity of thought, immediacy over mediation and interpretation, judgment over understanding, efficiency over contemplation, technique over response, construction over participation, and mastery over communion.[9] Ellul pins these prioritizations on a triumph of images over the word, and his perspective is well supported by McLuhan's research. In Chesterton's work, we find a priority of the right hemisphere over the left, and of the sacramental word over the decontextualized image. The point is not to humiliate the left hemisphere and its visual bias but to note important limitations and to stress the centrality of context for understanding content. The point is also not, as McGilchrist makes clear, to reduce the mind to the brain; it is to notice what sort of attention we are paying the world. The whole, when apprehended as a whole, is greater than

---

7. See Baudrillard, *Simulacra and Simulation*.
8. McGilchrist, *Matter with Things*, 28–30.
9. Ellul, *Humiliation of the Word*, 7–12.

the sum of its parts. As McLuhan suggests, Chesterton's insightfulness is because he does not perceive things as the typical person does.

Even with access to older and less robust neuroscientific research, McLuhan intuits a sense of how the West has neglected more right-brained modes of attending to the world. On observation, he notices that the visual order "has regard for the *figure* and not the *ground*."[10] For this reason, the audience, a key component of the ground or formal cause, tends to be overlooked as an aspect of communication and the communication of being. Creativity and understanding are impossible without something of an awareness of how formal causality intersects with the other causes, already suggested above by the fact that Plato's idea is composed, from an Aristotelian perspective, of three of the four causes, although they are not yet undifferentiated. Some awareness of how figure and ground interact is essential for art and philosophy. McLuhan contends that Chesterton has far more than a rudimentary understanding of this. "It might be argued," writes McLuhan, "that the abrupt and bumpy and grotesquely sprockety contours of Chesterton's prose are very much a response of his sensitivity to a perverse and misbegotten public that he earnestly but good-naturedly was determined to redeem from its banalities."[11] As an aside, I find it amusing that McLuhan is so critical of Chesterton, especially given his own tendency towards an even more rickety, chaotic, sprawling, tangled, meandering style of prose. I appreciate both writers, however, and see a certain method in their meandering. It is an expression of their awareness of formal causation.

In any case, Chesterton's first and most essential concern was with his public, and especially with the public's need to be supported and corrected.[12] This is a curious claim because it attributes formal causality not to a strictly objective pattern but to the very people Chesterton is writing for. And they are anything but a simple, homogeneous mass. What becomes important is a mode of interactions and processes. A formula detectable in this contention is that the formal cause may be defined as *everything with the primary object of attention* (almost entirely) *subtracted*. This means, with regard to Chesterton's writings, that the audience is a significant component of the formal cause of his work. "So pervasive is this feature in Chesterton," McLuhan suggests, "that it scarcely matters at what page one opens in order to illustrate it."[13] Formal causality as this concern with that which surrounds any object of enquiry is so important to Chesterton that it is to be

---

10. McLuhan and McLuhan, *Media and Formal Cause*, 76.
11. McLuhan and McLuhan, *Media and Formal Cause*, 76.
12. McLuhan and McLuhan, *Media and Formal Cause*, 75.
13. McLuhan and McLuhan, *Media and Formal Cause*, 75.

found everywhere in his work. Picking a page at random, McLuhan refers to Chesterton's *Charles Dickens: A Critical Study* (1906):

> Much of our modern difficulty, in religion and other things, arises merely from this: that we confuse the word "indefinable" with the word "vague." If someone speaks of a spiritual fact as "indefinable" we promptly picture something misty, a cloud with indeterminate edges. But this is an error even in commonplace logic. The thing that cannot be defined is the first thing; the primary fact. It is our arms and legs, our pots and pans, that are indefinable.[14]

McLuhan concludes from this that "Chesterton is quite aware that the problems of his time are not without a strong affinity for each other."[15] This fact is further exemplified by St. Thomas Aquinas in any of his opening objections. As an exemplar of an expansive awareness of the formal cause, the writer, whether Chesterton or St. Thomas, cannot conceive of any thing or issue apart from how it might be taken up by others. As in the above paragraph, "Chesterton usually gives strong indications of the kinds of people and the kinds of problems with which he is dealing."[16] Although not stated outright by McLuhan, Chesterton is preoccupied with what his audience is probably missing. In his example regarding what is "indefinable" versus what is "vague," in the sentence beyond what McLuhan directly quotes, Chesterton writes, "The indefinable is the indisputable. The man next door is indefinable, because he is too actual to be defined. And there are some to whom spiritual things have the same fierce and practical proximity; some to whom God is too actual to be defined."[17]

Here, as in Chesterton's parable of the roots of the world, reality transcends articulation. It takes priority over conceptual formulations and functions like negative feedback, reestablishing its ontological priority as that which is intensified through language and understanding. As Catherine Pickstock writes, reclaiming an ontological view of truth over an epistemological one, "truth is not found exclusively in things or in the mind."[18] If truth were to be found only in things, it would seep imperceptibly back into being without our noticing, which is to say that the very idea of truth would become redundant. But if truth were only in the mind, there would be no way to tell if that supposed truth were not just "one's contingent

---

14. Chesterton, *Charles Dickens*, 1.
15. McLuhan and McLuhan, *Media and Formal Cause*, 73–74.
16. McLuhan and McLuhan, *Media and Formal Cause*, 73.
17. McLuhan and McLuhan, *Media and Formal Cause*, 73.
18. Pickstock, *Aspects of Truth*, 256.

perspective."[19] For truth to be truth three things are needed: an "inherent connection between objects and subjects," a more than arbitrary connection "between things and spirits," and a connection "between things known and knowing minds."[20] These connections are found in the between and, as I have already suggested, this betweenness is at the heart of formal causality.

Formal causality is not therefore primarily what we regard as understood but is rather the truth of being that exists in and beyond understanding. Truth is in reality itself, first, before existing in the mind. And yet, the author, Chesterton in this case, must contend with the environment of what is (guessed to be) known by his audience. On the second page of his *Charles Dickens* (1906), quoted by McLuhan, Chesterton "focuses this larger awareness of the audience on Dickens itself."[21]

> In everyday talk, or in any of our journals, we may find the loose but important phrase, "Why have we no great men today? Why have we no great men like Thackeray, or Carlyle, or Dickens?" Do not let us dismiss this expression, because it appears loose or arbitrary. "Great" does mean something, and the test of its actuality is to be found by noting how instinctively and incisively we do apply it to some men and not to others; above all how instinctively and incisively we do apply it to four or five men in the Victorian era, four or five men of whom Dickens was not the least. The term is found to fit a definite thing. Dickens was what it means.[22]

What is Chesterton up to here? Simply, he wants his audience to see something. He takes a common phrase and draws attention to it to get to the concrete, which was previously articulated as indefinable. What is indefinable is not impossible to locate; it is found in the exact instantiation of greatness Dickens represents. By implication, Chesterton draws attention to "a defect in his readers" that he intends to "supply and to repair."[23] This reconfigures the "public as a formal cause in the sense that the public is in need of some help in some area of concern, an area in which it is ignorant, or mistaken, or confused."[24] The way McLuhan phrases this implies that Chesterton is inadvertently insulting his audience. True, Chesterton's often combative argumentation may be regarded by some as insulting. He

19. Pickstock, *Aspects of Truth*, 256.
20. Pickstock, *Aspects of Truth*, 256.
21. McLuhan and McLuhan, *Media and Formal Cause*, 74.
22. Chesterton, *Charles Dickens*, 2.
23. McLuhan and McLuhan, *Media and Formal Cause*, 74.
24. McLuhan and McLuhan, *Media and Formal Cause*, 75.

exasperated many of his readers, as McLuhan is quick to point out. But such a cynical reading is not necessary since clearly there is a reciprocal benefit to Chesterton's didacticism. He depends on his audience as much as his audience depends on him. He makes it his aim to find out what is overlooked because he owes it to his audience to do so. Chesterton's reader is a significant feature of his formal cause; the reader, including his future reader, plays a part in his prescience.

This is not to imply that the relationship between the formal cause and its figures is always symmetrical and mutually beneficial. McLuhan suggests, for instance, that the fall of man is the formal cause of the incarnation.[25] At least, it is a significant component of it. The fall and the incarnation are not linked through a straightforward sequence of cause and effect. They are linked in the back and forth of questioning and answering. The fall calls for an answer. The incarnation exposes the nature and the severity of the fall even as it answers and solves the fall. Crucially, however, formal causality reveals itself through and often as its effects; by implication. Indeed, Chesterton's prescience is always a matter of what is *by implication*. There is, in other words, an analogical continuity between the figure and the ground, even if there is no obvious cause-and-effect relationship. As McLuhan notes, however, a paradox exists in this: "because the effects come from the hidden ground of situations, the effects usually appear before their causes."[26] This strange twist of logic is not clearly explained by McLuhan in his essay on "Chesterton and Formal Cause," and more clarity is needed.

Eric McLuhan notes that in the electronic age in particular, the "vortex of effects of any innovation always precedes its causes."[27] His examples of this are poetic: "we see on every hand the effects of antigravity in the form of airplanes and spacecraft and submarines," for instance, and so it "is easy to predict that actual antigravity will soon be a feature of everyday life."[28] With regard to technological innovations, the effects of any new invention often arrive before the innovation itself.[29] The presence of radio, telephones, wireless computing and the like suggests that telepathy is on the way. The effect in the shape of some physical or material object, while the cause, meaning the formal cause, is somewhat more abstract and thus already helps us to understand something of what the reversal of cause and effect is meant to achieve. For starters, it disrupts any conception of cause and effect as sequential

---

25. McLuhan and McLuhan, *Media and Formal Cause*, 76.
26. McLuhan and McLuhan, *Media and Formal Cause*, 77.
27. McLuhan and McLuhan, *Media and Formal Cause*, 89.
28. McLuhan and McLuhan, *Media and Formal Cause*, 89.
29. McLuhan and McLuhan, *Media and Formal Cause*, 87.

events and reframes the two as being in a paradoxical relationship with one another, as mediating themselves to one another. We can therefore rethink effect and cause outside of the narrow frame of contracted efficient causality and resituate the two as being analogous to the relationship between figure, or effect, and ground, or cause. The reversal of cause and effect also recovers the Aristotelian emphasis on cause as concerning intelligibility and, in doing this, helps us to expand the breadth of this intelligibility so that we can make better sense of things in general. Finally, as this implies, it helps us to see things atmospherically—*by implication*. This is suggested by the above categories of *antigravity* and *telepathy*. The connection between being and intuition is restored.

The original formulation of cause and effect often divides the causal relationship along the following lines: cause, here meaning the form and agency implied by any particular object, is split off from effect, here meaning the resultant changes or aim in material givens. This reveals a narrowing of focus to the apparent blueprint provided by a given object under examination. But, as I have already noted, the blueprint metaphor so often used for the formal cause may just be an attempt to rationalize what does not conform perfectly to rationality. In other words, the formal cause is misinterpreted in this scenario to be no longer environmental but figural. Effects, meaning consequences in the usual understanding, are likely to be seen, in this case, in the wrong light. To refer to one of Eric McLuhan's examples above, we would see the effect of the invention of an airplane, for instance, to be only about moving people around in the air. We know that this is the typical way of understanding the meaning of the airplane, but it misses the context or formal cause within which a more expansive sense of intelligibility can be accessed. One reason why a few examples are set alongside each other—"airplanes and spacecraft and submarines"[30]—is that this allows for a wider intuition concerning what is happening. This intuition is named *antigravity*, which is less about a new kind of physics than it is about an adjusted way of interpreting the world, evidenced in the trend, since the advent of electricity, towards discarnation. It reveals the hermeneutic, adopted according to a newly disproportionate arrangement of human sense-ratios, that makes airplanes, spacecraft, and submarines comprehensible, as well as the prevalence of digital media and even political abstractions. It is a newly disproportionate arrangement of people even more immersed in artificiality than before. A similar collection of events and things as metaphors is echoed in my above assessment of Chesterton's use of parallelism to seek out connections and ultimately arrive at the law of the situation. The meaning of

---

30. McLuhan and McLuhan, *Media and Formal Cause*, 87.

efficient causality is therefore altered. It is no longer misattributed to material objects and is resituated within the realm of analogies and interpretations.

To further understand the contextual priority of cause over effect, and of the temporal precedence of effect over cause, is to notice that many inventions would not have been possible had it not been for the psychological and philosophical shifts that preceded them. Heidegger notices this when he makes the following claim, considering certain devastating events during World War Two, which we find echoed in certain fears in our time: "Man stares at what the explosion of the atom bomb could bring with it. He does not see that the atom bomb and its explosion are the mere final emission of what has long since taken place, has already happened."[31] Heidegger suggests that the obliteration of being took place before the bomb arrived on the world's stage, although he means the word *being* slightly differently than I do in this book. To better understand the analogous Chestertonian view, consider his view on how best to interpret technological innovation. The "proper view of machines" refuses to let "science" dominate our perspective; the "power of seeing" human inventions clearly "is not given by science, or by any advances in science; it is given by art, by poetry, and by religion."[32] Myriad "social influences modify the use" of any invention, "as they modify all other social practices."[33]

Chesterton makes the claim that "no scientific instrument has ever transformed society. It was always the soul of the society that transformed the scientific instrument."[34] Even if we think he is exaggerating here, it is clear that the search for the formal cause is, for him, a search for the soul of society. If it were not essentially this, we could talk very excitedly about inventions like the radio and the internet for the "wonderful opportunity which this machinery will give us to send our words to a remote continent, as if it were in the next street."[35] But this would be at the expense of asking "whether we have anything particular to say even to the next street, let alone to the remote continent."[36] He is rightly concerned that if people attribute too much magic to machines, they will fail to attend to the soul. "It is the beginning of all true criticism of our time to realise that it has really nothing to say, at the very moment when it has invented so tremendous a trumpet for

---

31. Heidegger, *Poetry, Language, Thought*, 164.
32. Chesterton, *Illustrated London News*, 10 February 1923.
33. Chesterton, *Illustrated London News*, 10 February 1923.
34. Chesterton, *Illustrated London News*, 10 February 1923.
35. Chesterton, *Illustrated London News*, 10 February 1923.
36. Chesterton, *Illustrated London News*, 10 February 1923.

saying it."[37] How true this is for us today. If we are to come to terms with the meaning of any medium or mediation today, it is important not to get stuck thinking that cause means only what *produces* effects. Causality is a matter, primarily, of *explanation* or *accounting for* the meaning of things rather than just a statement or restatement of how one thing leads to another.

Chesterton's awareness of his audience, and of people in general, is thus central to his understanding of formal causation. To misconstrue this priority would be to consider the audience dialectically as something to be subordinate to self-mediation. The effect would not precede dialectic but would stem from it. Rhetoric works similarly, although the focus is on changing the audience itself by modifying *what* and *how* people in the audience think. Both dialectic and rhetoric risk conflating what communication aims to achieve with formal causality. In other words, for shoddy dialecticians and rhetoricians, as for bad poets and other creators, the formal cause is the communication itself, even if there is some awareness of an audience.[38] The significance of the audience's participation is diminished.

While gifted in dialectic and rhetoric, Chesterton is keenly aware of his audience, even to the point of recognizing that it is not a homogeneous one. As I have already argued in the second chapter, he is aware of mediation in his work but stresses the metaxological middle voice, which suggests a subject be both actively engaged and passively receptive. He is therefore also aware that surpluses of otherness must be accounted for in any communication. He consistently maintains a tension *between* self-mediation and other-mediation. Most notably, he does not attempt to achieve an effect as someone overcommitted to efficient causality might. Because he is a good journalist, he recognizes that his audience, being far from strictly homogeneous, is likely to respond in many and various ways that have little to do with his writing. Where there is an "effect" on an audience, as typically understood, perhaps this is because it is responsive to it and its mode of intelligibility. The cause (figure) might be better understood as revealing the effect (ground) that predates it, the way a bud and flower reveals a plant. Indeed, the trouble usually is that the cause (figure) is taken to be more significant than the ground (effect), when the opposite is true. People are unlikely to agree with him without reservations, and he does not expect them to even believe he is right. Being a poet, he is willing to allow for a certain open-endedness even while committing to definiteness. He loves limits but refuses to reduce everything to his understanding of those limits. He is certain but he is also humble in his certainty.

37. Chesterton, *Illustrated London News*, 10 February 1923.
38. Chesterton, *Collected Works, Volume 3*, 150.

To put it more playfully, Chesterton's formal cause allows for a certain informality, even as it informs. There is also a conformality or hospitable accommodation that cannot be reduced to replication. Chesterton is not just thinking of the formal cause in relation to his audience. Every analysis he undertakes is pervaded by his awareness of formal causality. He is always mindful of the so-called "law of the situation," in that he is not merely looking for how different matters interact in any given scenario.[39] He is searching for, and often finds, the governing principle of the situation. An earlier example can be revisited here. "You cannot see the wind," writes Chesterton, "you can only see that there is a wind. So, also, you cannot see a revolution; you can only see that there is a revolution."[40] In fact, "there never has been in the history of the world a real revolution, brutally active and decisive, which was not preceded by unrest and a new dogma in the reign of invisible things. All revolutions began by being abstract. Most revolutions began by being quite pedantically abstract."[41]

This is an excellent example of how certain effects precede the cause in the sense that we can account for the consequences of various revolutions better if we have some sense of the principle and consciousness that governed what made them possible. Although we can see cause and effect procedurally, Chesterton is aware that looking at the world through sequences or temporal successions does not suffice to explain things. Adding two incomprehensible things together does not make a comprehensible thing, even if it creates the impression of comprehensibility.[42] What is needed is an understanding that the wind "is above the world before a twig on the tree has moved."[43] There must "always be a battle in the sky before there is a battle on the earth."[44] This defies the materialist thinking of our age, which insists that everything evolves, emerges, and adds up. What Chesterton is after is the philosophical principle that accounts for how and why things happen.

McLuhan notes, "Chesterton's awareness of the figure/ground consequences pervades his studies of history and human thought in general," and this, McLuhan contends, "made it easy for him to enter the field of detective fiction."[45] As Chesterton knew from experience, detective fiction is written backwards by working from effects towards causes. This works on several

39. McLuhan and McLuhan, *Media and Formal Cause*, 77.
40. Chesterton, *Tremendous Trifles*, 61.
41. Chesterton, *Tremendous Trifles*, 61.
42. Chesterton, *Collected Works, Volume 1*, 255.
43. Chesterton, *Tremendous Trifles*, 61.
44. Chesterton, *Tremendous Trifles*, 61.
45. McLuhan and McLuhan, *Media and Formal Cause*, 79.

levels. In keeping with the above, the story is responsive to the sense of an audience, and especially to the sense of engaging the audience through the questions and predictions it makes while reading. But, then, within the story itself is the fact of the crime, an explicit effect with only an implicit cause—a cause or account that must be figured out by the detective and/or the reader. The criminal in any detective story "is the person who is entirely concerned with *effects*. He considers the situation as one to be manipulated, both *figure* and *ground*."[46] This sense of the mind of the criminal is one reason why Chesterton's most famous detective, Father Brown, is so brilliant. As explained in the first Father Brown story, *The Blue Cross*, Father Brown knows the minds of criminals because he knows how people think.[47] He knows how people think because he has listened to them confess their sins in the confessional booth. His conception of cause is therefore not mechanical but metaphysical. He knows to look for an account and not just a sequence of events. Detective fiction, perhaps more than any other genre, is concerned with right understanding; its focus is truth, via explanation.

It is typical of Chesterton, as noted by Jorge Luis Borges, to propose a supernatural cause as the most believable explanation for a crime before replacing it with a more ordinary this-worldly explanation.[48] Importantly, he does this without sacrificing the possibility of the supernatural. Paradoxically, it is his supernaturalism, his belief that reality ought to present itself as a coherent whole, that makes his more mundane materialistic explanations so brilliant. Chesterton is more logical than, say, Arthur Conan Doyle, whose chief subject Sherlock Holmes relies on a particularly unruly guesswork, which makes sense only because Doyle forces it to. "Sherlock Holmes is not really a real logician," writes Chesterton, but "an ideal logician imagined by an illogical person. [He] is an ideal figure, and in an imaginative sense a very effective one. He does embody the notion which unreasonable people entertain of what pure reason would be like."[49] This does not render Doyle's stories any less enjoyable or entertaining. But it is worth having in mind since Chesterton's sense of formal causality, in the sense of knowing what principles are apparent, guides him towards noticing concrete particulars with remarkable perceptiveness. And yet, he does not sacrifice reason in the name of achieving a rhetorical or aesthetic effect. His Father Brown reveals a desire to reconnect appearances with metaphysical depths.

46. McLuhan and McLuhan, *Media and Formal Cause*, 79.
47. Chesterton, *Innocence of Father Brown*, 1–32.
48. Borges, *Perpetual Race of Achilles and the Tortoise*, 53.
49. Chesterton, *Illustrated London News*, 1 May 1927.

In this, Chesterton is aware of formal causality less as the explanation of a point of view than as a statement of the total situation. This is explained by Father Brown in his story, *The Queer Feet*. "A crime," he says, "is like any other work of art. . . . [E]very work of art, divine or diabolic, has one indispensable mark—I mean, that the centre of it is simple, however much the fulfilment may be complicated."[50] He continues to explain that the center of any crime is a fact that is no real mystery. The explanation of the crime, as Borges explains, needs to be both "necessary and marvelous."[51] The explanation should feel absolutely inevitable, even while it aims to surprise us. The real mystification will be, as Chesterton's Father Brown explains, in the way that the crime is covered up. The minds of people, both readers and characters in the story, will be led astray by details in the story. The author knows this in constructing a wild tale, and it is part of the fun of reading detective fiction to see past the details that point in so many different directions.

Another way to see the "covering-up process" in detective fiction is to notice that it involves the inclusion by the author of points of view that are mistaken about the meaning of the moment.[52] Such points of view are ultimately shown to be foreign to the principle that governs the situation, "leading men's thoughts away" from it.[53] They are distractions from the formal cause. "Points of view," McLuhan writes, "are always reserved for the police and the slow-witted" in the detective story.[54] The so-called "rational point of view, with its plodding accumulation of evidence," is reserved for those in the story, like Lestrade in Doyle's fiction, who stand no real chance of solving the crime.[55] Attending to formal cause *includes* an awareness of the limitations inherent especially in points of view dominated by the rationality of decontextualized efficient causality.

This throws some light on Nietzsche's doctrine of "perspectivism," which has shaped so much discourse after him. Arguably, the current philosophical paradigm of so many humanities subjects in so many universities across the globe cannot be understood without some sense of what this doctrine means and entails. Nietzsche radically dismissed any philosophical desire for some transcendent, impartial truth as a fool's errand. Knowledge is perspectivist, he claims, entangled in different, highly subjective perceptions of the world. This in itself is by no means a new claim. People have always

---

50. Chesterton, *Innocence of Father Brown*, 90.
51. Borges, *Perpetual Race of Achilles and the Tortoise*, 53.
52. McLuhan and McLuhan, *Media and Formal Cause*, 80.
53. Chesterton, *Innocence of Father Brown*, 91.
54. Chesterton, *Innocence of Father Brown*, 91.
55. Chesterton, *Innocence of Father Brown*, 91.

known that our perspectives differ. What Nietzsche adds to this common-sense understanding is the idea that our perspectives cannot be separated from our interests. His critique of philosophers—all of them—was largely that they seemed oblivious to the role that their own interests and personalities played in shaping their ideas.[56] By implication, philosophers do not make their claims apart from some often-unrecognized psychological need. For Nietzsche, everyone adopts an optics of cognition through which he interprets the world, often resulting in exaggerations and reversals of given assumptions.[57] There is, this suggests, no proverbial view from nowhere. All perspectives are perspectives within a given situation.

There is no getting completely beyond the drama. There is much to agree with here. Our own personal points of view no doubt play a significant role in shaping our ideas and doctrines. Indeed, our claims are often informed by our interests. However, to declare this perspectivism as universally true is to miss the fact that Nietzsche speaks equivocally. He cannot, by his own philosophical commitments, adhere to perspectivism without making the mistake made by tellers of that ancient myth about the blind people who are trying to tell their way around an elephant. The mistake in question is to assume that there is a new universal truth, namely the truth of perspectivism. I am not convinced Nietzsche makes this mistake even if many of his interpreters and those influenced by this idea do. Nietzsche's sense of truth is equivocal, but he does not deny that truth exists. However, the most obvious danger of taking this perspective on radical equivocity with even a hint of seriousness—thus radicalizing Nietzsche by univocalizing his equivocal philosophy—is that it tempts us to substitute will for knowledge; it replaces knowing with the will to power. To put it more strongly, it is in the *interests* of particularly egotistical people to believe this because it allows them to simply claim that what matters most is not what is true, intelligible, and real but rather what they want. As Chesterton predicts, this offers a rationale for having people seek out a mad consensus only to oppress those who do not agree with them. This has happened so often in history and in our time. When unanimity is turned into an "absurd assumption . . . a man may be howled down for saying that two and two make four" and persecuted for "calling a triangle a three-sided figure" and hanged "for maddening a mob with the news that grass is green."[58] This can only happen when the formal cause has been entirely occluded by an alienated efficient cause in a state of mimetic crisis.

56. Nietzsche, *Beyond Good and Evil*, 6–7, 12–13.
57. Nietzsche, *On the Genealogy of Morals*, 97–99.
58. Chesterton, *Illustrated London News*, 14 August 1926.

Nevertheless, Chesterton's awareness of the law of the situation, which includes a profound awareness of the interplay of perspectives, shows that it is possible to hold to a somewhat disinterested perspective, interested in being disinterested. We do not have to abandon our personal points of view so that we can hold only to some transcendental abstraction. There is no competition between the real and the ideal, because the quiddity of things is the form they participate in. It is possible to hold to a suspended middle of a kind that is both sufficiently detached and sufficiently near to things to perceive them clearly.[59] One can find the principle or law of a situation without becoming caught up in a dualistic battle between subjectivity and objectivity, without abandoning the metaxological. Is there anything that might help us to do this?

Above, I have accounted for the essence of what McLuhan says regarding Chesterton's relationship with formal causality in his article on "Formal Causality in Chesterton." But McLuhan provides a further way to consider Chesterton's work through his fourfold or tetrad, which he refers to as the four laws of media. These laws are set out as ways to describe the nature of formal causes, a way to see formal causality at work without tempting us to reduce things to only one perspective. McLuhan's tetrad offers a way to consider the proportions, ratios, and paradoxes at work within the formal cause.[60] It offers a way, in other words, for us to develop a metaxological sense of reality. These laws focus on the grammar and syntax of any artifact or medium. However, considering the centrality of mediation itself, I interpret each law as a matter of any form of mediation, especially as Chesterton discusses it in his work.

Any formal cause, McLuhan posits, has four main features that exist in analogical proportion to each other. These are enhancement, obsolescence, retrieval, and reversal.[61] Firstly, every mediation enhances, extends, and/or exaggerates something; it operates as a prosthetic for thought and action. Secondly, every mediation obsolesces, downplays, and/or removes something; it acts as an amputation of thought and action. Thirdly, every mediation retrieves, if only by analogy, something that was perhaps previously obsolesced and establishes it in a new form. Finally, every mediation, when pushed to the limits or extremes of its potential, reverses or flips into its opposite. "All extensions of man," McLuhan writes, whether "verbal or non-verbal, hardware or software, are *essentially* metaphoric in structure."[62]

59. Chesterton, *Everlasting Man*, 9–11.
60. McLuhan and McLuhan, *Laws of Media*, 127.
61. McLuhan and McLuhan, *Laws of Media*, 129.
62. McLuhan and McLuhan, *Laws of Media*, 7.

This insight furthers what I have already discussed regarding metaxology, for it reiterates the importance of attending to the tensions and relationships between things. It especially furthers what I have discussed regarding analogy as emphasizing both similarity and difference. Every metaphor (or analogy) "has four terms which are discontinuous, yet in ratio to one another."[63] On the one hand, "Retrieval is to obsolescence as enhancement is to reversal."[64] On the other hand, "Retrieval is to enhancement as obsolescence is to reversal."[65] This four-part analogy takes into account both the figure and the ground; it suggests two figures (enhancement and reversal) and two grounds (obsolescence and retrieval) through which we can better come to terms with the formal cause. As McLuhan notices, keeping with the Thomist philosophy that Chesterton also echoes, "the mind of man is structurally inherent in all human artifacts and hypotheses whatever."[66] To attend to and to be true to being, to participate in the real, means that theoretical reason is also attuned to the good and therefore also capable of guiding practical reason.

McLuhan regards his tetrad as intensifying an awareness of inclusive structural process even as it obsolesces or downplays sequential logical analysis and the exaggeration of efficient causality. It retrieves metaphor but can flip into another mere abstraction or technique of control if taken too far, that is, if taken too dialectically.[67] The nature of a metaphor can also be interpreted through the tetrad. Metaphor enhances our awareness of relationships while obsolescing fragmentary and overly linear logic; it also retrieves understanding and the way that meaning can be replayed in another mode while reversing into allegory when overextended.[68] It should already be clearer how this helps to elucidate the formal cause; the patterns and proportions according to which things relate and interact. Still, there is room to clarify how this pertains specifically to Chesterton's vision of the world, and so it is to this task that we can now turn our attention by turning to one of the most prescient essays Chesterton ever wrote.

The First Law of Mediation: Extension

Clearly, Chesterton regards the world not just as a place of things but as an arena of communication. Being is communication and revelation, set

63. McLuhan and Powers, *Global Village*, 8.
64. McLuhan and Powers, *Global Village*, 8.
65. McLuhan and Powers, *Global Village*, 8.
66. McLuhan and McLuhan, *Laws of Media*, 8.
67. McLuhan and McLuhan, *Laws of Media*, 10.
68. McLuhan and McLuhan, *Laws of Media*, 9.

against a backdrop of mystery. To attend to formal causality thus means considering how patterns in the world affect our relationship with the primal ethos and primary communication of being. What has our attunement to reality got to do with it? Everything. As St. Paul writes, echoing while preceding Chesterton's concern with formal causation: "And be not conformed to this world: but be ye transformed by the renewing of your mind, that ye may prove what is that good, and acceptable, and perfect, will of God."[69] In other words, there is a lot going on, so seek to know the roots of the world. In an uncollected essay first published in *G. K.'s Weekly* in 1926, Chesterton turns his attention to another of St. Paul's remarks: "Evil communications corrupt good manners."[70] He sees this as prophetic of a problem in the modern world, if not the chief problem. What are commonly referred to as "good communications" are not so good after all. Modern communications rest on the glorification of two things, namely efficiency and scale. "I mean," writes Chesterton, "rapid communications, efficient communications, elaborately organised communications, communications by petrol and electricity and machinery which go to every corner of the earth."[71] Moreover, "in every corner of the earth today," we can see how these rapid and far-reaching communications are "corrupting good manners."[72] Communications may deny mystery by hampering revelation. This he takes to be the law of a global situation. A figure, an efficient cause that has become a counterfeit formal cause, has kept us from the ground.

Seeing this, Chesterton stresses again how being is grounded and how we are grounded in it by a sense of proportion received through our senses. How we relate to the proportions in the world is crucial to what we are able to receive. This affects our thoughts and actions. Given that we are tool-using creatures by nature, it is reasonable to consider how our tools might echo our sense ratios; they affect how we engage with reality. Every medium we use functions as an extension of ourselves into the world. By implication, every medium stems from, intensifies, and affects our consciousness of the world.[73] If I pick up a pen to write on a piece of paper, I attend to the world differently than when I pick up a fly swatter to murder a bothersome insect. My involvement in the world changes as I interact with it through my tools. The world presents itself to me differently at one time or another depending on what media I take up, even as my consciousness gravitates towards

69. Romans 12:2.
70. 1 Corinthians 15:33.
71. Chesterton, *G. K.'s Weekly*, 19 June 1926.
72. Chesterton, *G. K.'s Weekly*, 19 June 1926.
73. McLuhan, *Understanding Media*, 3.

certain tools. Tools are not merely modes of personal control but are forms of mediation. They represent, each in its own way, a metaxological meeting point between subjectivity and objectivity, self and other. This means that they mediate the world for me just as I mediate the world and mediate myself to the world through them. The path of communication goes both ways or even in all directions, just because of the tools I use to cope with the world I am in.

Every medium is a metaphor or epistemological filter; every metaphor or epistemological filter is an intensification of being. This idea subverts the modern tendency to consider being univocally through various categorizations and conceptual divisions. The modern mind misconstrues being through the heuristic of control or manipulation.[74] But being is a forum of participation. Control and receptivity may be emphasized differently by different ways of interacting within it but at all times both are in play. We are receptive to the world while also actively involved in it. A necessary distance is essential for perceiving rightly, although this may vary depending on what needs to be perceived. This is analogous to finding the right visual distance from a specific object of attention. Being either too close or too far creates distortions of meaning. An example of the former, for Chesterton, is the idea of something being too big to be seen.[75] An example of the latter, for him, is the philosopher of the ego (who is also an egotistical philosopher), who sees all things foreshortened as if he is looking at them from a balloon.[76] Chesterton often discusses various processes of attempting to stand at the right distance from things to perceive them well.[77] Much of his work exemplifies a keen interest in restoring to the reader a proportional perspective on things. Nevertheless, he is aware that new technologies have the potential to perpetuate terrible distortions as we attend to the world. Having a sense of formal causality means becoming aware of what a normal or clear perception of things would be, as well as what has been and is still being thrown out of proportion. It is possible to notice the exaggeration on its own sometimes but this does risk having us think backwards instead of forwards, as I discuss in the next and final chapter.

It is possible to have a sense of what normal, human-scale communication would be, one which allows, firstly, sufficient depth in our participation without having us drown in a flood of uninterpretable information and, secondly, sufficient detachment to be able to reflect reasonably on the

74. McLuhan, *Understanding Media*, 7.
75. Chesterton, *Illustrated London News*, 7 December 1907.
76. Chesterton, *Defendant*, 101.
77. Chesterton, *Everlasting Man*, 204.

world we are in or to be able to contemplate our involvement in reveries or prayers. A metaxological tension is ideal. Some activities require depth while others require reflective distance. Our participation in the world allows for many variations, none of which ought to destroy our ability to understand things well. But some of our mediations exaggerate things in unhelpful and unhealthy ways without ever abating to allow us to restore a sense of order to our worlds. We can and often do cut ourselves off from our original participation. We often make use of our tools to worsen this severance.

Chesterton notices, for example, the accelerationist and expansionist tendencies of modern communication. Impressively, he sees this as a potential disaster since, even to his mind a century ago, it is likely to create various distortions that will destroy much good in any society. While he is, as I have said, not in favor of inevitability, he is aware of the force of human decisions and human habits, and he knows that human inventions tend not to be so easily undone. Even if he does not quite predict the advent of the internet, he is not far from imagining what such a thing would do to the world. What he says about technologically mediated mass communication describes the internet perfectly. "I mean," he writes, "rapid communications, efficient communications, elaborately organised communications, communications by petrol and electricity and machinery which go to every corner of the earth."[78] He is right to see a connection between such communications and ethical degradation: "In every corner of the earth today, we can see them corrupting good manners."[79] This begins in the soul of man, and Chesterton wants to throw his audience back onto itself to encourage a sense of their part in the drama of being. He wants to encourage responsibility.

When looking at McLuhan's examples of the first law concerning how media extend or exaggerate certain things, many have drawn the conclusion that he is a technological determinist. But he is a Thomist-like Chesterton. He notices how distorted sense ratios are revealed by media, which is to say that his focus is primarily on what media mean for perception, as well as what the psychological and social consequences of this might be. So, for instance, he sees that telephones enhance speech in dialogical form, the written word enhances visual communication and a sequential sense of temporality, the press enhances a concern with the day-to-day, and hermeneutics enhances clarity and an awareness of textual difficulty.[80] McLuhan sees each form of mediation as a way of revealing a paradoxical interplay between people and the world that exists before the mediation. His focus, like Chesterton's, is

78. Chesterton, *G. K.'s Weekly*, 19 June 1926.
79. Chesterton, *G. K.'s Weekly*, 19 June 1926.
80. McLuhan and McLuhan, *Laws of Media*, 140, 149, 152–55.

not on inevitability but on meaning. He notices what every medium does. But given his Chestertonian attunement to being, his attention to both the intimate and the universal, as well as his attention to the tensions between things, he notices not just what is done but also what is undone.

The Second Law of Mediation: Obsolescence

Before discussing Chesterton's understanding of what the human selection of rapid communications is undoing, let us consider his awareness of how different ways of mediating the world have an obsolescing function in something far less dramatic. Chesterton takes aim at the arguments of those who want to encourage "spelling-reform."[81] He acknowledges a problem, namely that much of our everyday speech consists of "dead words," of things that do not in any obvious way refer to what we are familiar with. He notices that entire worlds are suggested by common terms, although these worlds are now lost to us. "Half our speech," he says, "consists of similes that remind us of no similarity; of pictorial phrases that call up no picture; of historical allusions the origin of which we have forgotten."[82] So much of our verbal communication, for example, consists of what may be called dead metaphors—words that we use without noticing that they are metaphors. We see the figures but forget the ground.

By highlighting the forgotten within the remembered, Chesterton notes the threat, although not necessarily the inevitability, of the disintegration of meaning, where meanings can exist apparently without form; without formal causation. He recognizes that figures may not merely subdue the ground but utterly annihilate the ground in the mind of any communicator. However, while the ground can be forgotten or even obliterated, and this must happen even before spelling reform can be seriously proposed by anyone, this does not mean it has ceased or will cease to function. Having a metaxological awareness, which allows for the failures of self-mediations, he notices that the problem is perceptual. To forget the ground means simply that we see by and from it even if we cannot see it. The ground is more like an invisible conceptual forcefield that organizes our perceptual content into a prearranged design such that we take what we are viewing as obvious rather than acknowledging that the apparently obvious figure has been mediated by some ground. Chesterton's idea of the "symbolism of syntax" is worth recalling; the idea that the unarticulated and undefined tends to have much more sway

---

81. Chesterton, *Selected Essays*, 43.
82. Chesterton, *Selected Essays*, 43.

than we ordinarily acknowledge.[83] It is even possible to deny a certain belief while simultaneously expressing that very belief by our actions.

Having drawn attention to our forgetting, Chesterton asks his reader to pick any example that the eye might rest on and to pay close attention. He asks the reader to actively allow figures to stand out from the ground and so to allow them to point beyond themselves. He asks the reader, in other words, to bypass pre-decided expectations and to notice what has probably receded from conscious awareness. Perhaps what has receded from our awareness is something as yet unknown. But even in this, there is the question of the meaning of the thing, perhaps along the lines of something that Aristotle's fourfold might elucidate. Perhaps we have taken something for granted and have attributed to it a univocal meaning. But the thing itself poses questions. If it is an idea, at least four questions are foundational. Where did the idea come from? What are its implications? Can the idea be supported and how? Is there any criticism we might offer the idea? As Chesterton explains elsewhere, the object of his school of thought is to show us how many extraordinary things even an ordinary person can encounter simply by paying attention.[84] He wants us to see what we have unseen.

If we were to pay attention to something as simple as how words are spelt before reformers get their way and change everything, we might discover what has been subdued or obsolesced. The word *talented* is a good example and it is one Chesterton refers to. It comes from the New Testament.[85] The word implies not only a single concept but an entire history and tradition. As Chesterton suggests, altering the word's spelling would very likely eradicate the figure-ground dialogue completely; the figure would become fully transparent to consciousness and the ground would become completely invisible, perhaps irretrievable. Readers may find seeing beyond the obvious even more impossible if an active attempt is made to eradicate the very thing that makes the discovery of meaning possible. A simple change, which would be allowed for only by a certain receptivity to it, alters our relationship not just with that particular intensification of meaning in being but with an entire world of meaning.

This is central to Chesterton's entire argument against phonetic spelling, but it represents a much larger theme in his writings. The problem is not with mere alteration, with, say, making adjustments on the basis of some present concern for ease of use and for the sake of memorability. The problem is with the mindset that adopts such a change and the result of

---

83. Chesterton, *Illustrated London News*, 2 April 1932.
84. Chesterton, *Tremendous Trifles*, 6.
85. Matthew 25:14–30.

perpetuating such a change. A thing is extended or intensified but at what cost? To rip a word from its own story would render its meaning arbitrary and would therefore also destabilize its connection with truth. To do so would be to play a trick on the mind. It might rid the school child of the tiresome and potentially annoying task of learning how to spell things, but it would do away with far more than inconvenience. Arguably, it would likely generate more inconveniences than it solves. What would get lost in such a case is the potential to enter into a deep, experiential connection with reality through formal causality. The word would still have a meaning but it would mean less than what it once did. It would shrink the analogical resonances of the word to conform to a constricted self-mediation. Meaning would be policed and imprisoned; it would resolve to be built entirely upon a deliberate act of brutal reduction. With something as seemingly frivolous as changing the spelling of any word, allowing a word to be disconnected from its own lineage, the communicator would enter more deeply into a world of fragments without any connection to truth.

This example is instructive because it shows Chesterton's awareness of how a small change, with even a hint of obsolescing the wrong thing, suggests a larger distortion of form. It suggests deforming meaning. It is with this same awareness that he attends to the question of how rapid communication might affect something as simple as the way that a Castilian peasant in Spain conducts himself. He wears the crown of culture that we call good manners. His existence is marked by a combination of freedoms and obligations. He is able to defend his home against enemies even while he is able to welcome strangers. If he were to welcome a king from some other country, his pride in his miniature kingdom would not necessarily be diminished. But Chesterton imagines the arrival of a particular American who has the habit of treating another man's home as if it is just an "inferior hotel."[86] His mind has been corrupted by a view of the world warped by excessively fast communication. Everything has turned into a process of importing and exporting. Efficient causality has come to dominate his mind at the expense of gratitude and teleology. His consciousness has therefore shifted from participation to attending to the speed of the communication itself. Communication becomes a matter of mere transaction. What is nearby, one's neighbor and the obligation to love one's neighbor, is rendered distant. What is distant, namely the process of importing and exporting, is rendered near. The relational world is thrown entirely out of order and reconfigured by this intrusion of electricity—although, arguably, electricity is the cause that appears after the effect.

---

86. Chesterton, *G. K.'s Weekly*, 19 June 1926.

The realm of values is soon degraded to become a mess of potentials without any sense of actualizing form or purpose.

Having had his perspective on the world so altered, the American figure that Chesterton uses as a symbol here is therefore prone to being less friendly, perhaps even rude; and where he is not rude, he strains to retain any sort of subtlety. Bad communication has indeed corrupted his manners and his mannerisms. For Chesterton, it would therefore be "a benevolent and agreeable act to cut the communications," just as it would be good "to cut the cads."[87] What is wrong is the entire situation and not merely the new invention. "It is a stupid and irrational act merely to rejoice in the fact that the communications do communicate," since it is obvious that this is not all that is happening.[88] Merely willing is not enough to alter the situation since nothing does only one thing. Our will may guide us to understand things in only one way but the effects of things go beyond our intentions and thoughts. We need to understand what is going on to know what to do. Most importantly, we need to notice that "the science of communications" is a "tangle of communications: a system of perpetually passing on packages and never opening them."[89]

In this tangle, human beings themselves become packages of a kind. One can think of this along the lines of email or some form of social media. That American tourist or businessman, for example, is sent to Spain like a package. His very being is reduced to a function. Unfortunately, he is not really "opened" there. Having succumbed to the modern category of a project, he is likely to be a closed box even to himself. By this act of reducing the human being to a package, together with all the bureaucracy required to get the package transferred from one side of the world to another, he becomes a mere image or sign. And the meaning of that image or sign is up for grabs because it has been removed from its own world. This is an early indication of what is now known as context collapse, which refers to the way that multiple audiences or formal causes are reduced to a single context, the typical result being a whole host of misunderstandings. The figure becomes replanted in different soil without any consideration of whether it can thrive there. Even his original location stops mattering much. But then, in addition to this, the place he is sent to seems to become equally irrelevant. A sense of the local itself is diluted by a flood of cosmopolitanism.

Indiscriminate cosmopolitanism negates intimacy. It fails to sustain love because it denies boundaries, individuality, and locality. Genuine

---

87. Chesterton, *G. K.'s Weekly*, 19 June 1926.
88. Chesterton, *G. K.'s Weekly*, 19 June 1926.
89. Chesterton, *G. K.'s Weekly*, 19 June 1926.

universality is only accessible to us when we are convinced that the best relationship we can have is with our immediate world. According to a metaxological posture, we cannot be truly universal when we strive for mere universals. A father who loves his own children is far more universal and so also far more attuned to the general order "than the man who dandles the infant hippopotamus or puts the young crocodile in a perambulator."[90] Cosmopolitanism "gives us one country, and it is good," Chesterton writes. But "nationalism gives us a hundred countries, and everyone of them is the best."[91] Against the love of the local, and even a love of the neighbor in terms that appreciate his location in a different world, the new communication technologies confirm a consciousness that would shift people away from intimacy with being and so also move them away from real universality. It is not possible to be universal without attending to the particular. One cannot be global without being local.

Because of the obsolescing of the local, Chesterton thinks the personal world is destined to be diluted in a flood of jumbled customlessness. Wherever high-speed global communications reach, they will be "mischievous" in their destructive power but also "monotonous."[92] Whatever harm they do in one place will be the same harm they do in every place. "Unless local liberty and experience and instinct and invention can again be given a chance, the whole life of the world will be withered," Chesterton writes, and he is right.[93] What is primarily at issue here is not that superior things will be defeated by inferior things. Rather is "a question of a hundred things that are superior being defeated by one that is inferior."[94]

Chesterton offers a very simple example, again with reference to Spain. He notes how many Spanish women wear a traditional lace or silk shawl called a mantilla and contrasts this with women who wore "hats of the uniform and rather dull pattern dictated by Paris to New York."[95] This may seem like a frivolous example, but it is profoundly instructive since the mantilla is, or perhaps was, indicative of a tradition of local customs and loves. The trouble is, the business of importing and exporting fashions insists upon stylistic and rhetorical commonplaces that are commonplaces only because they are copies. Everything gets standardized to fit some aggregate

---

90. Chesterton, *Collected Works, Volume 20*, 597.
91. Chesterton, *Collected Works, Volume 20*, 597.
92. Chesterton, *Collected Works, Volume 20*, 597.
93. Chesterton, *Collected Works, Volume 20*, 597.
94. Chesterton, *Collected Works, Volume 20*, 597.
95. Chesterton, *G. K.'s Weekly*, 19 June 1926.

of acceptability determined by "American commerce and progress."[96] As a consequence, the "fine Spanish ladies look much less Spanish, they look much less fine, and (as is natural when the motive is snobbery) they look much less like ladies."[97] Unfortunately, even more important things get annihilated than traditional clothing. What matters is not "the headdress" but "the heart."[98] "Spanish customs do stand for traditions of dignity and domesticity; and these more serious things are also liable to be destroyed by that spirit of commercial communication, which everywhere destroys what it is too ignorant to understand."[99]

Understanding the form of things, as the above implies, means coming to terms with their limits. Chesterton constantly returns to the issue of limits. "All my life I have loved frames and limits," he writes, "and I will maintain that the largest wilderness looks larger seen through a window."[100] In *Orthodoxy* (1908), he imagines children who love playing on the flat, grassy top of a small island in the sea. "So long as there was a wall round the cliff's edge," he says, "they could fling themselves into every frantic game and make the place the noisiest of nurseries."[101] But what happens when the walls get knocked down to expose the brutal peril of the precipice? He suggests that there is not often any obvious danger when limits are done away with, but he pictures the children "huddled in terror in the centre of the island."[102] They no longer feel the same joy and the same sense of play. That seemingly minor alteration in and to the environment has changed both the environment and the figures in it.

In the same vein, he discusses an idea that we now know as Chesterton's fence, which can be simply stated: *Don't remove a fence before you know why it was put up in the first place.* This principle is articulated in one of Chesterton's essays in *The Thing* (1929). He suggests the possibility there of a fence, representing an institution, principle, custom, or law. But the "modern type of reformer" would declare that since he cannot see the use of it, it should be cleared away.[103] In response, "the more intelligent type of reformer" should answer, "If you don't see the use of it, I certainly won't let

---

96. Chesterton, *G. K.'s Weekly*, 19 June 1926.
97. Chesterton, *G. K.'s Weekly*, 19 June 1926.
98. Chesterton, *G. K.'s Weekly*, 19 June 1926.
99. Chesterton, *G. K.'s Weekly*, 19 June 1926.
100. Chesterton, *Autobiography*, 41.
101. Chesterton, *Collected Works, Volume 1*, 350.
102. Chesterton, *Collected Works, Volume 1*, 350.
103. Chesterton, *Collected Works, Volume 3*, 157.

you clear it away. Go away and think. Then, when you can come back and tell me that you do see the use of it, I may allow you to destroy it."[104]

Chesterton observes the core gesture of modernity, the inversion of act and potency, which rests on allowing will to usurp understanding. This inversion is captured in the proclamation of the modern reformer, "I don't see the use of this; let us clear it away."[105] Against this demonstration of sheer will, Chesterton proposes an alternative: give the "fence" considered thought instead of judging it negatively and tearing it down.[106] He proposes interpretation as an antidote to the arrogant display of power. This echoes something implied by the biblical story of the Tower of Babel.[107] The people who build that tower give no thought to the consequences of their desire to be equal to God. In response, the divine command creates a scenario where immediate univocal agreement is impossible. He splits people up into nations speaking different tongues, making interpretation a vital aspect of living in the world. The meaning of this story is later echoed at Pentecost, which is less about subsuming meaning under the reign of a single language than it is about stressing the importance of interpretation and mediation.[108] It is, in this case, the Holy Spirit, the formal cause, who mediates. Chesterton demonstrates the importance of this in his interpretation of modern technologies of haste and excess scale. He refuses to take them at face value and instead considers something of the "fence" that such things unthinkingly tear down. Every "doing" is a "displacing."[109] A central component of this interpretation of formal causality is an understanding of custom and history. Every medium, meaning every metaphor, retrieves something from history. This assumes that examples of what will happen now and in the future are already discoverable in the past. To be able to understand the present and the future, in other words, requires an understanding of history, which is not "one thing" but "twenty thousand things."[110] While not all of the things in history can be loved and appreciated, we can make some attempt to understand them and what they mean for us today.

---

104. Chesterton, *Collected Works, Volume 3*, 157.
105. Chesterton, *Collected Works, Volume 3*, 157.
106. Chesterton, *Collected Works, Volume 3*, 157.
107. Genesis 11:1–11.
108. Acts 2:1–13.
109. Chesterton, *G. K.'s Weekly*, 19 June 1926.
110. Chesterton, *Illustrated London News*, 14 June 1924.

The Third Law of Mediation: Retrieval

To understand the formal cause of anything requires attending, again with deference to the analogical structure of being and consciousness, to how both the present and the possible future retrieve something of the past. By now it should be clear that Chesterton already exemplifies a retrieval of the neglected principle of formal causality. He wants to retrieve a sense of how forms shape the world and also of how the rejection of form might shape the world now and later. He wants to understand how the world imposes itself on us at every moment, even while its impositions might escape our conscious awareness. History is one vital aspect of this imposition. We should imagine history, in this case, less as a formal field of study than as a search for form. History is no surface of cognitive constructions but is the environment within which the shape of reality can be discovered. History becomes a way to get beyond the many mechanical ways in which the world may be considered. It is a way to seek out and find "the homeward path again."[111] It may well lead us to repent of so many errors that we have mistaken for answers.[112] "Tradition," writes Chesterton, "means giving a vote to the most obscure of all classes, our ancestors. It is the democracy of the dead."[113] Tradition does not submit only to those of us who happen to be alive; it objects to people "being disqualified by the accident of death."[114] Tradition recognizes that the dead must not be forgotten but resurrected, just as wise people who live now must be listened to and not ignored, if we are to gain their wisdom.

This does not mean we should negate novelty, that endless obsession of moderns, but should recognize that even novelty is situated.[115] Novelty does not emerge out of nowhere and is far from being sufficient to account for itself. Novelty cannot even be understood without tradition. Chesterton notices this and wants an "intuitive and holistic approach to understanding the historical past."[116] For him, even originality does not mean, as it does for many moderns, generating a new point of origin or a new beginning. It does not mean severing one's connection with what has gone before. It means retrieving something of the origin. We can retrieve clues into the deeper forms of things. Many of our technologies, for instance, are echoes of

---

111. Chesterton, *Collected Works, Volume 5*, 71.
112. Chesterton, *Collected Works, Volume 5*, 73.
113. Chesterton, *Collected Works, Volume 1*, 251.
114. Chesterton, *Collected Works, Volume 1*, 251.
115. Chesterton, *Illustrated London News*, 28 June 1924.
116. McCleary, *Historical Imagination of G. K. Chesterton*, 117.

ideas that originate in a previous time. They are analogies and non-identical repetitions of previous intensifications of being. Everything, by its participation in form, retrieves something.

In the modern era, there are those for whom going back to anything of the past would be like staring back at Sodom and Gomorrah and turning into a pillar of salt like Lot's wife.[117] For Chesterton, however, the past is not something to retreat to. It is a teacher to learn from. Going back, for him, means getting past the "débris of effects" to better understand the "causes" we do not know.[118] In our time, too often, "fire is choked with its own ashes, the fountain is sealed with its own ice; the original purpose of the thing does not pierce through."[119] Often, the only way to see past the chaos of effects with no apparent causes is to seek to understand what any given thing "was primarily supposed to be."[120] "Nine times out of ten," he suggests, "the only way of really building the future is to imagine oneself in some much ruder society in the remote past."[121] To be clear, this act of imagination, this intentional attempt to see around things, rather than just looking at them, is not only about seeing history as something that happened long ago or once upon a time. It is vital for extending one's analogical awareness as far as possible beyond abstract reduction. To attend to history, as Chesterton does, is to attend to it as a symposium of specifics, with real implications for the present and future. This would help to protect us from any inclination we may have to reduce any happenings to rigid patterns. It would help us to get beyond mechanical repetitions and into non-identical repetitions; to see patterns in connection with pictures. Indeed, it would free us from being at the mercy of history and restore to us a sense of our own power to choose and to act.

One of the stranger eventualities of modernity is found in its obsession with novelty, as I have said. Losing Platonist realism turns novelty into something not simply enjoyed but into an obsession and even a principle of life. It starts to become unfashionable to follow form. In the work of Nietzsche, who has influenced so many philosophers after him, an unreasonable fear begins to emerge that metaphysics itself is a source of violence. For Nietzsche, truth is violent. This apparent violence emerges, as Hannah Arendt contends, from a misappropriation of the Greek notion of *techne*, where any human craftsman uses a perception of a form to beat reality into

---

117. Genesis 19:26.
118. Chesterton, *Illustrated London News*, 22 July 1911.
119. Chesterton, *Illustrated London News*, 22 July 1911.
120. Chesterton, *Illustrated London News*, 22 July 1911.
121. Chesterton, *Illustrated London News*, 22 July 1911.

its shape.¹²² Matter becomes wholly subject to a reductionist's version of form—a deformed cause.

It is not difficult to see why the fear of metaphysics might emerge. Totalitarian regimes, for instance, have been seen to set up false ideals that go against the order of creation, and then attempt to mangle the world into conforming with those false ideals. Some have considered Platonism, for instance, as a kind of proto-fascism because it suggests that things must conform to a form. However, this view emerges from a nominalist misunderstanding of Platonism, which includes a misunderstanding of Christian Platonism. It assumes an exact, univocal copying of a certain diminished conceptualization of form rather than a participation in transcendent form. This is to say that the fear of metaphysics is owed to a loss of metaphysical wonder; a loss of metaxology. For the Christian with a Platonist awareness, forms are participated in. They are not meant to be mechanically doubled in the material dimension. There is a dynamism in being that allows for much variation and creativity. Form and matter are in a dramatic relationship. Non-identical repetition is the rule, not identical, mechanistic repetition. Ironically, however, one of the surprising consequences of modernity's preference for novelty is that it renders repetition more predictable. The loss of participation makes imitation an absolute value. This is perhaps one reason why Chesterton refers to fashion as fatigue. "The future" becomes a "refuge" into which people can flee, often out of fierce and resentful competition with their ancestors.¹²³ "The modern mind is forced towards the future by a certain sense of fatigue, not unmixed with terror, with which it regards the past."¹²⁴

But fear subsides when we realize that the aim of being mindful of the past is not to merely replicate it, as if the past was necessarily better at imitating the forms than we can be in the present. When fear subsides, it becomes possible to see the past in a better light and not seek to reimagine it to fit contemporary biases. We ought to attend to history carefully, not trying to whitewash or blackwash it.¹²⁵ History is a means for understanding, not a mere ideological tool in the modernist's toolbox. "There is a trick of thought," Chesterton observes, that especially learned people often fall for. It is "the trick of giving parallels without proportions."¹²⁶ A good example of this is the Marxian division of the world into bourgeois oppressors and the proletarian oppressed. This division has taken on new names. More

---

122. Armitage, *Philosophy's Violent Sacred*, 11–12.
123. Chesterton, *Collected Works, Volume 4*, 54.
124. Chesterton, *Collected Works, Volume 4*, 54.
125. Chesterton, *Illustrated London News*, 10 May 1913.
126. Chesterton, *Illustrated London News*, 23 February 1918.

recently, the division has been repurposed by so-called conflict theories. Now, the privileged, whoever they are, are assumed to be oppressors, while those lacking in privilege, whoever they are, are assumed to be oppressed. If we were to read such a division as generously as we can, which is not easy to do given how obscenely simplistic it is, we might find some way for it to be instructive and even insightful. But the trouble, as Chesterton notes, is that a narrow generalization is soon applied so widely that it utterly obscures the truth of anything. "There is no harm," Chesterton observes, in identifying and naming "a resemblance," as long as we realize that "there is also a difference—and that the difference is always one of proportion."[127] Simply put, all things involve retrieval and history is a way to ensure the proper understanding of proportion. There are gradations in meaning that should not be too quickly disregarded.

There happens to be, let us say, a tradition that claims that jumping off a cliff is bad for your health. This, as long as the tradition holds, is why no one does it. But then along comes "a progressive prophet and reformer" who suggests that no one can claim that jumping off a cliff is bad for anyone's health.[128] After all, he notes, no one does it; no one he knows of. He might fuel a mass movement and a series of scientific experiments to support people jumping off cliffs. The movement may grow at an alarming rate, especially after it has started trending on social media and in mainstream media. Eventually, after some deaths and much irreversible damage done to people, a discovery will be made. Many people will agree, once again, that jumping off cliffs is bad for your health. Unfortunately, this sort of thing is likely to happen only after jumping off cliffs has become something of a new tradition. An awareness of *retrieval*—some understanding of history, in other words—would prevent so much harm and so much evil from being done. It would be like remembering why a fence was put up to prevent it from being torn down. This would ensure a better understanding of our current condition.

Retrieval therefore means not only that we know what happened once upon a time but that we see history as analogically connected to the present and the future. We have surveillance cameras, for instance, but these are analogies and recollections of the castle watchtower, which is an echo of the ancient practice of being on the lookout for wild animals and foes, or perhaps extends the more pleasant activity of bird watching. Similarly, republicanism retrieves tribal democracy, sports retrieve both war and dialogue, spectacles retrieve average vision, mirrors retrieve the mode of

---

127. Chesterton, *Illustrated London News*, 23 February 1918.
128. Chesterton, *Illustrated London News*, 9 March 1918.

Narcissus, the written word retrieves elitism, windows retrieve the outdoors, and cameras retrieve the past as present.[129] In everything, there is an echo of something else. Sometimes the echo is approximate, close to a non-identical repetition, like the daisies that Chesterton says God makes individually only because he has never grown tired of making them.[130] At other times, the echo is less than identical, where the gap between similarity and difference is wider than in a non-identical repetition.

The aim of noticing retrievals, as with the other aspects of McLuhan's tetrad, is not to arrive at a univocal literalism. Formal causality remains metaxological. It obsolesces figures and specialization even as it enhances the ground.[131] This is particularly important to consider with Chesterton. He is by no means a specialist. This much is obvious when we consider the sheer range of his work. Yet, it is this lack of specialization—which does not exclude expertise, although it perhaps risks diluting it—that allows him to be so well attuned to the formal cause. His knowledge of history follows this, being somewhat more generalist than it is specialist. It is a kind of knowledge that is also fundamentally creative. The power of creativity, Chesterton notices, is a "power of combination."[132] It is an ability to transform the given through anamnesis. All invention is recollection. All events involve retrieval. The example of phonetic spelling mentioned earlier symbolizes Chesterton's desire to ensure that we remain mindful of retrieval, as a dimension of analogy. To rid words of their associations with the past is to chip away at the poetic and formal coherence of the world. The past remains one of the strongest guides to interpreting both the present and the future.

Belloc notes how Chesterton goes against the trend towards becoming oblivious to history. The severe presentism of our age is a retrieval of the presentism of previous ages, including his age. Even the common obsession with novelty today is not new. Chesterton was not officially educated in many of the subjects he dabbled in, from sociology to history to philosophy and theology, but he was an autodidact. He knew that understanding anything well required understanding the past in all its complexity.[133] It is terrible to look at things divorced from their contexts and interpret them only in relation

---

129. McLuhan and McLuhan, *Lost Tetrads of Marshall McLuhan*, 13, 44, 46, 50, 52, 56.

130. Chesterton, *Collected Works, Volume 1*, 264.

131. Chesterton, *Collected Works, Volume 1*, 235.

132. Quoted in Ward, *Gilbert Keith Chesterton*, 258.

133. Chesterton, *Illustrated London News*, 21 July 1923.

to the most immediate associations and projections we have of them.[134] This causes association to replace analysis. It blocks the way to retrieval.

Chesterton is not saying that we should resort to cold rationalism to replace rampant emotionalism. It does not do to solve one mistake by substituting it with another. "We should not regard one poison as an antidote to [another] poison," he writes.[135] Reason and feeling ought to be allied. Arguably, a vital component of Chesterton's attention to formal causality, and especially to retrieval, is not just in his desire to know the world abstractly but is in his willingness to feel the world. A romance of the real needs to be retrieved and not merely an abstracting mode of reasoning. Formal causality ought to be deep as well as broad, and feeling is essential for this. Already this has been intimated. For instance, if we are to enter into an awareness of the material cause, we should feel matter brimming with possibility and not just regard it as an inert, dead, spiritless given—as just there for theoretically driven instrumentality. Even matter is felt and not merely abstractly thought.

While the univocalizer risks turning the past into something that can be mechanically reproduced, the metaxological thinker, attuned as he is to reality in its analogical and paradoxical character, is able to see patterns without necessarily presuming immediate identity. It is not wrong, for example, to perceive patterns and disproportions in totalitarian thought, with its zero-sum strategies, its simplistic allegiances, and its scapegoats, and then notice how such patterns might be somewhat evident today even in so-called free societies. It is one thing to claim that the world is like Zamyatin's nightmare *We* (1924), or Huxley's nightmare *Brave New World* (1932), or Orwell's nightmare *1984* (1949), when it is not, and quite another to claim that Zamyatin, Huxley, and Orwell highlight some things that we would do well to avoid, which is fairly reasonable. As I have noted, thinking analogically means being attuned to difference, as well as similarity. Thus, while attuned to being in its horizontality and verticality, we can think beyond any assumption that the past will merely reoccur identically in the present. Nevertheless, to make sense of the present and the future, which is the aim, requires a feeling for the past. We feel our way through time as we reason through it.

In his reflection on global communication, while noting that certain facets of communication echo history, Chesterton stresses the importance of focusing on the process. As I've already said, during the modern era, efficient causality has been emphasized in particular, to the exclusion of final

---

134. Chesterton, *Illustrated London News*, 4 March 1933.
135. Chesterton, *Collected Works, Volume 5*, 67.

and formal causality, and this has obsolesced a sense of simultaneous causality.[136] In other words, instead of co-participating with the other causes, efficient causality chips away at awareness. One consequence of this is the unhaloing of the world. If the formal cause welcomes the poetry of being, allowing all things to live and breathe through all other things, an amplification of efficient causality drowns out the polyphonic music of being and renders it monotonous. Everything is soon perceived as merely sequential, if not as always alienated from everything else. History itself is transformed into a series of discrete stages.

What is evident to Chesterton is that this disproportionate focus on efficiency is directly connected, perhaps surprisingly, to capitalism. Tradition is sacrificed especially to the god Mammon, as is evidenced by the fact that "the mind of the millionaire" governs so much of what the "mind of the poor man" is exposed to.[137] Already back then, journalism was fast becoming "a conspiracy of a very few millionaires," who by being of a "sufficiently similar" type felt that it should be within their power to dictate to others what "ought" to be known by the public.[138] Still now, this problem persists. Much journalism today tends to resist viewpoints that are too different while the corporations that fund mainstream media agree on the same ideological coordinates. Reporters will be reluctant to provide a perspective that differs from that of their primary source of funding. No dog wants to bite the hand that feeds him if does not want to be thrown out of doors. In this, certain external and superficial concerns might override more nuanced understandings of the world. Efficiency tends to render depth as yet another surface. This amounts to rendering as indifferent those aspects of tradition that encourage human flourishing. Chesterton takes aim at capitalism as a system and as a way of thinking about systems that threatens traditions and so also threatens history. It frames the world along the lines of speed and expansion. It represents "the spirit that is proud of having sold a hundred Paris hats to Spanish peasants without thinking of what it is doing or what it is displacing."[139]

Chesterton has in mind especially the Yellow Press, a term used to refer to journalism that paid little attention to well-researched news and went instead for eye-catching headlines and sensational content. Signs were already evident in his time, with commercial success as the dominating motivator, that scandal-mongering and various exaggerations and distortions

---

136. McLuhan and McLuhan, *Lost Tetrads of Marshall McLuhan*, 235.
137. Chesterton, *Collected Works, Volume 5*, 500.
138. Chesterton, *Collected Works, Volume 5*, 500.
139. Chesterton, *G. K.'s Weekly*, 19 June 1926.

could become the norm in new media. Around the time, Charles Rowley said of the Yellow Press, "You pay your penny and you get your harm's worth."[140] Chesterton notices that this functions as something of a principle when communication extends too far and moves too quickly. Such communication is, in a sense, very cheap; and that is why it is so very costly. The cheaper our words, the more impoverished our sense of meaning becomes. The more we have, the more alienated from the world we become.

Christ asks the question, "What shall it profit a man, if he shall gain the whole world, and lose his own soul?"[141] But the capitalist does not bother to even offer the world; he tries to push an agenda that would have people trade their souls for things of barely any significance. It profits a man less than nothing to lose his own soul for the sake of a few momentary pleasures and cheap trinkets. Most apparently, it is people who are forgotten. Every emphasis selects certain meanings and so also reflects certain meanings. But other meanings are thus deflected. And the meaning left out of impersonal systems is the meaning of the person. In response to the overstatement of efficiency, Chesterton recommends a retrieval of a different kind: "We must get back to the man behind the machines, and the desire behind all systems; and the simpler the man and the more direct the desire, the better."[142]

Historically speaking, Chesterton understands that the tradition to which he belongs has often been and is still accused of being behind the times. In truth, this is because of a tendency to deal "with the last heresy rather than the next one."[143] However, the accusation says more about the fickleness and inconsistencies of various enemies and critics of the church than it says about the church. Modern modifications of the world can be conceived of as heresies.[144] They derive whatever moral force they have from forgotten foundations laid by Christianity. They are heresies not because they are novel forms but because they are corruptions of an older and truer form. But such heresies "die faster than they can be killed."[145] Conforming to a form keeps things alive. Sticking to an essence ensures sustainability while negating an essence in one way or another ensures decay. This is why so many ideological movements cannot last. Still, the Catholic who defended almsgiving against the madness of Malthus would be found defending ownership against Marx or progressive capitalism. The Catholic who would

---

140. Chesterton, *G. K.'s Weekly*, 19 June 1926.
141. Mark 8:36.
142. Chesterton, *New Renascence*, 84.
143. Chesterton, *G. K.'s Weekly*, 19 June 1926.
144. Chesterton, *Illustrated London News*, 31 August 1912.
145. Chesterton, *G. K.'s Weekly*, 19 June 1926.

defend the joys of sex against puritanical excesses will also defend chastity against the excesses of hook-up culture and pornography. Today, there is a need to recover the form, and history can help us to do this so that we can defend "morality against monopoly."[146]

We need history to prevent what Chesterton refers to as spiritual kidnapping.[147] Such spiritual kidnapping, which implies ripping people away from God and his bride, the church, is easier when people are divorced from their contexts. Propaganda, the manipulative use of language in service of the will and not of truth or understanding, is made more digestible when people have no sense of how to make sense of things, especially when they have no sense of how to situate things within a larger world of meaning. Without context, a concern with truth is replaced by a concern with plausibility; and a concern with understanding is replaced by a concern with opinion. Plausibility and opinion are at their most corrupted when they block the path to reality. When removed from all historical context—not just history as a field of study but history or tradition as the form that gives shape to life—the result can only be deformations. Nevertheless, such deformations cannot hold indefinitely. Under the tyranny of opinion, truth remains generously intact. One way to recognize this is in McLuhan's fourth law of media, which refers to the idea that built into being is a natural mechanism that prevents distortions from holding their shape. There is elasticity in being, a sense in which things desire to return to their original form. When we act against reality, reality bites back.

The Fourth Law of Mediation: Reversal

The final component of McLuhan's tetrad, through which we can better understand Chesterton's attention to formal cause, rests on the observation that every mediation reverses or flips into its opposite when it is pushed to its extreme. This component of McLuhan's tetrad is arguably the most Chestertonian in that it is entirely paradoxical. As McLuhan notes, Chesterton's attention to paradox implies, among other things, his refusal to see only one side of an issue: "he always saw more than one aspect in a question."[148] It is only a discarnate view of things that can maintain the integrity of its abstractions in non-paradoxical form because reality is not discarnate for us.

The principle of reversal is found in many traditions. In the Judeo-Christian Scriptures, for instance, the story of the Tower of Babel in the

---

146. Chesterton, *G. K.'s Weekly*, 19 June 1926.
147. Chesterton, *Illustrated London News*, 29 October 1932.
148. McLuhan, *Medium and the Light*, 49.

book of Genesis is perhaps the most striking symbol of this principle.[149] There, an attempt to generate an idolatrous unity and power through a technology collapses into malfunction and disunity. A similar idea is found in the *Dao De Jing*, which in its ninth poem suggests that withdrawal tugs even within every extension and that collapse is found lurking within every exaggeration.[150] Limits within the world, says the writer of those poems, are not entirely malleable and will alert us to their presence soon enough. Carl Jung takes this idea as a psychological principle, rooted in the work of Heraclitus, in the form of *enantiodromia*.[151] This is the idea that what is unconscious gradually turns into its opposite. Sensation and intuition are interlinked in a continuum, for instance, as are thinking and feeling. Moreover, psychological chaos flips into order.[152] Extended periods of excitement, for instance, quite naturally produce in people a more downcast demeanor and physical engagement with the world translates into higher levels of intuitive insight. The beatitudes reflect the same principle such that poverty of spirit is no barrier to the welcome of heaven and mourning invites comfort because it is not so proud that it would seek to conceal basic human vulnerability.[153] However, this principle of reversal, one of the meta-laws of any situation, does not mean, in all cases, that what mediation flips into is necessarily in harmony with an original or archetypal form. The reversal of mediation, instantiated in particular beings and events, suggests the underlying form of things. Reversal is an analogy, like all of the above aspects and lenses on formal cause, including the formal cause itself. It indicates something beyond the obvious that is not the thing itself. If there is any truth to the fact that reality is governed by real forms, it is arguably most perceptible in this principle. Attempts to escape this reality by imposing imaginary abstractions onto it soon reveals the inescapability of reality. Ideologies prove to be terribly mortal and transient, while the church endlessly resurrects when constantly crucified.[154] "A dead thing can go with the stream," says Chesterton, "but only a living thing can go against it."[155] In other words, it is by no means certain that modern heresies must necessarily continue to become more and more entrenched while Christian orthodoxy is increasingly

---

149. Genesis 11:1–9.
150. Kim, *Reading Jesus' Parables with Dao De Jing*.
151. Jung, *Psychological Types*, 87.
152. See Schwartz-Salant, *Order-Disorder Paradox*.
153. Matthew 5:3–12.
154. Chesterton, *Everlasting Man*, 250.
155. Chesterton, *Everlasting Man*, 256.

sidelined. Contact with reality cannot be eradicated because heresies rely on reality for their existence.

One example that Chesterton notices of something destined to flip into its opposite is the ideology of futurism already touched on. This offers a case study not only of a particular modern frame of mind but also of how Chesterton manages to see through it into its more bothersome consequences. Perhaps the most forthright statement of the nature and character of futurism is found in Filippo Tommaso Marinetti's *Futurist Manifesto* (1909), which, although reliant on the zero-sum logic of Karl Marx and Freddie Engels's *Communist Manifesto* (1848), acts as something of an archetype of the hundreds of art manifestos that would follow it. The logic of this manifesto is made explicit in Tristan Tzara's *Dada Manifesto* (1916), which says, "To put out a manifesto, you must want ABC to fulminate against 1, 2, 3. To fly into a rage, and sharpen your wings to conquer and disseminate little ABCs and big ABCs."[156] To possess an "ABC," for the avant gardist, is explicitly named as a rejection of form. It is the modernist negative spirit, its obsession with falsification and demythologization, translated into artistic terms.

Marinetti sees this rejection as the source of renewal in art and so praises the rejection of history and tradition. This merely mimics the modern elevation of efficient causality over formal and final causality. The mere process becomes the aim. If at first this suggests a retrieval of the equivocal qualities of material causality and gives rise to some interesting creative possibilities, defaulting to a mere process of rejecting the past soon becomes slavery, not unlike the slavery of free verse.[157] It becomes nearly impossible to determine not only what is *art* but what is *good*. It is unsurprising that Marinetti connects his movement to violence and therefore also that his thinking around art intersects so well with his commitment to fascism. The futurists are as mad and practical and progressive as fascists because they are fascistic. The rejection of form causes real violence, first to any representative of history, but ultimately also to the avant-gardist.

Chesterton argues that "the Futurists" do not "really have much to say that we cannot all of us say without being Futurists. All that these novelties do is narrow the mind to what is novel, when it was already in possession of what is universal."[158] What the futurist ends up with is not ultimately novelty but mere negation. "It is not so much that speed is beautiful" for the futurist "as that stillness is not beautiful" to him. "A more universal poet" would not feel the need to negate the relational nature of being for the sake of one small

156. Danchev, *100 Artists' Manifestos*, 137.
157. Chesterton, *In Defense of Sanity*, 154–58.
158. Chesterton, *Illustrated London News*, 23 December 1922.

element of being. He would be perfectly capable of admiring "thunderbolts and wild horses at one time, without losing the power to admire lakes and lilies at another."[159] But the futurist fails to see that exaggerating one element of a form at the expense of its own formal cause can only lead to a reversal. This may be perceived as a pendulum-like oscillation from one alternative to another. What speeds up must eventually stop; what becomes more focused ends up losing all perspective; and the obsession with novelty soon grows old and stale.[160] The movement's antagonism towards tradition ends up as violence against itself, and this inadvertently supports the very tradition it rages against. Violence against the other transforms into self-annihilation. Art ceases to be artistic without form. Indeed, so much art today, thankfully not all of it, seems to be caught in a dialectical trap set by the futurists. In a perpetual search for authenticity, art becomes ensnared in an endless game of imitation, rivalry, and resentment. The pursuit of originality apart from formal causality has made so many artworks utterly banal.[161]

This is only one example. Chesterton is aware that similar reversals can be found anywhere attention to the formal cause is ignored. He notices, for instance, that abandoning morality leads to moralism; that abandoning God leads to fundamentalisms; that modern so-called emancipations, exemplified in certain expressions of feminism, leads to slavery; that a loss of form in poetry leads to a loss of poetry. This is not to say, once again, that such reversals are inevitable. Form acts on us beneath the level of our conscious awareness, after all, and so may have an influence on us without our being fully of it. However, an overt and rebellious rejection of form will have consequences, usually of a negative kind. We can act as if form is not real but that does not mean that it is not real.

It is on the basis of the above—a profound sense of certain proportions between extension, obsolescence, retrieval, and reversal—that Chesterton goes on, in that same article in *G. K.'s Weekly*, to make one of his most often cited predictions. He notes, on recognizing the capitalistic emphasis on efficiency, that "the next great heresy is going to be simply an attack on morality."[162] More specifically, probably because of an observation that ends disappear thanks to an overemphasis on pure efficiency, "sexual morality" will be the prime target.[163] When sex and sexuality are tied to specific ends, namely the nurturing of children and developing their full capacities,

---

159. Chesterton, *Illustrated London News*, 23 December 1922.
160. Chesterton, *Illustrated London News*, 23 December 1922.
161. Reyburn, "Repetitions Repeatedly Repeated."
162. Chesterton, *G. K.'s Weekly*, 26 July 1930.
163. Chesterton, *G. K.'s Weekly*, 26 July 1930.

families and traditions will be upheld. But when divorcing sex and sexuality from procreation, means are transformed into ends in themselves. As Chesterton notices, the attack on sexual morality will come from "the living exultant energy of the rich resolved to enjoy themselves at last, with neither Popery nor Puritanism nor Socialism to hold them back."[164]

While various heresies of the past have relied on generating a consensus with a very thin foundation and barely any roots at all, the next heresy is "as deep as nature itself, whose flower is the lust of the flesh and the lust of the eye and the pride of life."[165] It is a heresy that exaggerates very "natural" things into a very unnatural proportion, obsolesces chastity and holiness, and retrieves the pride and envy that went before the fall of man, and overextends even, as Chesterton writes elsewhere, into absolute "sexlessness."[166] "I say," writes Chesterton, "that the man who cannot see this cannot see the signs of the times; cannot see even the sky-signs in the street, that are the new sort of signs in heaven. The madness of to-morrow is not in Moscow, but much more in Manhattan—but most of what was in Broadway is already in Piccadilly."[167] Today, we live in a world that has carried on in the aftermath of this very eventuality. Chesterton's predictions here have proved right, and the grim results of what he foresaw are indeed terrible. We have seen, and many of us have experienced, the profound loneliness and alienation of a world in which families have been sacrificed to fashionable but nonsensical ideological whims. We have seen people attempt to live out the lies of so-called new moralities, as if there is no natural law, only to reap the whirlwind as the truth of being reasserts itself. The fact of Chesterton's foresight on this one matter proves again that he is worth paying attention to. At the very least, we can see that his attention to formal causality might be retrieved for today.

---

164. Chesterton, *G. K.'s Weekly*, 26 July 1930.
165. Chesterton, *G. K.'s Weekly*, 26 July 1930.
166. Chesterton, *G. K.'s Weekly*, 26 July 1930.
167. Chesterton, *G. K.'s Weekly*, 26 July 1930.

6

Being Transformed

Chesterton's (Formal) Cause

IN HIS ESSAY "THE Man Who Thinks Backwards" (1912), Chesterton considers the person who is utterly beguiled by whatever fashion happens to dictate to him. He is "the man who thinks backwards."[1] Chesterton understands this person as perpetually confused about "all our current discussions" even while he seems to be in the know.[2] The man who thinks backwards conforms even when he has no clue about the meaning of his conformity. But his mode of thought—the way that this backwards-thinker considers things—can be explained by a simple analogy. Chesterton picks a common poker as an example. To figure out the meaning of the poker "well and wisely," the sage will follow a process that places form and aims at the center of his inquiry.[3] He will seek to think forwards, beginning first with the creature called man, who "has to go outside himself for everything that he wants."[4] The human being would be absolutely at the mercy of the world if it were not for his ability to intelligently understand the world and then craft tools to ensure that he is safer and more capable than he would otherwise be. Man without his tools is quite literally, and often embarrassingly, naked. He has not even been able to "keep his hair on."[5] As a consequence,

1. Chesterton, *Miscellany of Men*, 14.
2. Chesterton, *Miscellany of Men*, 14.
3. Chesterton, *Miscellany of Men*, 15.
4. Chesterton, *Miscellany of Men*, 15.
5. Chesterton, *Miscellany of Men*, 16.

just as external need "has lit in his dark brain the dreadful star called religion, so it has lit in his hand the only adequate symbol of it: I mean the red flower called Fire."[6] Man has to keep warm. For this reason, he has made for himself hearths and altars. But there is about this thing called fire "an alien and awful quality: the quality of torture. Its presence is life; its touch is death."[7] To avoid serious injury, man needs a mediator between himself and the blaze, just as he needs a priest to intercede with the gods. "That priest," Chesterton writes, "is the poker."[8] It may seem at first a very frivolous thing to consider the poker at such length. Well, it is frivolous, and that is why it is important. Chesterton's point is that the essence of something as commonplace as a poker cannot be understood without understanding its relation to the place of the man in history, even if it is only very roughly sketched out. The thing cannot be understood apart from its formal cause.

The above, he says, is the right way to think about pokers. Without thinking about pokers like this, it is not difficult to reimagine them as ideal for hurting people, whether behind closed doors, shuttered windows, at home, or in public. "He who has thus gone back to the beginning, and seen everything as quaint and new, will always see things in their right order," Chesterton writes.[9] We would see one thing as depending on others things "in degree of purpose and importance: the poker for the fire and the fire for the man and the man for the glory of God."[10] This he regards as "thinking forwards."[11] Unfortunately, in the modern world, thinking forwards appears to be so uncommon as to be abnormal. It is also less contentious than thinking backwards. The modern man, prone to modern childishness, will look at the poker and consider it as univocally determinate. He may see, for example, that the poker is crooked. He may feel sorry for it. In a therapeutic age, this is especially likely. He may then wonder how it got to be so crooked. Surely it was not always so crooked? His thinking, having been shaped by the narrow dialectical logic of cause and effect, will lead him to discover that fire made it crooked. He will think how terrible fire must be, if that's what it does to pokers. And so he will say, "Let us abolish fire! Then we will have perfectly straight pokers."[12] Although not explicitly said by Chesterton, the man who thinks backwards will have, in his mind, created

---

6. Chesterton, *Miscellany of Men*, 16.
7. Chesterton, *Miscellany of Men*, 16.
8. Chesterton, *Miscellany of Men*, 16.
9. Chesterton, *Miscellany of Men*, 17.
10. Chesterton, *Miscellany of Men*, 17.
11. Chesterton, *Miscellany of Men*, 17.
12. Chesterton, *Miscellany of Men*, 18.

a poker without a purpose; and without a clear purpose, the tool may then be understood as, say, a weapon. Abuses become much more likely when uses are not rightly considered. And abuses are only understood when uses are understood. The man who thinks backwards sees cause and effect but he cannot see formal causation. He cannot see things in context. This is why his conclusions are wrong. Thus, Chesterton asks his readers to consider things in their right place, in the best light possible, in the right order. He wants us to look backwards but not to think backwards.[13] He suggests that we ought to defend our beliefs, not on the basis of their immediate obviousness or seeming popularity but on the basis of whether or not they are right.

When it comes to political reforms, for example, "Let us ask ourselves first what we really do want, not what recent legal decisions have told us to want, or recent logical philosophies proved that we must want, or recent social prophecies predicted that we shall some day want."[14] In the end, for Chesterton, history is like a deeply planted tree. Its roots are deep and its trunk is large, although it "tapers away at last into tiny twigs."[15] Right here where we are, we "are in the topmost branches."[16] If we think from the wrong end, each of us is only too likely to try "to bend the tree by a twig."[17] But a wiser person "resists this temptation of trivial triumph or surrender," and a happier person "remembers the roots of things."[18] The aim of Chestertonian prescience, in a word, is to be rooted. Predicting the future with fair accuracy is, at best, a byproduct of being true. This is how we will best help things, ourselves included, to grow. We ought to be as rooted as Chesterton was. But what does that mean? Below I briefly recapitulate some of what I have already covered to articulate how Chesterton attunes himself to formal causality. Afterwards, I offer detail on the nature of his prescience. And, finally, as I conclude the chapter and this book, I explore what it might mean to be part of a Chestertonian renascence.

First, understanding Chesterton's attunement to the formal cause means noticing his profound sense of immersion in the world. Chesterton resisted the many labels that people would want to attach to him and insisted that he was merely a journalist. While the term may have decidedly negative connotations in our time, it is impossible to side-step the fact that Chesterton favored the ordinary. This was by no means to denigrate

---

13. Chesterton, *Collected Works, Volume 5*, 78.
14. Chesterton, *Miscellany of Men*, 18.
15. Chesterton, *Miscellany of Men*, 21.
16. Chesterton, *Miscellany of Men*, 21.
17. Chesterton, *Miscellany of Men*, 21.
18. Chesterton, *Miscellany of Men*, 21.

the lofty achievements of others or to assume that what is taken as normal ought to be used to excuse abolishing higher standards. For Chesterton, this means embracing standards. The ordinary presumes an order. It assumes that reality, and our interaction with it, ought to be composed in a certain way. Chesterton's sense of the normal is shaped by his faith. Christianity really is "Platonism for the people"[19]—Nietzsche uses this phrase to denigrate Christianity, but it is high praise indeed. Christianity presumes that the life of faith is not for only elites but is meant for everyone. It is this sense of immersion in being, in seeing the word made flesh, that Chesterton develops a journalistic metaphysics—a philosophical theology of the between—that sees contact with reality as its aim. He often resorts to paradox, not because it offers opportunities for rhetorical and aesthetic skill, but because it resonates with reality. Being is analogical, and paradox fits with the analogy of being. The analogical structure of being is evident in the analogical structures of thought. Thought and things correlate and cooperate but not in any way that suggests that one can be reduced to the other or that all mystery disappears when non-identical repetitions are observed and uttered. The deterministic gaze is overcome in metaxological awareness.

There can be no doubt that this may give rise to some nervousness among, for instance, theologians who have arrived at a perspective that tends to be more determinate. Scientists and others with more literalistic inclinations are likely to be even more nervous. However, we should remember that the metaxological sense of being does not rid us of all determinacy. It does not denigrate the lessons of univocity, equivocity, and dialectic. It awakens us to the ways in which being is genuinely other to thought; it demands the subservience of univocity, equivocity, and dialectic to transcendence. It is for God to be absolute, not for us. We interpret things in accordance with the contingent being that we ourselves are. We interpret things as relative to things and, ultimately, as relative to God. The metaxological sense of being is not equal to the equivocal sense of being. It wrestles, or perhaps dances, with God and angels and the created order to deepen dialogue. The metaxological is *interested—inter esse*. We are meant for adventure. We are meant for a home. We are meant for God.

In the preceding pages, keeping in mind our tendency to forget being, I have attempted to build a telescope of sorts by lining up several lenses that help us to better see what Chesterton is up to. Through William Desmond's work, I highlighted Chesterton's metaxological posture towards being as seeking to maintain the tension between home and adventure. It attends to the between in its limitations and frictions, taking into account

---

19. Nietzsche, *Beyond Good and Evil*, §193.

the univocal, equivocal, and dialectical postures while admiring the limitations of immediacy and self-mediation. I highlighted the importance of intermediation in being true to reality. Apart from considering its wider implications for metaphysics, if we are not mindful of intermediation, we are likely to fall into the trap of wrongly regarding Chestertonian prescience as siding with some overly self-confident science of history. After discussing Desmond's fourfold in relation to Chesterton, I turned to Plato. Through Plato, I stressed Chesterton's attention to ideals and ideas, as echoes of the first and ultimate cause of being. For Chesterton, God accounts for things best. It is through the ideas in God's mind that God orders the world, and it is our task to know these ideas and to know the one in whom these ideas originate and cohere. Unfortunately, for various reasons, people misinterpret God's design. And yet the very intelligibility of anything, even of what goes against God's good design and his divine ideas, is only possible against the backdrop of the ideal. Distortions of things rely on a sense, articulated or not, of the proportions of things. Chesterton assumes no Utopia in his attention to the idea but he insists on the possibility of thinking of things according to what is right. He insists that the best way to know what is wrong is to know what is right first.

Through Aristotle, I attended to Chesterton's mindfulness of the various dimensions of causation. In connecting Chesterton to Aristotle's fourfold nexus, I have clarified the intertwining and tense togetherness of mind and being, and especially how the different facets of causality blend somewhat together. We cannot artificially separate the material, efficient, final, and formal causes without generating a wrongheaded view of how to account for what is happening in the happening of being. Keeping in mind Desmond's metaxology and Plato's doctrine of participation, the idea in all this has been to encourage and retain a somewhat loose and playful perception, one that is not too rigid in its analytic of being and can therefore make room for the imagination; our viewpoint must allow for intuitions and insights that transcend detailed and careful analysis, even while attending closely to what is going on. In all of this, however, the precise role of paradox in formal causality was not yet as fully articulated as it needed to be, even if I had gestured towards the importance of keeping paradox in mind. Although I had covered certain conceptual tools, like parallelism, up to this point, which partially explained some of Chesterton's predictions, I had not yet detailed how we might be mindful of the multifacetedness of the formal cause. If Aristotle asks us to home in on the causes of individual changes, another way of attending, echoing Desmond's metaxological posture, could allow for a more expansive sense of the interplay of various other causal relations.

For this reason, I brought the work of Marshall McLuhan into the conversation. McLuhan's tetrad allows us to see how mediations both give and take away, how they retrieve the past and flip into their opposites in the future when taken to the extreme. McLuhan allows us to retain the specificity of the Aristotelian perspective while also allowing us to widen our gaze somewhat. Much of what McLuhan notices is an echo, a retrieval, of Chesterton's intuitive attunement to formal causality. With the above in mind, I should mention, however, that it would be wrong to consider each of the lenses supplied by each of the philosophers discussed above as implying that Chesterton's attunement to formal causation is found only in the articulated. In truth, I have made an attempt here to articulate what is largely implicit. What I have parsed out is evident in Chesterton's work as simultaneous; his perception of the details was in keeping with a peripheral vision of the whole. Anyhow, in the end, to put this Chestertonian telescope to the eye, having adjusted and polished the lenses with the help of other thinkers, is not to see the lenses themselves. What we see, what we *hopefully* see, is what Chesterton wants us to see, namely *the truth*. This is only possible, and the main reason for this book, if we restore to its rightful place, against certain modern misunderstandings, the vital importance of the formal cause. Chesterton's sense of the formal cause, I have argued, is what granted him a clearer perception of the world; it is what allowed him to guess, with profound perspicacity, what might happen next.

In the exploration of formal causation, causality emerges primarily as a concern with intelligibility. This is not say, however, that we can reduce causation to only what we understand. Certainly, events and qualities, as figures, can be said to have been caused when brought into being by a certain pattern or configuration, an actualizing ground, within the drama of being; and my stress on formal causation, especially evident in my analysis of Chesterton's fondness for parallelism, suggests that certain synchronicities and acausal elements, including miracles and revelations, may also likely be present. Any prediction, when rooted in a sound understanding of principles and causes, remains, in a certain sense, a guess; this is so even if the guess happens to prove right. Chesterton's prescience gestures to the future actions and activities of people whose actions are not necessarily reducible to the rational, and inevitably include non-rational and irrational elements. People in the future may, for instance, repeat the errors of their ancestors without knowing it, simply because they are caught in a similar pattern of thought and action. To perceive a relation—which is necessary for accounting for any given thing, which is what causality is all about—does not mean we can fully articulate everything about the nature and meaning of that relation, as Chesterton clearly understood. If I say, echoing St. Thomas, that the formal cause of the incarnation is God's care of man, I cannot therefore conclude that I have come close to fully comprehending or even appreciating God's care of man. I have seen something but not everything in the between.

Before I summarize and conclude my reflections on Chesterton's prescience, I want to pay attention to two ideas that further articulate his attunement to formal causation. The first comes from Plato in the form of his idea of *reminiscence* or *anamnesis*, also translated as *recollection*. The second comes from Søren Kierkegaard in the form of his pseudo-metaphysical notion of *repetition*. Regarding the first, Plato suggests the idea in his *Meno* and *Phaedo* as a way to overcome the paradox of knowledge.[20] The paradox concerns how it is possible to be certain of how we can seek out what we do not apparently know. This paradox is not irrelevant to the question of how we might anticipate certain future happenings. It is one thing to anticipate a discovery that is in keeping with one's expectations but can the soul be taken by surprise?[21] This is not about novelty-seeking; it is about being surprised by the truth.

The answer suggested by Plato is that a moment of encounter recalls what was already somewhat known. In this way, the anticipation is fulfilled. But more than that, in the moment of encounter, the anticipation of discovery is suddenly and dramatically reframed. To put it paradoxically, the effect precedes and adjusts the cause just as the cause reveals the effect. The future, or perhaps the present, transforms and reveals the past. Thus, even while the anticipation is answered, it is also surprised. The anticipation, which was incomplete in itself, is completed. Contact with reality occurs in the encounter and involves both grasping and being grasped by what we are attending to. True knowing does not dissolve the between but sustains it. The desire for home and the desire for adventure are not conflated, therefore, but are supported in their difference. The same applies to the cruciform intersection of horizontal and vertical orders; we grasp the world as we are grasped by it and know God as we are known by him. However, knowledge can be distorted by memory, and especially by grief, as both Chesterton and Kierkegaard notice.[22] Sometimes our recollecting is indistinguishable from mourning, given our capacity for forgetting even while remembering. For this reason, the second idea may be of some value for better understanding Chesterton's attunement to formal causality.

Kierkegaard offers the idea of *repetition* as an antidote to the mourning that may accompany reminiscence. He sees repetition as having the same

---

20. Schindler, *Catholicity of Reason*, 39.
21. Schindler, *Catholicity of Reason*, 39.
22. Chesterton, *Autobiography*, 44.

movement as reminiscence, only it occurs in a different temporal direction.[23] Reminiscence looks back and therefore risks falling into a state of nostalgia or regret. Things are now not as they once were. Repetition, however, looks forward and attempts to ask what of the present can be gathered up and repeated non-identically in and for the future. This is an act of love that seeks to endlessly renew and rejuvenate "old clothing" so that it fits always perfectly comfortably.[24] If reminiscence tends to focus more on knowing, repetition stresses will, although it does not thereby usurp knowing.[25] If reminiscence, as an act of faith, has nothing to lose and only much to gain, repetition, as an act of hoping, risks loss.[26] If reminiscence tarries more with the actual, repetition lingers on the possible; on what does not necessarily conform to self-mediation.[27] Repetition seeks to accommodate and transpose what is recalled into a different key, one that takes into account the way the world changes.[28] It is artful and creative, which is to say it does not conform to any formula.[29] But repetition does not mean exact mechanical reproduction.[30] Difference emerges even within the realm of identity. Each repetition requires a moment of truth and decision. It demands a response and responsibility. Every repetition is, in a way, a crisis. It concerns how an ideal may be incarnated and given concrete form.

Arguably, there is no need to choose between reminiscence and repetition. In a way, they are, as even Kierkegaard intimates, the same idea. The suggestion that the two can be neatly split up by categorizing them as having different orientations in time potentially forgets that our sense of time is not as neat and tidy as it appears on a calendar or timeline. Time folds in on itself. As much as the past shapes the future, our sense of the future shapes the past. Our anticipations inform our receptivity in the present. Still, it can be illuminating to consider how reminiscence and repetition play off each other in much the same way that extension, obsolescence, retrieval, and reversal play off each other. Repetition is a non-identical repetition of reminiscence; it reveals a certain posture towards the given. It happens also to be an idea entertained by Chesterton, who does not choose between reminiscence and repetition. He asks us to recollect a great deal and also

---

23. Kierkegaard, *Repetition & Philosophical Crumbs*, 3.
24. Kierkegaard, *Repetition & Philosophical Crumbs*, 3.
25. Kierkegaard, *Repetition & Philosophical Crumbs*, 4.
26. Kierkegaard, *Repetition & Philosophical Crumbs*, 8.
27. Kierkegaard, *Repetition & Philosophical Crumbs*, 20.
28. Kierkegaard, *Repetition & Philosophical Crumbs*, 22.
29. Kierkegaard, *Repetition & Philosophical Crumbs*, 24.
30. Kierkegaard, *Repetition & Philosophical Crumbs*, 27.

invites us to ponder what sort of future we want to create. However, we must consider, as Chesterton does, how what might be repeated is not the ideal repetition, which retains a strong link to the truth in the way that reminiscence does. If perhaps also non-identically, false remembrances, mistaken identities, and the like may be repeated. Lies, always parasitic on the truth and how the truth functions, may also be recapitulated. If at one time and place, it has been illegal not to smile in public, for instance, such a prohibition (a certain figure) may resurface at another time and place, given certain contextual factors (a certain discernible ground, shaped by the organizing principle, form, or law of the situation). If specific social conditions are sufficiently replicated, it would make sense to make some kind of prediction, although we ought to be careful to note aspects of non-identity in the play of identities. The question nevertheless remains: what do we *want* repeated, given what we can remember?

If the future turns out the same as the present, only more so in its plodding adherence to various shaky gestures of decline or progress, we can be sure that we have fallen asleep to the world we are in. Gently gesturing to the many silly predictions of his friend H. G. Wells in the book *Anticipations* (1901),[31] Chesterton suggests that we can be sure that we have "lost faith in revolutions."[32] But what sort of revolution does Chesterton want? He suggests the need for an eternal revolution.[33] About this revolution, he declares that we need a fixed ideal, provided by Christianity, which is also an "artistically combined" ideal.[34] The ideal should also be a lofty one, capable of inspiring in us a desire of Utopia or, better, heaven. It does us no good to be progressive if this presumes an impossible hope for betterment apart from an ideal.[35] Being progressive does not stop anything from getting worse. Without a fixed, picturesque, lofty ideal, you can always claim that things in general are getting better even if they are not, just as you can claim that things in general are getting worse, even if they are not. What are we measuring ourselves by? What form are we, and should we be, conforming to?

It is no good to be conservative, if conservatism means leaving things as they are. If you "leave a thing alone you leave it to a torrent of change. If you leave a white post alone it will soon be a black post."[36] What is needed is a healthy combination of reminiscence and repetition, and Chesterton

---

31. Clark, *G. K. Chesterton*, 12.
32. Chesterton, *Napoleon of Notting Hill & The Man Who Was Thursday*, 16.
33. Chesterton, *Collected Works, Volume 1*, 307–28.
34. Chesterton, *Collected Works, Volume 1*, 320.
35. Chesterton, *Collected Works, Volume 1*, 320.
36. Chesterton, *Collected Works, Volume 1*, 321.

suggests such a combination in his conception of a revolution. A revolution combines wise understanding and willful determination to ensure that the best of the past is recovered and repeated for the sake of a better future. Chesterton preempts this idea in a theological mode and in the process further links recollection with repetition. He suggests that the fall of man means that "every man has forgotten who he is."[37] He goes on: "All that we call common sense and rationality and practicality and positivism only means that for certain dead levels of our life we forget that we have forgotten. All that we call spirit and art and ecstasy only means that for one awful instant we remember that we forget."[38] It is to the latter that Chesterton devotes much of his energy. He wants us to remember, in gratitude, the many good gifts we are given. Even repetitions in nature suggest something willful. Children can tolerate endless repetitions because they possess abundant vitality. If grown-ups fail to do the same, it is because they are probably "not strong enough to exult in monotony."[39] The innocent child is a reminder of the innocence of God, who similarly may make "every daisy separately" because he "has never got tired of making them."[40] Nature's repetitions are an encore. God wants the show to go on because it is his show.

By weaving recollection and repetition together using the thread of gratitude, Chesterton mocks modern worshippers of cause and effect. He suggests that what we may see so often as separate events—first cause and then effect—are very likely simply mental connections. Cause and effect are not as separate or as linear as moderns may want them to be. In the natural sciences, for instance, we find many logical identities and relations. However, science cannot give us realities.[41] Chesterton wants to restore to us a sense that causality is not separate from the haloing of the world. We see this more clearly when we start to notice, as I have attempted to show throughout this book, that causality is relational and so seeks out complementarity and conformity to form. This means, among other things, and perhaps surprisingly, that there is no incontestable relation, logically speaking, between causation and prediction. What is necessary is the relation between beings and their ground; and the true ground of all things is God. When we find patterns in the world, the point is not to pridefully assume that we can therefore know how things will turn out. Ultimately, the aim is to know God. We ought to "cheat the prophet," in the sense of refusing to treat as inevitable what is only

37. Chesterton, *Collected Works, Volume 1*, 257.
38. Chesterton, *Collected Works, Volume 1*, 257.
39. Chesterton, *Collected Works, Volume 1*, 264.
40. Chesterton, *Collected Works, Volume 1*, 264.
41. Jaki, *Chesterton*, 26.

possible.[42] We ought to attempt to live in keeping with the principles of faith and faithful reason. We should do this because we ought to be faithful to the God on whose behalf the prophet, Gilbert Keith Chesterton, speaks.

Chestertonian Prescience

"The one really rousing thing about human history," says Chesterton, is that "the prophecies always go wrong. The promises are never fulfilled and the threats are never fulfilled"[43] Even "when good things do happen, they are never the good things that were guaranteed. And even when bad things happen, they are never the bad things that were inevitable."[44] If a pessimist claims that his country is going to the dogs, it is almost certain that it will go to any other animal except "the dogs."[45] It may go, symbolically speaking, to ducks, lions, or dragons. This may come across as a somewhat perplexing assertion when read towards the end of a book that examines Chesterton's penchant for prediction and even considers his self-conscious references to his predictions as prophecies. We know now, after all, that many of his prophecies were right. At first, what he says above would seem to upend my aim here to explore and explain Chesterton's prescience by his attention to formal causality. But such a conclusion would be too hasty. My focus has not been on the question of what we can expect to happen next; my focus has been on what Chesterton is doing in asking the question of what is going to happen next. What we find is a metaphysics that does not invoke a neat vector pointing to a clear outcome. Its point is not merely predictive. Chesterton encourages us to account for the world of meaning that we inhabit. We need to come into contact with reality. We need wisdom. As I have already suggested, Chesterton's predictions often function less to pinpoint a specific result or possibility than to engage the imagination of his readers to further consider the implications of what he is talking about.

In his predictions, Chesterton's intention remains to be true to being, which is something one can do in jest as well as in all seriousness, with playful analogies as well as more focused and deliberate ones. In brief, it is in the very nature of Chestertonian prescience to suggest that we come to terms with formal causation. What he demonstrates for us is a desire to do this in the profoundest way possible. Prescience is a byproduct of an immersive engagement with the world, through body, mind, and spirit. Where it hits the

---

42. Chesterton, *Napoleon of Notting Hill & The Man Who Was Thursday*, 9.
43. Chesterton, *Illustrated London News*, 17 April 1926.
44. Chesterton, *Illustrated London News*, 17 April 1926.
45. Chesterton, *Illustrated London News*, 17 April 1926.

nail on the head, we see how deep the engagement goes. Indeed, one might reasonably contend that Chesterton did not predict the future; he reported what he saw in his time, given that he was paying particularly close attention to it, sometimes exaggerating it slightly to highlight certain incongruities, absurdities, and possibilities. He noted, often by analogy, that what starts as a spark in a forest in the present may give rise to a forest fire later. Perhaps he did this to help his audience to see more clearly what was already going on. One consequence of this is that we can often, through Chesterton, see more clearly what is going on right now.

Whatever view we may conclude with regarding Chesterton's prescience, especially with respect to its relevance to our own situations, whether local or global, we should be clear on what he thought of attempts to draw lessons from futures that did not yet exist. We should be clear, for instance, that he did not take his forecasts of the weather of the future very seriously. There is an equivocation in his pronouncements on possibility. This was inevitable given his posture towards the world in general. He never claimed to know the future with univocal certainty. It is not unreasonable to think, therefore, that he had some other purpose in mind while making his predictions. One likely aim was that he was generating ephemeral, trifling figures, miniature comparisons and anti-environments, through which his readers might be able to more clearly perceive the environment in its present condition. If the world is in "permanent danger of being misjudged," as Chesterton claims, we need to find ways to judge it rightly.[46] If the world is in danger of becoming invisible to us, we need to find ways to see it more clearly. It is no wonder Chesterton would seek to relativize all prophesying. The ultimate point is not to grasp the objective ends of things as being somehow separate from our own participation in reality. We are as much a part of the formal cause as things supposedly out there beyond us.

Elsewhere, Chesterton wonders "why the game of Scientific Prophecy has become so dull and stale. Why does not some liar say something fresh and fanciful about the future of humanity, instead of going on perpetually repeating that things will be as they are, only more so?"[47] People may predict that we will soon be on Mars. Many people from the past would be shocked to discover that we are not there already. But to Chesterton, this is similar to saying that we will soon find ourselves in Margate, only more so. So much prediction is, as he recognizes, rooted in a belief that the future is a plagiarism of the present, albeit with minor tweaks of scale and proportion. In one sense, this is right. Just having a "good general knowledge

---

46. Chesterton, *Defendant*, 24.
47. Chesterton, *Illustrated London News*, 23 June 1932.

of science, or even a good general knowledge of social tendencies, will tell anybody of sufficiently sound judgment what practical problems men are likely to attack next, and in what department their success will probably be nearest."[48] In an article from the early 1930s, Chesterton declares that no "supernatural inspiration" was needed "to say that television would certainly be attempted, and probably achieved" quite a while before it was attempted and achieved.[49] The problem is in assuming that prescience merely involves identifying and exaggerating certain possibilities already evident from certain actualities. For Chesterton, this amounts to developing foresight that "can only predict one sort of thing."[50] This is the sort of foresight that was popular in his own time.

In the end, Chesterton was not interested in looking only at technological improvements and developments. He was not interested, in other words, in figures at the expense of the ground. He wanted to know the form and not only the content. This is why he could speculate about the possibility that the future may also involve developments in "good manners" and an appreciation for "epic and heroic poetry."[51] Indeed, in our time, we have seen many such developments, even if the mass of culture is more concerned with fancies and fads. Again, it is important to remember Chesterton's refusal of historicism. He never claimed to know the inner meaning of history. He was acutely aware that history is replete with contingencies. What happens at any given moment depends on more things than we can account for. What may happen in the future can therefore never be made completely certain. This awareness would banish any thought that Chesterton's prescience was rooted in egotistical certainty. He would have been untroubled by early Christian teachings about the potential for the idolatry of omen-seeking.[52] He was not trying to be right about what was going to happen but about how we might reorient ourselves around the good.

In the above, Chesterton is not denouncing prophecies in total. He is not declaring the end of all prophesying. We find that he wants to question any expectation of exactness in prophesying in much the same way that he wants to throw into question any scientific expectation that we ought to write in literalisms only when writing poetry. Prophecies do not generally achieve univocal precision and perhaps our expectation of any such precision should be questioned. Being includes ambiguities. And so, if we predict

---

48. Chesterton, *Illustrated London News*, 23 June 1932.
49. Chesterton, *Illustrated London News*, 23 June 1932.
50. Chesterton, *Illustrated London News*, 23 June 1932.
51. Chesterton, *Illustrated London News*, 23 June 1932.
52. Stewart-Sykes, *On the Two Ways*, 37; Didache, ch. 3.

that China should expect a revolution in the fairly near future, say, or that biotechnologies will make it possible to resurrect extinct animals, or that the abuse of employees by employers will return as a matter of course, we cannot be certain how such things will play out—even if such things could happen, given what is happening in the world today. The future doesn't exist; not yet.

Chesterton's prescience, as with what he thinks of as ideal poetry, is part of a holistic way of mediating the world. Time, as we experience it in our real lives, is enfolded on itself. We do not experience past, present, and future in linear fashion. On closer inspection, it becomes evident that our experience of time is filled with overlaps. Past and future are folded into the present and unfold in the present.[53] In a sense, the past is created for us by our encounter with an imaginary future. When I look ahead at what could happen, it is this act of looking ahead that poses a question to the past that has shaped me. As the question is posed, I cannot avoid considering how to answer it in the present. The future shapes how my past is lived out right now. I once imagined that at some point in the future this book would be completed, and now it is. The effect preceded the cause. Consider, for instance, the much more common experience of wanting to leave your office at work and return home after a day filled with astounding and wondrous banalities. The forecast opens up a possibility and shapes actuality, because actuality can be shaped by such a forecast. Even where a forecast is wrong, it calls us beyond the present and the past into unrealized possibilities. The future molds history. One might even say it *causes* history, even if only partially.

As this suggests, our experience of time is an experience of constantly reframing the world. We may therefore find ourselves in a state of nostalgic reverie from time to time, or absentmindedly pondering what might happen in the future. We may not always be present to the present. Prescience, as a phenomenon, suggests that it is impossible to completely separate from the past or the present. This is another way to say that prescience is not as much about prediction as we may initially assume it is; instead, as I have endeavored to argue in this book, it is another expression of mediation. As such, it always raises the question of *relevance*. I cannot help but notice, in this regard, that many who call attention to Chesterton's remarkable prescience do so to highlight how what he is saying is pertinent for us today. If at one time Chesterton's voice was growing softer, it is a striking feature of our time that his voice is now so widely recognized as worth listening to now. He is more relevant now as a metaphysician than he used to be as a journalist.

---

53. Merleau-Ponty, *Phenomenology of Perception*, 434.

But there is something else we need to consider, namely that Chesterton's world may not have been so different from our own as we may sometimes suppose. Perhaps chronological snobbery is endemic nowadays such that it is easy to think that more has changed than has changed. Still, Chesterton remains relevant to us, just as Shakespeare or Homer or the Christian tradition remain relevant. They offer counter-environments through which we might gain a clearer sense of our own environment.

In any case, declaring the end of prophecies would be futile. We are all soothsayers and predictors and prophets of a kind, if only middling ones. We naturally, almost instinctively, cast ourselves into the future, even if it is only the very near future. Sometimes the future appears to us like a dream or an atmosphere, a feeling of something approaching, whether to welcome or threaten us. We all wonder about what's going to happen next or what we plan to do next. We all have dreams and fears for ourselves and for those we love. Even the fact that we set up schedules and calendars is indicative of this capacity. However, our fortune-telling is not always so neatly formalized. Everything we do involves looking ahead in time, not just the more organizational aspects of our lives. We imagine and guess and plan. We intuit and hypothesize. We build our ordinary experiences on conjecture. We throw ourselves ahead of ourselves. We may even cast ourselves into the lifetimes of others who will live long after we are gone. But we cannot know for certain what is not yet. Our plans for the future are, at best, written in sand and not stone.[54]

The philosopher Martin Heidegger paid close attention to this ability and how it illuminates something of the nature of human experience. He called it *projection*.[55] At a glance, it might seem that we are the products of the past, living in the present, and orientated towards the future. As I have already noted, we fairly easily consider our experience of time as broken up into segments: what was is followed by what is, which is followed by what will be. But this does not capture our experience. At best, it points to how we think of time abstractly, after we have forgotten the experience. We tend to represent time chronologically but the representation is not the hermeneutical reality. To exist, as Heidegger holds, means to be continuously confronted with the possible. And it is through confronting possibility, always shimmering with equivocities, that we make decisions about how to live.

Considering the future always means considering what we decide in the present. What happens shows up more clearly for us because of what is yet to be. This fact affects and shapes us at every moment of our lives. How

---

54. James 4:13–16.
55. Heidegger, *Being and Time*, 185–88.

we live depends on what sort of future we find imaginable. But this capacity for pondering the future—this mode of being that Heidegger calls *projection*—is not just about the concrete particulars of daily life. When we think of what could be, we are not restricted to pondering only the things we have immediate access to. We are prone to wondering what life itself is and ought to be. This is manifest also in how our view of the past is transformed by the present. This can help us to see that Chesterton's prescience is not merely projection. It reflects an incarnational mode of awareness. This is why his attention to formal causality takes up more pages in this book than his predictions about the future. The real question is, how can we enact the giant humility of the incarnation and descend into the flesh to become human?

In keeping with his distrust of univocal exactness, Chesterton was ready for his predictions to be proven wrong. "Like all healthy-minded prophets," Chesterton writes in *Utopia for Usurers* (1917), "I can only prophesy when I am in a rage and think things look ugly for everybody. And like all healthy-minded prophets, I prophesy in the hope that my prophecy may not come true."[56] In *The Well and the Shallows* (1935), he writes, "The world is what the saints and the prophets saw it was; it is not merely getting better or merely getting worse; there is one thing that the world does; it wobbles. Left to itself, it does not get anywhere; though if helped by real reformers of the right religion and philosophy, it may get better in many respects, and sometimes for considerable periods."[57] As this suggests, Chesterton is clear that "in itself," the world cannot merely be thought of as "progress" or even as any mere "process."[58] It cannot be understood along the lines of mere cause and effect because the destiny of the world is bound up in the shape of human life. It is up to us to search for this shape as Gabriel Syme searches for, and eventually finds, Sunday; and as Job searches for, and eventually finds, God.[59]

A Chestertonian Renascence

In his short story, *A Descent into the Maelstrom* (1841), Edgar Allan Poe tells the story of a sailor who, after a fishing expedition went horribly wrong, ends up in desperate danger out at sea. His fishing boat gets caught in the powerful death grip of a seething, swirling mass of water. In the midst of this maelstrom, his doom becomes clear to him. "Our progress downward, at

---

56. Chesterton, *Collected Works, Volume 5*, 405.
57. Chesterton, *Well and the Shallows*, 35.
58. Chesterton, *Well and the Shallows*, 35.
59. See Chesterton, *Man Who Was Thursday*.

each revolution," says the sailor, "was slow, but very perceptible."[60] He is surrounded by fragments also caught up in the velocity of the vortex, "masses of building timber and trunks to trees, with many smaller articles, such as pieces of furniture, broken boxes, barrels, and staves."[61] Surprising himself, however, he accepts his death and in an instant is unburdened of all fear. He starts to look for amusement. He begins to speculate about the various velocities at play in the maelstrom. Given the slowness of his descent and the unexpected time he has to look carefully at what is going on around him, he starts to predict what will happen to some of those fragments and then tests the rightness of his predictions. Suddenly, amusement gives way to hope. He sees, right there in the midst of all that chaos, that there are clues that point to the possibility of survival. Patience welcomes insight.

He sees that some things disappear into the maelstrom. But there are also things that reappear. He notices a pattern of death and resurrection, a pattern of absorption and expulsion, as some things dip down into the abyss, while others are yielded up. This, he explains, is directly related to noticing the "forms" of things.[62] Some things, because of their specific forms, are destined for a watery grave. Others, because of their forms, are destined to stay afloat. He comes to believe that if he attaches himself to those things that reappear, he will be saved. This requires him to abandon the ship, so this is what he does. As McLuhan suggests while reflecting on this tale, the man lives because of an act of pattern recognition. He sees the forms of things and understands the form of the environment and so finds a way to endure. "By studying the patterns of the effects of this huge vortex of energy in which we are involved," writes McLuhan, "it may be possible to program a strategy of evasion and survival."[63]

It is not difficult to see through this story a symbol that is more than relevant to our times. We live in a particularly turbulent age. We live in an age of metacrisis, in the midst of a crisis of meaning. We find ourselves looking at not just one or two but many problems and concerns, at almost every level of life, at varying degrees of scale. The world can seem to us like that maelstrom in Poe's story. Signs of precarity around us crackle with negative possibilities. They may give way at any moment to a destructive force that will drag us down, away from light, love, and laughter. Yes, there are richer values than mere survival, which is the apparent focus of Poe's story. Bare life is never the point of life. However, a similar kind of attention to what we

60. Poe, *Tales of Mystery and Imagination*, 98.
61. Poe, *Tales of Mystery and Imagination*, 98.
62. Poe, *Tales of Mystery and Imagination*, 99.
63. McLuhan, *Understanding Me*, 285.

find exemplified in that sailor could make a difference to us. We might see not only a chance of surviving but also of fullness and flourishing. What we see depends on what we are looking for, as well as how we go about looking for it. While I have been working on this book, there have been wars and rumors of war, constant outbreaks of protest and upheaval, a global pandemic, unusually vicious political squabbles, polarizations, both global and local economic instabilities, and more. This age can be interpreted as an age of anxiety, anger, and catastrophe, even while so many conditions around the world have improved. It may well be an age of burnout and malaise.[64] In my own lifetime, a sense of imminent collapse has increasingly grown. Decline is in the air, even if it is not the only air we breathe.

Most obviously, liberalism, the dominant ideology of the West, is somehow both, if the mixed metaphor might be excused, a maelstrom and a sinking ship. We are in a world of troubles, personal, social, environmental, economic, and spiritual. And what we are to make of various vortices and sinking ships in our time is perhaps not so easy to discern. How this maelstrom-like environment of ours functions is not self-evident. Many of us are wondering, understandably, where today's happenings will lead in the future. How are things going to turn out given what is going on now? The future is mixed up in the present. It hides, waiting to emerge, waiting to reveal how it was already evident. Should we be worried? Should we be hopeful? Even if pessimism dominates our age, perhaps there are reasons to see more positive possibilities. There are, after all, many signs of good things, positive happenings that reflect the claims of a Christian hope. Even Poe's sailor finds hope in the midst of an awful situation and many of us are hardly in a worse position than he was. It would be tragic if we notice only what sinks into the maelstroms of our time and not what emerges. All is not doom and gloom. But we need to be able to see more clearly what spells disaster and what spells blessing. We need to know what to hold onto.

While reflecting on a different shipwreck to Poe's, albeit with a related meaning, Chesterton sees in it a symbol of civilization. He recognizes the risk of using such a terrible event, the sinking of the RMS Titanic in April of 1912, in this case, as an analogy. It was a tragedy only a month old in the minds and hearts of people when Chesterton's first reflection on the event was published. But there is something in the story he feels his readers should be aware of. The sinking of a supposedly unsinkable ship is an image of how easy it is to mistake size for invulnerability. "Our whole civilisation is indeed very like the *Titanic*; alike in its power and its impotence, its security and its

---

64. See Han, *Burnout Society*.

insecurity."[65] There were obvious technical problems that caused the ship to sink, not just the lifeboat shortage. Characteristically, Chesterton's concern was not with mere logistics and mechanics. "Quite apart from the question of whether anyone was to blame," writes Chesterton, "the big outstanding fact remains: that there was no sort of proportion for luxury and levity and the extent of the provision for need and desperation. The scheme did far too much for prosperity and far too little for distress—just like the modern State."[66] This is the essence of the sunken ship as a symbol. It speaks of a failure of perception and intellect. We attend to specific figures, but we miss the ground. Wonderful and terrible things will happen in life. It matters that we are receptive to understanding them.

Chesterton notices a world around him growing weary of considering proportions. It is a world that forgets the forms of things and the forms of the environment. It is a world in the throes of forgetting that we are never just dealing with impersonal things like ships and lifeboats and the separation of social classes. We are always dealing with meanings. We are dealing with organizing principles and laws of situations. We are dealing with what people make of the truth. We are all governed not only by what we think but by what we choose to think about, by what we choose not to think about, and "the sights that sink into us day by day colour our minds with every tint between insolence and terror."[67] Poe's hero sees patterns in the maelstrom. He attunes himself to the environment, and this ensures his salvation. In contrast, the Titanic promoters and builders were overly self-assured and failed to attune themselves to those things hidden in the shadowy depths of the environment. This was to invite doom. When faced with a crisis like that of a sinking ship or even the mere possibility of a sinking civilization, what should we be considering? What should we be on the lookout for? Is there a way to avoid being dragged down by the vortex? Is there a possibility of a new renascence?

A clue to answering such questions is found in another reflection by Chesterton on a different shipwreck. The image of the wreckage did not always disconcert him. To him, a shipwreck can even hint, as it does even in the case of the Titanic, at a "poetry of limits" and the "wild romance of prudence."[68] He draws attention to Daniel Defoe's novel *Robinson Crusoe* (1719). The "best thing about the book," writes Chesterton, "is simply the

---

65. Chesterton, *Illustrated London News*, 11 May 1912.
66. Chesterton, *Illustrated London News*, 11 May 1912.
67. Chesterton, *Illustrated London News*, 11 May 1912.
68. Chesterton, *Collected Works, Volume 1*, 267.

list of things saved from the wreck. The greatest of poems is an inventory."[69] Crusoe ends up with only a few minor comforts to support him on that island in the form of those things he manages to salvage from the ship he was sailing on. Chesterton uses this image to reflect on the world he lives in. He asks his reader to take notice of anything in one's environment and appreciate it as if it had been rescued from a sinking ship. Indeed, he says, everything has already been "saved from the wreck" of its own possible nonexistence.[70] At every moment, everything we are and perceive is called into being out of nothing. Everything hovers miraculously above the possibility of being absorbed into nonentity. The whole world might not have been, and yet here it is and here we are. Chesterton is astonished at this simple truth. In a way, he asks us to look not just at the vortex before us or the apparently sinking ship we are on but at the shape of reality itself. He asks more of us than Poe does and even more than Defoe does. We must see being itself emerge from the maelstrom. We must see things not just saved from a shipwreck but saved from nonbeing. After attending to this, we will be better able to notice what we have perhaps overlooked and need to restore to its rightful place. This becomes a clue to a specific attention to the world evident in all of Chesterton's writings.

While studying Chesterton's attention to the formal cause, it becomes clear that he is strongly motivated by a desire to clear away various modern habits of thought that mechanize perception. This is partly why he resists offering anything like a formula for how we ought to best interpret history or the present, as well as for how we might best discern what is likely to happen in the future. He is aware of a trend in his time to transform the world, and people along with it, into a machine. Such an eventuality results from speeding life up and narrowing and flattening perception to fit pre-decided formulas. Such a trend is still with us. Formal causation is therefore a symbol of his intention to recover a sense of the personal dimension of being through contemplation and a more open and creative mode of perceiving. Two concerns are implied by this. The one is, perhaps, mundane. We should be able to look at everyday happenings and comprehend something of the story they are telling. On the one hand, like Poe's sailor, we should do our best to understand the world we are in. We live within the realm of beings within which particular existences interact in various ways. We ought therefore to be able to perceive and interpret the signs of our times. On the other hand, we should see through things and their trivial meanings. We should see behind the face of things what is hidden and forgotten. This second

---

69. Chesterton, *Collected Works, Volume 1*, 267.
70. Chesterton, *Collected Works, Volume 1*, 267.

concern is of a higher order. It is the true aim of the first concern and does not negate the first concern. If anything, it points to its real value. Depth cries out to greater depth. To switch to a Platonic metaphor, the shadows recall and repeat the substance.

In this time of ours, especially, the greatest threat is arguably less in the turbulences of civilizational crisis than in the forgetting of the depths of being and the forgetting of the God from whom the gift of being originates. We may see the trees too easily while missing the forest, and we especially fail to notice the hidden roots of the forest that keep it standing, its branches raised like arms in praise of our Creator. Ours is an age of shallowness. This seems to underlie so many of the troubles we see around us. The richness of existence is too often traded for a world of smooth surfaces and instant gratifications. But we do not have to be stuck believing that the trend to flatten and literalize being cannot be reversed. We do not have to believe that we cannot return to a way of perceiving in which wonder is restored to its rightful place. Chesterton is proof of this. He proves that what we are looking for and how we look for it matters.

What sort of attention we pay to the world shapes what sort of world we find. We should be able to look at being itself, beyond the claims of specific beings, and wonder at what sort of world God has set up. Like the sailor in Poe's story and the sailor in Defoe's story, we should be able to look at little things and marvel at how they live in a drama of veiling and unveiling. And like Chesterton, who was always so appreciative of little things, we should also be able to marvel at being and how it plays against a backdrop of nonentity, given to us by God. We should be able to discern the signs of our times, as Chesterton did, but we should also, more importantly, be able to discover a vision of the signs that transcend the times. In this, there is a chance of being at the forefront of a new renascence, which retrieves that proclamation of repentance and renewal uttered by Christ.[71] We will be transformed, all the better to participate in transforming the world. Chesterton observes that the "Thing" that keeps emerging from various vortices and maelstroms, the "Thing" that keeps dying and rising from the dead, is what he simply calls "the Faith," which "gives a man back his body and his soul and his reason and his will and his very life."[72] It is Christianity, expressed in the Catholic tradition, in the bride of Christ, the body of Christ, the church. Of Catholicism, in particular, he says: "When the hammer hits the right nail on the head a hundred times, there comes a time when we

---

71. Matthew 4:17.

72. Chesterton, *Collected Works, Volume 3*, 145; Chesterton, *Everlasting Man*, 250–61.

think it was not altogether an accident."[73] And so he leaves the ship of modernity, which is doomed for a watery grave, and swims to grab hold of that bridge to life and redemption. He more than suggests that this is the way to live, in truths that have stood the many tests of the ages. We need to be rooted. As the Psalmist writes: "Blessed is the man that walketh not in the counsel of the ungodly, nor standeth in the way of sinners, nor sitteth in the seat of the scornful. But his delight is in the law of the Lord; and in his law doth he meditate day and night. And he shall be like a tree planted by the rivers of water, that bringeth forth his fruit in his season; his leaf also shall not wither; and whatsoever he doeth shall prosper."[74]

---

73. Chesterton, *Collected Works, Volume 3*, 190.
74. Psalm 1:1–3.

Bibliography

Agamben, Giorgio. *The Signature of All Things: On Method*. Translated by Luca D'Isanto and Kevin Attel. New York: Zone, 2009.
Ahlquist, Dale. *G. K. Chesterton: The Apostle of Common Sense*. San Francisco: Ignatius, 2003.
Ahmari, Sohrab. "Foreword." In *What's Wrong with the World*, by G. K. Chesterton, ix–xii. Manchester: Sophia Institute, 2021.
Armitage, Duane. *Philosophy's Violent Sacred*. East Lansing, MI: Michigan State University Press, 2021.
Aquinas, Thomas. *Selected Philosophical Writings*. Oxford: Oxford University Press, 1993.
Aristotle. *Metaphysics*. Translated by H. Lawson-Tancred. London: Penguin, 2004.
Barfield, Owen. *Poetic Diction: A Study in Meaning*. 3rd ed. Middletown, CT: Wesleyan University Press, 1973.
———. *Saving the Appearances: A Study in Idolatry*. 2nd ed. Middletown, CT: Wesleyan University Press, 1988.
Baudrillard, Jean. *The Perfect Crime*. Translated by Chris Turner. London: Verso, 2008.
———. *Simulacra and Simulation*. Translated by S. F. Glaser. Ann Arbor: University of Michigan, 1994.
Belloc, Joseph Hillaire. *The Great Heresies*. 1938. Reprint, San Francisco, 2017.
———. *On the Place of Gilbert Chesterton in English Letters*. London: Sheed & Ward, 1940.
Berenson, Alex. *Pandemia: How Coronavirus Hysteria Took Over Our Government, Rights, and Lives*. Washington, DC: Regnery, 2021.
Borges, Jorge Luis. *The Perpetual Race of Achilles and the Tortoise*. London: Penguin, 2010.
Boersma, Hans. *Heavenly Participation*. Grand Rapids: Eerdmans, 2011.
Brague, Rémi. *Curing Mad Truths: Medieval Wisdom for the Modern Age*. Catholic Ideas for a Secular World. Notre Dame: University of Notre Dame, 2019.

Cammaerts, Émile. *The Laughing Prophet: The Seven Virtues of G. K. Chesterton.* London: Metheuen, 1937.

Campbell, Bradley, and Jason Manning. *The Rise of Victimhood Culture: Microaggressions, Safe Spaces, and the New Culture Wars.* London: Palgrave Macmillan, 2018.

Chesterton, Cecil. *Gilbert K. Chesterton.* New York: Lane, 1909.

Chesterton, G. K. *Alarms and Discursions.* 1910. Reprint, London: Dodo, 2011.

———. *All Things Considered.* 1908. Reprint, Sioux Falls, SD: NuVision, 2009.

———. *All Is Grist: A Book of Essays.* New York: Dodd & Mead, 1932.

———. *The Annotated Innocence of Father Brown.* Edited by Martin Garner. Mineola, NY: Dover, 1998.

———. *Appreciations and Criticisms of the Works of Charles Dickens.* London: Dent and Sons, 1911.

———. *Autobiography.* 1936. Reprint, San Francisco: Ignatius, 2006.

———. *The Ball and the Cross.* 1910. Reprint, Nashville: Torode, 2010.

———. *Charles Dickens: A Critical Study.* London: Dodd & Mead, 1906.

———. *Chesterton Day by Day: The Wit and Wisdom of G. K. Chesterton.* Edited by Michael W. Perry. Seattle: Inkling, 2002.

———. *The Club of Queer Trades.* London: Hesperus, 2007.

———. *Collected Works, Volume 1: Heretics, Orthodoxy, The Blatchford Controversies.* San Francisco: Ignatius, 1986.

———. *Collected Works, Volume 3: The Catholic Church and Conversion, The Thing: Why I Am a Catholic, The Well and the Shallows, The Way of the Cross, and Others.* San Francisco: Ignatius, 1990.

———. *Collected Works, Volume 4: What's Wrong with the World, The Superstition of Divorce, Eugenics and Other Evils, and Others.* San Francisco: Ignatius, 1987.

———. *Collected Works, Volume 5: The Outline of Sanity, The End of the Armistice, Utopia of Usurers, and Others.* San Francisco: Ignatius, 1987.

———. *Collected Works, Volume 11: Plays, Chesterton on Shaw.* San Francisco: Ignatius, 1989.

———. *Collected Works, Volume 13: Father Brown Stories.* San Francisco: Ignatius, 2010.

———. *Collected Works, Volume 14: Short Stories, Fairy Tales, Mystery Stories, Illustrations.* San Francisco: Ignatius, 2012.

———. *Collected Works, Volume 20: Christendom in Dublin, Irish Imions, The New Jerusalem, A Short History of England.* San Francisco: Ignatius, 2001.

———. *Collected Works, Volume 21: What I Saw in America, The Resurrection of Rome, Sidelights.* San Francisco: Ignatius, 1990.

———. *Collected Works, Volume 27: The Illustrated London News, 1905–1907.* Edited by Lawrence J. Clipper. San Francisco: Ignatius, 1986.

———. *Collected Works, Volume 28: The Illustrated London News, 1908–1910.* Edited by Lawrence J. Clipper. San Francisco: Ignatius, 1987.

———. *Collected Works, Volume 29: The Illustrated London News, 1911–1913.* Edited by Lawrence J. Clipper. San Francisco: Ignatius, 1988.

———. *Collected Works, Volume 30: The Illustrated London News, 1914–1916.* Edited by Lawrence J. Clipper. San Francisco: Ignatius, 1988.

———. *Collected Works, Volume 31: The Illustrated London News, 1917–1919.* Edited by Lawrence J. Clipper. San Francisco: Ignatius, 1989.

---. *Collected Works, Volume 32: The Illustrated London News, 1920–922.* Edited by Lawrence J. Clipper. San Francisco: Ignatius, 1989.
---. *Collected Works, Volume 33: The Illustrated London News, 1923–1935.* Edited by Lawrence J. Clipper. San Francisco: Ignatius, 1990.
---. *Collected Works, Volume 34: The Illustrated London News, 1926–1928.* Edited by Lawrence J. Clipper. San Francisco: Ignatius, 1991.
---. *Collected Works, Volume 35: The Illustrated London News, 1929–1931.* Edited by Lawrence J. Clipper. San Francisco: Ignatius, 1991.
---. *Collected Works, Volume 36: The Illustrated London News, 1932–1934,* edited by Lawrence J. Clipper. San Francisco: Ignatius, 2011.
---. *Collected Works, Volume 37: The Illustrated London News, 1935–1936.* Edited by Lawrence J. Clipper. San Francisco: Ignatius, 2012.
---. *The Coloured Lands.* Edited by Maisie Ward. 1938. Reprint, Mineola: Dover, 2009.
---. *The Common Man.* New York: Sheed & Ward, 1950.
---. *The Defendant.* London: Dent & Sons, 1901.
---. *The End of the Armistice.* Edited by Frank Sheed. London: Sheed & Ward, 1940.
---. *Eugenics and Other Evils.* London: Cassell, 1922.
---. *The Everlasting Man.* 1925. Reprint, San Francisco: Ignatius, 1993.
---. *Father Brown: Selected Stories.* London: Collector's Library, 2003.
---. *G. F. Watts.* London: Duckworth, 1904.
---. *G. K. Chesterton at the Daily News: Literature, Liberalism, and Revolution, 1901–1913.* Vols. 1–8. Edited by Julia Stapleton. London: Routledge, 2012.
---. *In Defense of Sanity.* Edited by Dale Alquist et al. San Francisco: Ignatius, 2011.
---. *The Innocence of Father Brown.* New York: Dodd, Mead, and Company, 1911.
---. *Irish Impressions.* New York: Lane, 1919.
---. *Lunacy and Letters.* Edited by Dorothy Collins. London: Sheed and Ward, 1958.
---. *Manalive.* New York: Lane, 1912.
---. *The Man Who Was Orthodox.* Edited by A. L. Maycock. London: Dobson, 1963.
---. *The Man Who Was Thursday.* 1908. Reprint, San Francisco: Ignatius, 1999.
---. *A Miscellany of Men.* London: Methuen, 1912.
---. *The Napoleon of Notting Hill: The Man Who Was Thursday.* Peabody, MA: Hendrickson, 2011.
---. *The New Renascence: Thoughts on the Structure of the Future.* London: Omo, 2020.
---. *The Poet and the Lunatics.* 1929. Reprint, London: Dover, 2010.
---. *Saint Thomas Aquinas & Saint Francis of Assisi.* San Francisco: Ignatius, 2002.
---. *Selected Essays.* Edited by John Guest. 1936. Reprint, London: Collins, 1953.
---. *The Thing.* London: Sheed and Ward, 1929.
---. *Tolstoy.* http://www.gkc.org.uk/gkc//tolstoy.html.
---. *Tremendous Trifles.* 1909. Reprint, Mineola: Dover , 2007.
---. *Varied Types.* New York: Dodd & Mead, 1905.
---. *The Victorian Age in Literature.* New York: Holt, 1913.
---. *The Well and the Shallows.* 1935. Reprint, San Francisco: Ignatius, 2006.
---. *What's Wrong with the World.* 1910. Reprint, San Francisco: Ignatius, 1994.
---. *What's Wrong with the World.* Foreword by Sohrab Amari. Manchester: Sophia Institute, 2022.

Clark, Stephen R. L. *G. K. Chesterton: Thinking Backward, Looking Forward*. West Conshohocken, PA: Templeton Foundation, 2006.
Danchev, Alex. *100 Artists' Manifestos: From the Futurists to the Stuckists*. London: Penguin, 2011.
Davison, Andrew. *Participation in God*. Cambridge: Cambridge University Press, 2019.
Desmond, William. *Being and the Between*. New York: State University of New York Press, 1995.
———. *Desire, Dialectic, and Otherness: An Essay on Origins*. 2nd ed. Eugene, OR: Cascade, 2013.
———. *Ethics and the Between*. New York: State University of New York Press, 2001.
———. *God and the Between*. London: Wiley-Blackwell, 2008.
———. *The Intimate Universal: The Hidden Porosity Among Religion, Art, Philosophy, and Politics*. Insurrections: Critical Studies in Religion, Politics, and Culture. New York: Columbia University Press, 2016.
———. *Perplexity and Ultimacy: Metaphysical Thoughts from the Middle*. Albany: State University of New York Press, 1995.
———. *The William Desmond Reader*. Edited by Christopher Ben Simpson. New York: State University of New York Press, 2012.
Di Fuccia, Michael Vincent. *Owen Barfield: Philosophy, Poetry, and Theology*. Eugene, OR: Cascade, 2016.
Dupuy, Jean-Pierre. *How to Think About Catastrophe: Toward a Theory of Enlightened Doomsaying*. East Lansing, MI: Michigan State University Press, 2023.
Ellul, Jacques. *The Humiliation of the Word*. Translated by Joyce Main Hanks. Eugene, OR: Cascade, 1985.
Favale, Abigail. *The Genesis of Gender: A Christian Theory*. San Francisco: Ignatius, 2022.
Feser, Edward. *Five Proofs of the Existence of God*. San Francisco: Ignatius, 2017.
Fritzman, J. M. *Hegel*. Cambridge: Polity, 2014.
Galton, Francis. "On Men of Science, Their Nature and Their Nurture." *Proceedings of the Royal Institution of Great Britain*. 7 (1874) 227–36.
Gerson, Lloyd P. *Aristotle and Other Platonists*. Ithaca, NY: Cornell University Press, 2005.
Girard, René. *Evolution and Conversion*, London: Bloomsbury, 2020.
Grondin, Jean. *Introduction to Metaphysics*. Translated by Lukas Soderstrom. New York: Columbia University Press, 2012.
Haidt, Jonathan, and Gregory Lukianoff. *The Coddling of the American Mind*. London: Penguin, 2018.
Han, Byung-Chul. *The Burnout Society*. Translated by Erik Butler. Princeton: Princeton University Press, 2015.
———. *In the Swarm*. Translated by Erik Butler. Cambridge: MIT, 2017.
———. *Palliative Society*. Translated by Daniel Steuer. London: Polity, 2022.
———. *Psychopolitics*. Translated by Erik Butler. London: Verso, 2017.
———. *The Transparency Society*. Translated by Erik Butler. Princeton: Princeton University Press, 2015.
Harrington, Mary. *Feminism Against Progress*. Washington, DC: Regnery, 2023.
Hart, David Bentley. *The Experience of God: Being, Consciousness, Bliss*. New Haven: Yale University Press, 2013.

———. *The Hidden and the Manifest: Essays in Theology and Metaphysics.* Grand Rapids: Eerdmans, 2017.
———. *Tradition and Apocalypse.* Grand Rapids: Baker Academic, 2022.
Heidegger, Martin. *Being and Time.* Translated by John MacQuarrie and Edward Robinson. London: Harper Perennial, 1962.
———. *Poetry, Language, Thought.* Translated by Albert Hofstadter. London: Harper Perennial, 1971.
———. *The Question Concerning Technology and Other Essays.* London: Harper Perennial, 1977.
Hegel, G. W. F. *Phenomenology of Spirit.* Translated by A. V. Miller. Oxford: Oxford University Press, 1977.
Hofstadter, Douglas, and Emmanuel Sander. *Surfaces and Essences.* New York: Basic, 2013.
Huxley, Aldous. *Brave New World.* 1932. Reprint, London: HarperPerennial, 2006.
Illich, Ivan. *Limits to Medicine: Medical Nemesis: The Expropriation of Health.* London: Boyars, 2000.
Jaki, Stanley. *Chesterton: Seer of Science.* Pinckney, MI: Real View, 2001.
Jakobson, Roman. *Language in Literature.* New Haven: Belknap, 1987.
Jankunas, Gediminas. T. *The Dictatorship of Relativism: Pope Benedict XVI's Response.* New York: St. Paul's, 2011.
Jay, Martin. *Downcast Eyes: The Denigration of Vision in Twentieth-Century French Thought.* Berkeley: University of California Press, 1993.
Jung, C. G. *Psychological Types.* Translated by H. G. Baynes and R. F. C. Hull. London: Routledge, 2017.
———. *Synchronicity: An Acausal Principle.* Translated by R. F. C. Hull. Princeton: Princeton University Press, 2010.
Jünger, Friedrich Georg. *The Failure of Technology: Perfection Without Purpose.* Translated by F. D. Wieck. Hinsdale, IL: Regnery, 1949.
Jureidin, Jon, and Leemon B. McHenry. "The Illusion of Evidence-Based Medicine." *British Medical Journal* 376 (2022). doi: https://doi.org/10.1136/bmj.o702.
Kenner, W. H. *Paradox in Chesterton.* London: Sheed & Ward, 1948.
Kierkegaard, Søren. *Repetition & Philosophical Crumbs.* Translated by M. G. Piety. Oxford: Oxford World Classics, 2009.
Kim, Yung Suk. *Reading Jesus' Parables with Dao De Jing.* Eugene, OR: Resource, 2018.
Kołakowski, Leszek. *Why Is There Something Rather Than Nothing?* London: Penguin, 2004.
Lauer, Quentin. *G. K. Chesterton: Philosopher Without Portfolio.* New York: Fordham University Press, 1988.
Le Bon, Gustave. *The Crowd: A Study of the Popular Mind.* Macmillan: New York, 1896.
Legutko, Ryszard. *The Demon in Democracy: Totalitarian Temptations in Free Societies.* Translated by Teresa Adelson. New York: Encounter, 2016.
Lewis, C. S. *Essay Collection: Literature, Philosophy and Short Stories.* London: Harper Collins, 2000.
Liñán, Laura Trujillo. *Formal Cause in Marshall McLuhan's Thinking.* New York: Institute of General Semantics, 2022.
Mackey, Aidan. *G. K. Chesterton: A Prophet for the 21st Century.* Norfolk, VA: IHS, 2008.

Manent, Pierre. *Human Rights and Natural Law*. Catholic Ideas for a Secular World. South Bend, IN: University of Notre Dame, 2021.
Maycock, A. L. "Introduction." In *The Man Who Was Orthodox*, by G. K. Chesterton, edited by A. L. Maycock, 13–81. London: Dobson, 1963.
McCleary, Joseph R. *The Historical Imagination of G. K. Chesterton: Locality, Patriotism, and Nationalism*. London: Routledge, 2009.
McGilchrist, Iain. *The Master and His Emissary*. New Haven: Yale University Press, 2019.
———. *The Matter with Things: Volume 1*. London: Perspectiva, 2022.
———. *The Matter with Things: Volume 2*. London: Perspectiva, 2022.
McLean, George F. *Plenitude and Participation: The Life of God in Man*. Washington, DC: Council for Research in Values and Philosophy, 2004.
McLuhan, Marshall. *McLuhan Unbound*. Edited by Terrence W. Gordan. Corte Madera, CA: Ginko, 2005.
———. *The Medium and the Light*. Eugene, OR: Wipf & Stock, 1999.
———. *Understanding Me: Lectures and Interviews*. Toronto: MIT, 2003.
———. *Understanding Media*. London: Routledge, 1964.
McLuhan, Marshall, and Eric McLuhan. *Laws of Media*. Toronto: University of Toronto, 1988.
———. *The Lost Tetrads of Marshall McLuhan*. New York: OR, 2017.
———. *Media and Formal Cause*. Edited by Eric McLuhan. Houston: NeoPoeisis, 2011.
McLuhan, Marshall, and Bruce Powers. *The Global Village*. Oxford: Oxford University Press, 1989.
McCleary, Joseph. R. *The Historical Imagination of G. K. Chesterton*. London: Routledge, 2009.
Merleau-Ponty, Maurice. *Phenomenology of Perception*. Translated by Donald A. Landes. London: Routledge, 2013.
Milbank, Alison. *Chesterton and Tolkien as Theologians*. London: T. & T. Clark, 2009.
Milbank, John. "The Double Glory, or Paradox Versus Dialectics: On Not Quite Agreeing with Slavoj Žižek." In *The Monstrosity of Christ*, edited by Creston Davis, 110–233. Cambridge: MIT, 2008.
Nichols, Aidan. *Chesterton, Theologian*. Manchester: Sophia Institute, 2009.
Nietzsche, Friedrich. *Beyond Good and Evil*. Translated by R. J. Hollingdale. London: Penguin, 2014.
———. *On the Genealogy of Morals*. Translated by Douglas Smith. Oxford: Oxford University Press, 1996.
———. *Writings from the Late Notebooks*. Translated and edited by Rüdiger Bittner. Cambridge: Cambridge University Press, 2003.
Nisbet, Robert. *History of the Idea of Progress*. New York: Basic, 1980.
Nolde, O. Frank. *Freedom's Charter: The Universal Declaration of Human Rights*. New York: Foreign Policy Association, 1949.
Orwell, George. *1984*. 1949. Reprint, London: Penguin, 2018.
Perry, Louise. *The Case Against the Sexual Revolution*. Cambridge: Polity, 2022.
Pickstock, Catherine. *Aspects of Truth: A New Religious Metaphysics*. Cambridge: Cambridge University Press, 2020.
Philips, Jacob. *Obedience Is Freedom*. London: Polity, 2022.
Plotinus. *The Enneads*. Translated by Stephen MacKenna. London: Penguin, 1991.
Poe, Edgar Allan. *Tales of Mystery and Imagination*. New York: Brentano's, 1923.
Popper, Karl. *The Open Society and Its Enemies*. London: Routledge, 1949.

Reno, R. R. *The Return of the Strong Gods: Nationalism, Populism, and the Future of the West*. Washington, DC: Regnery, 2019.

Reyburn, Duncan. "The Death of the Feminine and the Homelessness of Man." In *Sacred Selves*, edited by Juliana Claasens and Stella Viljoen, 61–79. Griffel, 2012.

———. "Repetitions Repeatedly Repeated: Mimetic Desire, Ressentiment, and Mimetic Crisis in Julian Rosefeld's Manifesto (2015)." *Image & Text* 33 (2019) 1–22.

———. *Seeing Things as They Are: G. K. Chesterton and the Drama of Meaning*. Eugene, OR: Cascade, 2016.

Rieff, Philip. *The Triumph of the Therapeutic*. Wilmington, NC: Intercollegiate Studies Institute, 2006.

Schall, James V. *Schall on Chesterton: Timely Essays on Timeless Paradoxes*. Washington, DC: The Catholic University of America, 2000.

Scheler, Max. *Ressentiment*. Translated by Lewis B. Coser and William W. Holdheim. Milwaukee: Marquette University Press, 2007.

Schindler, D. C. *The Catholicity of Reason*. Grand Rapids: Eerdmans, 2013.

Schwartz-Salant, Nathan. *The Order-Disorder Paradox*. Berkeley, CA: North Atlantic, 2017.

Scruton, Roger. *The Uses of Pessimism and the Dangers of False Hope*. London: Atlantic, 2012.

Simpson, Christopher Ben. *Religion, Metaphysics, and the Postmodern: William Desmond and John D. Caputo*. Bloomington, IN: Indiana University Press, 2009.

Slaboch, Matthew W. *The Road to Nowhere: The Idea of Progress and Its Critics*. Philadelphia: University of Pennsylvania Press, 2017.

Stewart-Sykes, Alister, ed. *On the Two Ways: Life or Death, Light or Darkness: Foundational Texts in the Tradition*. New York: St. Vladimir's Seminary, 2011.

Tanabe, Hajime. *Philosophy as Metanoetics*. Translated by Yoshinori Takeuchi. Los Angeles: University of California Press, 1990.

Trueman, Carl. *The Rise and Triumph of the Modern Self: Cultural Amnesia, Expressive Individualism, and the Road to Sexual Revolution*. Wheaton, IL: Crossway, 2020.

Ward, Maisie. *Gilbert Keith Chesterton*. London: Sheed & Ward, 1944.

Whyte, Lancelot Law. *Aspects of Form*. 2nd ed. London: Lund Humphries, 1968.

Williams, Donald T. *Mere Humanity: G. K. Chesterton, C. S. Lewis, and J. R. R. Tolkien on the Human Condition*. Nashville: B&H, 2006.

Zamyatin, Yevgeny. *We*. 1924. Reprint, Translated by Clarence Brown. London: Penguin, 1993.

Žižek, Slavoj. *The Sublime Object of Ideology*. 2nd ed. London: Verso, 2009.

Zuboff, Shoshana. *The Age of Surveillance Capitalism*. New York: Public Affairs, 2019.

Index

audience, 56, 150–58, 165, 169, 197
act, actuality, 3, 20–22, 33, 54, 60, 82, 92–93, 115–17, 119, 122, 141–43, 151, 153, 169, 172
adequatio, 94
Agape, 62
Ahmari, Sohrab, 7
Ahlquist, Dale, 5
airplane, 153–54
America, American, 8, 23, 100–101, 104, 107–8, 135, 168–71
Ambrose, Saint, 75
analogy, 22, 35, 50, 70, 74–75, 93–101, 105–6, 109, 121, 140, 161–62, 177, 182, 186, 197, 203
analogy of being, see being, analogy of
anarchy, 8, 65, 81
Antichrist, 135
anti-environment, 145–46, 197
antigravity, 153–54
Apollo, 74
Apostle's Creed, 131
appearance, appearances, 3, 34, 45, 60, 76, 78, 116, 123, 158
Aquinas, Thomas, see Thomas, Saint
Aristotle, Aristotelian, 24, 28, 73, 82, 92, 110–20, 125–31, 145–46

attention, 2, 16, 17, 24, 26, 28, 32, 35, 38, 39, 43–46, 48–49, 51, 54, 57–58, 73, 76, 80, 97–98, 101, 104, 106, 112, 115, 121, 136, 149, 150, 152, 162, 164–66, 178–79, 181, 185, 190, 192, 196–97, 199–202, 204–6
Augustine, Saint, 28, 75, 81, 140

Babel, Tower of, 55, 172, 181
Baudrillard, Jean 142, 149
Barfield, Owen, 27, 33, 39
Belgium, 121
betweenness, (the) between, 14, 20–21, 27–28, 30–33, 38–41, 45, 47, 52–55, 57–59, 60, 62, 64, 66–67, 71–72, 92–97, 102–3, 110, 122, 152–54, 161, 177, 189, 192, 193, 195
Bolshevism, 12, 68
brain, 1, 40, 99, 148–50, 187
Bellamy, Edward, 2
Belloc, Hilaire, 97–100, 136, 177
Benedict XVI, Pope, 7
Bernays, Edward, 6

218 INDEX

being, 3, 14, 15, 21, 26–46, 52–72, 189–92, 194, 205–6
   analogy of, 80, 93–97, 100, 129, 189
   as agapeic community, 57, 59, 62, 91
   being between (See also metaxology, metaxological), 14, 20–21, 28, 30–31, 33, 38, 40–41, 45, 49, 52–55, 57
   equivocal sense of, 26, 33, 38, 40, 43–53, 55, 60, 70, 88, 96, 103, 119, 126, 160, 183, 189, 190
   question of, 26–29, 32, 34, 92
Bible, 84, 181
   Genesis 3, 14
   Psalm 1:1–3, 207
   Psalm 115:4–8, 28, 131
   Ecclesiastes 1:9, 66
   Matthew 4:17, 206; 5:3–12, 182; 16:2–3, viii; 25:14–30, 167
   Acts 2:1–13, 172
   Romans 5:6, 115
   1 Corinthians 13:2; 14:1, 14
   2 Corinthians 12:9, 115
   James 1:17, 14
Blatchford, Robert, 67
Bolshevism, 12, 68
Borges, Jorge Luis, 158–59
Brexit, 4
bureaucracy, bureaucratic, 4, 9, 115, 129, 133, 142, 169
Bury, J. B., 83

Cammaerts, Emile, 2
capitalism, 7, 10, 179–80
Carlyle, Thomas, 63, 152
Cartesian, 144
catastrophe, 4, 15, 68, 203
Catholic, Catholicism, 3, 24, 63, 74, 93, 97, 117, 132, 134–35, 147, 180, 206, 209
causality, cause, 11, 15, 16, 22, 24, 26, 30–31, 34, 37, 38, 40, 42, 44, 47, 54–59, 61, 64, 71, 73–74, 76, 79, 82, 91, 101, 103–6, 111, 121, 127, 130, 132, 134, 136–37, 144–46, 148–50, 152–54, 156–59, 161–64, 166, 168, 172, 177–79, 183–85, 188, 190–92, 195–96, 201, 205
   as account, explanation, 14, 34, 35, 40, 42, 50, 55, 56, 59, 74, 77, 78, 81, 91, 92, 95, 101, 103, 117, 120, 145, 156–58, 161–62, 173, 189–91, 193, 196
   cause and effect, 11, 16, 35, 40, 60–61, 111–12, 115, 127, 130, 145, 153–57, 168, 187–88, 192, 195, 201
   efficient cause, efficient causality, 40, 44, 54, 61, 74, 89, 91, 111, 116, 125, 126, 127, 128, 129, 130, 134, 145, 149–50, 154, 157, 164, 166, 179, 183
   formal cause, formal causality, formal cause, 26, 31, 37, 40, 42, 54, 56, 59, 61, 64, 73- 74, 76, 82, 91, 101, 103–6, 111, 113, 115, 116, 126, 131, 145–57, 162–63, 166, 173, 181–82, 184, 187, 190–91, 205
   material cause, material causality, 1, 91, 111–15, 118–25, 127, 128, 130, 131, 144–45, 178, 183, 190
censorship, 58, 105
Chaucer, Geoffrey, 27
Christianity, 9, 63, 75, 89, 115, 133–37, 180, 189, 194–95, 206–7
Chesterton, Cecil, 46–47
Chesterton, G. K., 1–207
   as autodidact, 9
   as journalist, 14, 28, 32, 51, 59, 74, 156, 188, 189, 199,
   as medievalist, 27
   as metaphysician, 3, 28, 199,
   as prophet, 2, 3, 4, 15, 18, 24, 27, 67, 68, 70, 196, 200, 201
   as theologian, 3
   as writer, 92, 150, 151
Chesterton's fence, 171–72
China, 18, 199
Christendom, 132, 135
Christianity, 9, 63, 75, 89 115, 133–37, 180, 189, 194, 206
chronology, 69, 83, 86, 145–46, 200
church, 132, 145, 180–82, 206

communication, 63, 129, 150, 156, 162–66, 168–71, 178–80
  of being, 33, 35, 57, 74
  hyper-communication, 143
communism, 4, 57, 87, 139, 183
computing, 153
contemplation, 21–22, 49, 82, 140, 149, 205
cosmopolitanism, 169–70
creation, 15, 26, 34, 74, 81, 91–95, 103, 107, 116–18, 138, 175

Dada, 183
Dao De Jing, 182
Darwinism, 84, 131
Davison, Andrew, 93
Declaration of Human Rights, 132–33
decline,15, 39, 66, 69, 85, 99, 129–30, 194, 203
decontextualize, decontextualization, 60, 140, 149, 159
defamiliarization, 48–52, 146
Defoe, Daniel, 204–5
Desmond, William, 24, 26, 28–72, 126, 147, 190
determinism, 12,13, 15, 23, 49, 129, 146, 165, 189
dialectic, 26, 33, 35, 44, 53–61, 63, 66–72, 86, 88–89, 93, 96, 102, 106, 112, 113, 124, 128, 140, 145, 156, 162, 184, 187, 189, 190
dialectical, 33, 35, 44, 53–59, 63, 67, 70–71, 79, 83, 88, 93, 96, 102, 106, 113, 124, 126, 128, 140, 145, 156, 162, 184, 187, 190
Dickens, Charles, 158–59
dignity, 90, 92, 102, 103, 133, 134, 171
distortion, 9, 41, 66, 79, 81, 97, 102, 109, 129, 164–65, 168, 179, 181, 190
disproportion, 71, 154, 178, 179
dogma, 12, 89, 91, 139, 143, 147, 157
dominion, 34, 138, 139
domination, 138
Dostoevsky, Fyodor, 8
Doyle, Sir Arthur Conan, 158–59
drama, 15, 22, 29, 49, 64, 65, 66, 70, 71, 89, 92, 102, 117, 136, 149, 160, 165, 166, 175, 191, 192, 206

Dupuy, Jean-Pierre, 68

education, 9, 88, 92, 122
efficient cause, see causality, efficient cause
egotism, 39, 55
eidos, 78–79
electricity, 86, 142, 154, 163, 165, 168
Ellul, Jacques, 149
Engels, Freddie, 57, 183
England, 67, 68, 74, 105
environment, environmental, 9, 10, 18, 71, 79, 90, 113, 117, 141, 145–46, 152, 154, 171, 197, 200–205
enworld, enworlded, enworldedness, 22, 138
eros, 62
essence, 2, 21, 28, 30, 41–42, 46, 81–82, 90–91, 94, 110, 116, 127, 130, 161, 180, 187, 204
eugenics, 19, 135
evil, 11, 77, 86, 125, 136, 163, 176

fall of man, doctrine of the, 86, 95, 109, 135, 153, 185, 195
family, 10, 63, 96, 100, 131
fascism, 22, 58, 175, 183
fashion, 6, 10, 11, 22, 29, 82, 86, 123, 170, 174–75, 185–86
Father Brown, 158–59
feminism, 7, 19, 184
figure/ground, 40, 42, 57, 60, 69, 83, 88, 100, 123, 126, 144–58, 162, 166–67, 177, 194, 198, 204
Francis of Assisi, Saint, 27, 146
Frankenstein, 149
Freud, Sigmund, 6, 63, 143
future, 1, 3–4, 9–10, 13–16, 23–27, 52, 58, 64–65, 68, 70–74, 83, 97–98, 101, 103–6, 108–9, 115, 117, 122, 126, 128, 130, 135, 138, 146, 153, 172–78, 188, 191, 192–95, 197–201, 203, 205
faith, 14, 46, 63, 68, 75, 77, 87, 97, 123, 143, 189, 193, 194, 196, 206
final cause, see causality, final cause
formal cause, see causality, formal cause

INDEX

Gabriel Gale, 50
Galton, Francis, 19
Germany, 22, 67
Girard, René, 24, 134
Great War, see World War One,
grace, 7, 14, 35, 59, 115, 131
Greek, 73, 74, 79, 174
groove, groovings, 71, 103, 106
Guinness Book of World Records, 11

habit, 36, 43, 46, 49, 68, 71, 96, 98, 130, 165, 168, 196
halo, haloing, 27, 37, 39, 59, 76, 179, 195
Han, Byung-Chul, 8, 142
happiness, 7, 87, 88, 131
harmony, 11, 55, 64, 65, 78, 82, 182
Hart, David Bentley, 94–95, 118
healing, 127–28, 135
health, 8, 15, 85, 105, 128, 130, 165, 176, 194, 201
Hegel, G. F. W., Hegelian, 53, 54, 55, 57, 58, 83, 88
Heidegger, Martin, 91, 118, 131, 144, 148, 155, 200–201
historicism, 12, 58, 60, 61, 84, 107, 129, 198
history, 12–15, 29, 58, 60, 61, 66, 69, 70, 73, 83–85, 103, 106, 107, 129, 143, 157, 160, 167, 172–79, 181, 183, 187
Hitler, Adolf, 4, 22
Homer, 200
hope, viii, 2, 15, 44, 59, 71, 77, 87, 105, 149, 201–3
Hopkins, Gerard Manley, 98
human dignity, 90, 92, 102, 103, 133, 134, 171
humanism, 8, 134
human rights, 130–34
humility, 14–15, 29, 201
Huxley, Aldous, 178

Ibsen, Henrik, 111
idealism, 21, 93
identity, 34, 37–38, 46, 56, 59, 76–77, 80, 88, 93, 95, 142, 145, 178, 193–94
identity politics, 7

idolatry, 5, 17, 39, 50, 130–31, 135–37, 140, 147, 182, 189
ideal, 74, 78, 80, 82, 86–93, 95, 103, 105–10, 114, 127, 132–33, 137–38, 158, 161, 165, 175, 175, 187, 190, 193–94, 199
ideology, 7, 12, 19–20, 47–48, 57, 60, 63, 82, 92, 104, 108, 122, 134, 136, 141, 175, 179–80, 182–83, 185, 203
imagination, 11, 52, 85, 87, 106, 107, 108, 146, 174, 190, 196
indeterminacy, 32, 34, 53, 91, 119, 125, 145, 151
individual, individuality, 20, 62, 63, 71, 79 87 96, 105, 113, 127, 132, 134, 138, 140, 143–44, 169, 177, 190
incarnation, 62, 75, 110, 139, 153, 192–93, 201
Innocent Smith, 92
instrumentalism, instrumental logic, instrumental reason, 40, 48, 80, 99, 118, 121, 130, 145, 155, 178
intelligibility, 17, 22, 36, 38, 42, 44, 50–51, 78, 80, 82, 90, 92–93, 103, 106, 112–13, 118–20, 126–27, 130–31, 134, 145, 154, 156, 160, 191
intuition, 10, 22, 26, 52, 56, 61, 73, 75, 93, 95, 97, 100, 106, 150, 154, 173, 182, 190–91, 200

Jaki, Stanley, 47, 195
Joseph, Saint, 63
journalism, 9, 14, 28, 32, 47, 51, 59, 74, 111, 156, 179, 188–89, 199
journalistic metaphysics, 28, 32, 51,189
Jünger, Friedrich, 2
Jung, Carl, 182

kairos, kairology, 69, 83
Kierkegaard, Søren, 192–93
Keats, John, 88
Kenner, Hugh, 26, 61
Kipling, Rudyard, 111

Lady Gaga, 11

Lauer, Quentin, 53, 58
law/s of the situation, 20, 102, 104, 154, 157, 161, 163, 182, 194, 204
laws, 11, 13, 17, 20, 49, 51, 67, 68, 84, 92, 100, 102, 104–5, 107, 126, 130, 133, 142, 161–62, 165–66, 171, 173, 181–82, 185, 204, 207
Le Bon, Gustave, 9
Legutko, Ryszard, 133
Lestrade, 159
Lewis, C. S., 12, 24
liberal-democratic, 7, 20
liberalism, 4, 8, 141, 142, 203
limit, limitation, 5, 17, 38–40, 47, 48, 53, 55, 59, 61, 64, 68, 76, 87, 89, 92, 95, 104, 110, 129, 138, 139, 140, 142, 143, 149, 156, 161, 171, 182, 189, 204
logic, 11–14, 16, 23, 26, 33, 37, 53, 56, 58, 60, 84, 88, 92–93, 96, 116, 118, 130, 145, 158, 162, 183, 187, 188, 195, 198
logos, 81, 135
love, 2, 14–15, 35, 46, 59, 62, 75–76, 87, 94–95, 106, 108–9, 117, 124–25, 145, 156, 168–71, 193, 200, 202

machine, 5, 12, 13, 70, 135, 140, 155, 163, 165, 180, 205
maelstrom, 44, 201–6
Marinetti, Filippo Tommaso, 56–57, 183
Marx, Karl, 13, 183
Mary, Saint, Blessed Virgin, 63, 121, 123
materialism, materialistic, 13, 16, 27, 47, 78, 84, 89, 104, 112, 157, 158
measure, 19, 30, 33, 69, 84–85, 105, 139
Medusa, 106
Merleau-Ponty, Maurice, 149, 199
metaphor, metaphors, 18, 36, 39, 64, 66, 69–71, 99–100, 115, 117, 154, 161, 162, 164, 166, 172, 203
metaphysical mindfulness, 29–30, 32, 34, 75
methexis, see participation
method, 13, 24, 39, 47, 49, 55, 60, 65, 69, 83–84, 100, 111, 127, 138, 150
Moses, 10

McLuhan, Eric, 145–54,
McLuhan, Marshall, 16, 148–57, 161–66, 173, 177, 181–82, 191, 202
McGilchrist, Iain, 136, 148–49
mediation, 21, 32, 33, 35, 38, 39, 40, 43, 45, 46, 51–62, 67–69, 71, 75, 78–79, 93–94, 106–7, 120, 127, 130, 139, 140, 149, 156, 161–84, 190–93, 199
  enhancement, 161–66
  obsolescence, 161–62, 166–72
  retrieval, 161–62, 173–81, 184
  reversal, 161–62, 181–84
Milbank, Alison, 49
Milbank, John, 57
modernity, 3, 5, 7, 40, 92, 133, 136–37, 139, 141, 143, 172, 174, 195, 207
material cause, see causality, material cause
metaxological, metaxology, 26, 33–34, 41, 49, 51, 53, 58–61, 63, 69–71, 75, 77–80, 88, 94, 97, 99, 101, 104, 107, 110, 124, 128, 146, 156, 161–62, 164–66, 170, 175, 177, 178, 189, 190
monocausality, 40
Morris, William, 87

Narcissus, 177
natural law, 17, 49, 67, 130, 134, 185
negative capability, 88
negative spirit, 17–18, 22, 66, 86, 147, 151, 172, 183
non-identical repetition, 11, 48, 58, 60, 65, 76, 98, 105, 174–75, 177, 189, 193–94
novelty, 57, 66, 86, 90, 173–77, 183–84, 192
nationalism, 4, 170
Newton, Sir Isaac, 13
nominalism, 3, 7, 20, 78, 82, 99, 109, 129, 131, 142, 175
Nichols, Aidan, 112
Nietzsche, Friedrich, 44, 63, 131, 159, 160, 174, 189
Nisbet, Robert, 83

222 INDEX

objective, objectivity, 31, 33, 58, 81, 113, 120, 122, 140, 144, 150, 197
ontotheology, 80
orthodoxy, 28, 31, 131, 136, 171, 182
original, originality, 2, 18, 32, 74, 121, 134, 154, 165, 169, 174, 181–82, 184
original sin, 12
overdeterminacy, overdeterminate, 32, 34, 66
oligarchy, 9
Orwell, George, 105, 178

paradox, 22, 26, 56–62, 64, 75–76, 93, 110, 115, 153–54, 158, 161, 165, 178, 181, 189–92
parallelism, 22, 97–96, 154, 175, 190–91
participation, participatory, 31, 51, 58, 75–81, 93–96, 100, 120, 123, 128, 131, 140, 149, 156, 164–65, 168, 175, 190, 197
pattern, viii, 16, 19, 21, 37, 40, 45, 49, 60, 62, 65–66, 69, 77–79, 82, 84, 99–96, 112, 115, 118, 126, 128, 129, 145, 147, 150, 162, 163, 170, 174, 178, 191, 195, 202, 204
Paul, Saint, 14, 18, 115, 163
pendulum, 12–13, 69–70, 184
perception, 2–3, 21, 27, 31, 38–39, 46–51, 60, 83, 95, 97, 102, 107, 112, 122, 130, 146, 159, 164–65, 174, 190–91, 199, 204–4
perspectivism, 159–60
Pessimism, 15, 67, 69, 71, 77, 133, 149, 196, 203
phenomenology, 17, 54, 58–59, 76, 148
photograph, photography, 22–23, 106, 107, 121, 123
photographic negative, 22–23
Plato, Platonism, 23–24, 28, 30, 53, 56, 59, 62, 72–82, 89–94, 106, 110, 113–14, 118–19, 130–31, 150, 174–75, 189–90, 192, 206
Poe, Edgar Allan, 201–5
poet, poetic, poetry, 31, 39, 41–43, 49, 57–59, 98–100, 107, 146, 153, 156, 177, 179, 183–84, 198–99, 204

Popper, Karl, 8
populism, 4, 9, 215
potency, potentiality, 3, 13, 20–22, 33, 47, 51, 54, 57, 60, 61, 79, 82, 92–94, 107, 113, 115–25, 128–30, 141–42, 161, 164–65, 168, 169, 172, 193, 198, 203
pragmatism, 21, 126
prediction, 3, 6–15, 26, 58, 67, 68, 73–74, 84, 100, 107, 108, 115, 116, 122, 135, 158, 185, 190 191, 194, 196–202
prescience, 2, 3, 11, 13, 14, 15, 20, 34, 37, 58, 64, 67, 188, 191, 196–200
progress, 5–7, 56–60, 64, 66, 69–71, 82–89, 92–93, 102, 109, 138–39, 145, 171, 176, 180, 183, 194, 201
project, 47, 71, 79, 126, 132, 137–44
projector, 137–41, 144
prophecy, prophetic, the, 2, 14, 15, 18, 20, 23, 24, 27, 67–69, 83, 101, 104, 163, 176, 195–97, 201
Prussia, 67
Puritan, puritanism, 115, 181, 185

radio, 153, 155
reader, 15, 42, 45–49, 51, 58–59, 73, 98, 100, 104–5, 121, 146, 152, 158–59, 164, 167, 188, 197, 205
redemption, 95, 135, 139, 207
relation, relational, relationality, 7, 11, 16, 17, 21, 28, 30, 45, 48, 64, 65, 66, 80, 81, 89, 93, 95–99, 102–3, 105, 111, 113, 118–23, 126, 128, 137–38, 140–41, 153–54, 157, 161–63, 167–68, 170, 175, 183, 187, 190–91, 195
resentment, *ressentiment*, 7, 89, 135, 184
romance, 19, 31, 46, 48, 178, 204
relativism, 7, 47, 50, 89, 130, 197
revolution, 4, 6, 13, 18, 21–23, 27, 68, 103, 109, 131, 146, 157, 194–95, 199, 202
reminiscence, 192–94
repetition, 11, 46, 48, 57–58, 65, 76, 78, 98, 105, 175, 177, 184, 189, 192–95
resonance, 17, 28, 97, 168

INDEX   223

Rieff, Philip, 6, 143
Russia, 4, 36

Sabbath, 45, 201
Sartre, Jean-Paul, 28
satire, 74
Scheler, Max, 89, 135, 148
Schindler, D. C., 74–75, 117, 143, 192
science, sciences, 2–3, 6, 12–14, 27, 46–48, 83, 114, 118, 123, 129, 130, 138–41, 158, 155, 190, 195
scientism, 42, 47, 48,
Scruton, Sir Roger, 133
sense-ratios, 154
Shaw, George Bernard, 47, 112
Sheed, Frank, 4, 19
Shelly, Mary, 149
Sherlock Holmes, 158
shipwreck, 201–5
significance, 3, 9, 14, 19, 28, 48, 66, 60, 67, 73, 74, 82, 83, 95, 98, 103, 106, 120, 140, 145, 150, 153, 156, 180
simulacrum, 45
skepticism, 44, 89, 129, 143
socialism, 74, 185
sophistry, 114
Soviet, 36
Spain, Spanish, 168–71, 179
speculation, 2, 4, 23, 27, 52, 104–5, 108, 198, 202
spelling reform, 166–67
Spengler, Oswald, 15
state, states, statecraft, 6, 8, 10, 67–68, 83, 104–5, 107, 125, 133–34, 204
standardization, 136, 170
subjective, subjectivity, 27, 33, 44, 57, 78, 95, 113, 159, 161, 164
submarine, 154–55
Sunday, 201
surveillance, 8, 68, 104, 105, 176
system, 52, 64, 82, 90, 108, 112–13, 115, 117, 140–41, 169, 179–80
synchronicity, 191

Tanabe, Hajime, 56
Tatehana, Noritaka, 11
techne, 174

telescope, 24, 189, 191
teleology, 129–36, 138, 143
telepathy, 153–54
telephone, 153, 165
tetrad, Marshall McLuhan's, 148–85, 191
Thomas Aquinas, Saint, 22, 26, 27, 28, 31, 75, 77, 92, 117, 191
tradition, 22, 81, 84, 96, 99, 118, 121, 167, 170–73, 176, 179–85, 206
Trinitarian, Trinity, 57, 75, 145
truth, 3, 10–13, 16, 18–19, 21, 25, 28, 30, 33–38, 42–46, 48, 51–55, 60, 65, 80, 89, 93–95, 98, 100, 105, 107, 118, 120, 122–24, 132, 136–43, 151–52, 159–60, 168, 174, 176, 180–82, 185, 191–94, 204–5, 207
technology, 5, 9, 18, 19, 84, 91, 105, 125, 127, 129, 140, 144, 153, 155, 164–65, 170, 172, 173, 199
Thackeray, W. M., 152
Tocqueville, Alexis, 8
transcendence, 29, 37, 54, 59, 62, 75–81, 94–95, 159, 161, 175, 189
Titanic, RMS, 203–4
tyranny, 7, 68, 81, 181
Tzara, Tristan, 183

Utopia, 13, 15, 87, 190, 194
univocal, 26, 33, 35–43, 46–53, 55, 60, 63, 67, 73, 79, 80, 88, 93–94, 96, 102, 106, 124–26, 142, 146, 160, 164, 167, 172, 175, 177–78, 187, 189, 190, 197–98, 201

Victorian, 152
violence, 4–5, 13, 29–30, 57, 100, 174, 183–84
vulnerability, 33, 182, 203
Vanity Fair, 15, 101–9.
virtue, 5, 13, 40, 68, 80, 82, 89, 109, 115, 122, 130, 136, 141
Verne, Jules, 2
Virgil, 22
vortex, 153, 202–7

wonder, 28, 32, 34–35, 52, 109, 175, 204, 206

Wells, H. G., 2, 112, 140, 194
World War One, 4, 101
World War Two, 4, 10, 155

Yellow Press, 179–80

zero-sum, 178, 183
zig-zag, zig-zagging, 70
Zamyatin, Yevgeny, 178
Žižek, Slavoj, 54, 57
Zuboff, Shoshana, 8

www.ingramcontent.com/pod-product-compliance
Lightning Source LLC
Chambersburg PA
CBHW020408230426
43664CB00009B/1239